THE OTHER
BOOK OF JOHN

REMEMBERING MY HOME AND NATIVE LAND

JOHN GEEN

LifeRich Publishing is a registered trademark of The Reader's Digest Association, Inc.

LifeRich Publishing books may be ordered through booksellers or by contacting:

LifeRich Publishing
1663 Liberty Drive
Bloomington, IN 47403
www.liferichpublishing.com
844-686-9607

Because of the dynamic nature of the Internet, any web addresses or links contained in this book may have changed since publication and may no longer be valid. The views expressed in this work are solely those of the author and do not necessarily reflect the views of the publisher, and the publisher hereby disclaims any responsibility for them.

Any people depicted in stock imagery provided by Getty Images are models, and such images are being used for illustrative purposes only. Certain stock imagery © Getty Images.

Scripture quotations are from the Holy Bible, King James Version (Authorized Version). First published in 1611. Quoted from the KJV Classic Reference Bible, Copyright © 1983 by The Zondervan Corporation.

ISBN: 978-1-4897-4505-7 (sc)
ISBN: 978-1-4897-4506-4 (hc)
ISBN: 978-1-4897-4507-1 (e)

Library of Congress Control Number: 2022920659

Print information available on the last page.

LifeRich Publishing rev. date: 11/22/2022

I dedicate this book to Nora, my late wife of sixty-five years. She was subjected to hardships that no person should have been expected to endure.

I know she rests in the hands of God!

CONTENTS

PREFACE

*I did not know myself until I began
to write my memoirs.
Now I don't like me nearly so much!*

This was written solely for entertainment and because, as my youthful capabilities fade, I really don't have much else to do. Readers will neither learn secrets of life nor gain insight into social protocols. I, the author, am not a life coach, a philosopher, a prophet, an academic, a clairvoyant, or an intellectual. I am, in fact, a high school dropout.

My life began before there were automatic transmissions in cars, ballpoint pens, televisions, miniskirts, pantyhose, Viagra, zippered flies on trousers, and many other amenities of modern living. In my early years, I lived without electricity, indoor plumbing, disease preventative medications, and a wristwatch. While I hesitate to call myself a pioneer, I have seen life changes that range from amazing to alarming. It is my hope that my life story will be read by a generation who can relate it to their great-grandparents, or even great-great-grandparents, who endured similar times to give them the legacy of life they enjoy today.

In my earlier days, the government was not a charitable organization. It did not provide for the welfare of its citizens. Citizens worked to provide for themselves. The government benefited.

In my story, names may have been misspelled or substituted because I forgot them—or deliberately changed to protect the guilty and deliver me from lawsuits.

INTRODUCTION

*For I am the voice crying in the
wilderness.—John 1:23*

This book is about me, John Geen, who as an unschooled boy emerged from poverty and the obscurity of a poor Ontario farm to eventually gain a measure of celebrity and accrue a small fortune in investment assets. This book is not to brag but simply to call attention to the fact that with reasonable effort, personal sacrifice, and a bunch of luck, it can be done.

The Other Book of John will dwell mostly on things long etched in my mind. One cannot select what one remembers, but I can select what I write about. I have tried to keep the line between factual memories and wishful reminiscences from blurring.

Writing memoirs is like entering a confessional with the cameras running. There are many specifics one does not wish to reveal about oneself, so I may forgo a few details. During my life, I was constantly led into temptation and not always delivered from evil. Suffice to say that during my sixty-five years of marriage to a wonderful and enduring woman, there was a time and a reason for each of us to stray from the expectations of a normal marital relationship.

My early career involved long-term absence from the home. A beautiful woman left alone without affection emits an aura of desire that will be detected by men with an instinct and strength to pursue.

The need to discard a chaste existence has been embedded into the nature of woman since Eve ate of the apple.

Likewise, a traveling man, upon entering geographically remote communities, will be perceived by local womenfolk as an opportunity to expand the tribal gene pool. A woman's will to stalk and entice is equal to a man's will to sow the seeds of life. The instincts of species survival are instilled in every living thing.

An understanding of these basics of nature is the needed foundation for forgiveness. Forgiving transgressions was an essential ingredient in our sixty-five-year marriage.

I will begin with a story about me and God. Religion has always played a part in my life, even though I do not subscribe to its rigid rules for communal behavior. The Bible is one of the greatest novels ever written, and its teachings and societal guidelines cannot be, nor ever will be, surpassed. Churches have held the Christian community in spiritual servitude for twenty centuries by demanding absolute belief in specifics that are, at best, questionable. This has resulted in the rejection of spirits, apparitions, and divine retribution by the masses.

Jesus was a courageous individual who obviously believed His self-sacrifice would benefit mankind for all time to come. Even as nails were being driven into Him, I doubt that He was aware of the improbable powers that would ultimately be attributed to Him in scripture. The gathered throngs of his time may have accepted the scriptural claims of mind-defying miracles; the scientific awareness of today's peoples does not allow for the same.

Witnesses to His many miracles obviously did not undergo any objective cross-examination.

Henceforth I call you not servants; for the servant knoweth not what his lord doeth: but I have called you friends; for all things that I have heard of my Father I have made known unto you.—John 15:15

CHAPTER 1

ME AND GOD

*Of one thing I am certain: I will be the
last to die during my lifetime.*

When people perceive that they do not have a great deal of
time left to look forward, they tend to look back.

I often muse about what I believe or what I don't believe,
and in both cases, I wonder why. I am never exactly sure when I did
or did not believe in this or that. I am not even sure when I became
an analytical, ecclesiastic cynic.

In early childhood, there were two books that competed for my
faith: the Holy Bible and *Grimms' Nursery Rhymes*. Yes, I had no
doubt that the cat played the fiddle and the cow jumped over the
moon. I really believed, without a doubt, that there was a little old
lady who lived in a shoe, and I had deep sympathy for Little Bo Peep
who lost her sheep. I truly had faith.

When we attended our little village church each Sunday, the
Reverend Beazer would proclaim the merits of Jesus Christ loudly
and forcefully. He seemed to believe that if the message was weak, he
should yell like hell. When he proclaimed how the blind were made
to see and the lame were made to walk, the congregation nodded
to indicate their unwavering conviction. There were no apparent
doubts. They, too, had faith.

Conflicting values were imposed upon me at a tender age. When an older sibling or the hired man uttered the name Jesus Christ or said "God damn" whatever, they were sternly admonished by my parents, who gave full approval when these same phrases were annunciated from the pulpit by the Reverend Beazer. Why this selective difference?

Even as my older sister read stories to me from *Grimms' Nursery Rymes* and Mother read me selections from her Bible, I did not perceive a significant distinction between Jack's slaying of the beanstalk giant and David's slaying of Goliath. Then another factor began to influence me: logic. There arose a conflict between what I was told and what I could see.

For instance, our chimney was small, and I was told that if I was good, Santa Claus would come down that chimney and bring me a new tricycle. I knew a tricycle was bigger than that chimney! Doubt was further fortified at a Santa Claus parade when I noticed that Santa's sleigh was towed by horses. I had expected a snow-cutter towed by reindeer. It was a logging sleigh camouflaged with Christmas decorations, and it was evident that behind the bearded mask of Santa, joyfully passing out candy with vocal *ho, ho, hos* to gleeful children, was my uncle Cecil. When bringing the subject up in conversation with adults, I was told with much authority to shush—*Don't tell; you must believe!*

Eventually, I began to question things I was told, and even some things I was to learn from books. I did not understand why books that brought unquestionable knowledge and hope to so many brought questions of fact to me. I did surmise that I was expected to believe stories of miracles in the Holy Bible and to forsake those of *Grimms' Nursery Rhymes*.

Time passed, and by my middle to late teens, my understanding of faith was maturing. Faith was a firm belief in something for which there was no proof. Faith was to believe without question. Faith was a belief in the traditional doctrine of religion. By nature, I, like St. Thomas, was one of little faith. I needed to see those hollows made by the nails and put my fingers in the wound from the lances.

I began to suspect that faith was merely a concept, and the image of God was in the mind of the beholder. After all, when Moses wrote Genesis, had not humans existed on earth for unknown ages? Could Moses possibly have perceived God in the image of man as of the time he wrote of creation? So did God make us in His image, or do we accept God as a reflection of humankind's image at the time of Moses?

Because I questioned my faith, when time came to study the catechisms for confirmation to the church, I dissented. I could not bring myself to believe that water could be turned into wine, that lepers could be cleansed, or that the dead could be returned to life. There was no supporting evidence or logical probability that any person could mandate a miracle.

I finally realized just how steadfastly my father had clung to his faith when a historical event inserted some doubts into his beliefs. On October 4, 1957, Sputnik went into orbit—far above the clouds and into the ether of space. I remember him sadly saying, "I guess there is nothing up there after all."

I wondered what he had expected. Our Bible constantly pictured God as far above those clouds as a bearded old man with long flowing hair sitting on a golden throne with a shepherd's staff in His right hand, surrounded by winged angels playing harps. Was this really his expectation? Did Sputnik soil this image? I felt a deep sense of sympathy for him.

Over many years, I have accumulated, bit by bit, information on scientific explorations and studies that have cast shadows on the likelihood of some biblical stories. I was having trouble accepting them on faith alone. Now let me share with you some further thoughts on the subject.

I believe there is an influence, a power, a force that is greater than

3

anything that mortal humans can ever begin to comprehend—a power that has created all that has ever been created and ever will be created. I have chosen to call this power, this phenomenon, God. Whether our little corner of the universe has been created by some powerful intelligence or by random acts of nature, I do not know. There are too many coincidences of likeness from species to species to ignore the possibility of some limited pool of early life, but again, maybe not. I have left room for that doubt because we simply do not know, and science has not yet solved all these mysteries. It is still a work in progress.

Having said this, I do not wish to express doubt on the need and purpose of the Bible. It is a masterful piece of literature, a fabled history of the Asia Minor region—the Holy Land. It is a history that recorded the troubles and tribulations of settlements and cultures of that region, the rise of powerful kingdoms, the building of cities and temples, the wars and destruction of nations. Archaeological discoveries have verified many of these biblical subjects.

Other questions have entered my mind, and I realize that there may already be answers to many of them that I do not know. In what language was the Bible written? On what and with what was it written? Where were the scriptures kept and by whom? Who translated them? How many times were they translated? Why were they translated, and how accurate were the translations?

Let me first address a theory of purpose. As enduring agrarian colonies and urban communities developed, they required law and order to achieve peace and purpose. For this, they needed leaders. Leaders need a convincing power of knowledge as well as strength to retain their rank. Surely there must have been an inquisitive curiosity among their subjects in the communities; therefore, leaders needed answers to questions that would satisfy this curiosity.

Questions for which their subjects sought answers may have included, *Why do we exist? Where did we come from? Why do tide waters rise and fall? Why does the sun rise in the east and set in the west? Does water flow off the edge of the world and come back as rain? Why does our settlement live by the rules we live by? Who made those rules and on what authority?*

The leaders needed answers. They needed, among other things, a confirmation of creation and a source of rules by which the community was governed. Genesis served this purpose. They needed the Bible.

We all concede that science comes into conflict with much of the Bible, but did the Bible not provide convincing material for the early leaders to hold and control their subjects? I have little doubt that threatening the wrath of God upon those who were reluctant to conform must have helped a great deal. It still works today!

Having said that, what would be my thoughts on Genesis today? I am not an astronomer. I have no extensive knowledge of the universe. I cannot employ the principles of physics or chemistry to astronomical objects, nor do I have any illusions about the accuracy of my convictions. I just know that the creation of where and what I am is above and beyond my comprehensive capacity. It is in the hands of some mysterious power I refer to as God.

Genesis speaks of the beginning of the universe, of the earth, of plants, animals, and humans—things of which the Hebrew nations had little knowledge, but leaders needed explanations to retain the respect of their subjects. Genesis met this need!

Literature I have read measures all time in years—a year being the time the Earth takes for one orbit of the sun. In the beginning, there was no sun and no Earth. There was no time! It did not exist! There was only space with no boundaries, no beginning, and no end.

A modern Genesis may well speak of a mass in space: matter with no shape and no structure. Was it a solid mass? Were components of this mass discreet? Was it gathered and compacted by its own gravitational forces? Were there active electrical energies? Were thermal nuclear temperatures generated in the presence of hydrogen and in sufficient quantities to cause that proverbial big bang we are told about? Who knows?

Obviously, matter was scattered, and stars were born. Stray

matter was captured by their gravity and became planets. Planets, having a gravitational influence of their own, captured fragments of matter, which became moons. Climates on planets ebbed, flowed, evolved, and eventually, somewhere, at some time, life was born.

———◆•◆•◆———

I will not go further into my theories of creation nor of my beliefs in the limited hegemonies of mortal man. I go to church on Sundays. I listen with great rapture to the history of the Holy Land, of how prophesies have come to pass, how further prophesies may one day apply to current earthly beings and foretell what is in store for us. I still reserve the right to harbor some doubts and form my own opinions. Of course, one of the messages in the Holy Bible is that we should live a good life and be rewarded by eternal peace in Heaven. Does my skeptical approach let me believe in such? Yes!

I have put some thought into that subject, based to some extent on the accounts of near-death experiences that have been documented. They speak of an approach of a brilliant light and life memories flooding forth across the mind, a feeling of loving comfort and peace, and so forth. Many accounts are too alike to ignore, and science provides some support for this.

When approaching death, bodily functions begin, one by one, to shut down. When digestive functions and such end, the heart will stop, and oxygen-rich blood will cease to flow to the one organ that records our life: the brain. As sight fails, the brain ceases to record visual images, and a blank screen of light appears. Hearing shuts down, smell turns off, and bodily nerve-end feelings are no longer transmitted to the still-living brain. At this point, a sensation of floating in weightless peace will engulf us.

Starved of life-sustaining oxygen and with no new input, the current thought chamber, the frontal cortex, will be flooded with recent memories. These fade, to be followed by the next most recent memory retentions that in turn vanish, replaced by those stored in more distant segments of the cerebral cortex. Some recollections may be those of actual experiences; some may be thoughts and fears ever warehoused in the imagination. They will continue to cascade back in time until, eventually, the synapses will diminish, then cease. There will be no more.

In our real world, there are beginnings and ends. Each and every venture and experience of our life is stored in some mysterious memory sector of our brain, of which modern science knows little. When our mind is no longer tethered to our body, life in the real world ends. Since we have no way of knowing life has ended, our closing recollections become eternal.

This, then, is our heaven, or perhaps a place of lesser appeal. There may be no man with a flowing beard on a golden throne surrounded by angels playing harps and passing judgments upon us. Our soul is that which we have lived and will evermore embrace or endure. Our afterlife is without end.

This is what I have chosen to believe.

CHAPTER 2

THE DAWN OF KNOWLEDGE

*A child has no concept of home. To a
child, home is but a nursery.*

This is the tale of three persons—all of them me. It is about the person I was, the person I wanted to be, and the person I became. While the tale is autobiographical, from time to time it may be a drama, a comedy, or even a tragedy. How will it end? I'm not there yet!

Now I could say that it was the indomitability of the human spirit that propelled me, the son of a poor dirt farmer working a hilly fifty acres littered with boulders, to achieve what many would consider a life of relative comfort and security. Perhaps I just lacked the intuitive sense to comprehend the consequences of failure. Perhaps I should have realized that I could not be the person I was never meant to be.

But in truth, much of my success in life was not due to my own efforts but the oversights of others. I have had a wonderful journey that has taken me from my sheltered preschool life to the here and now. In short, I have been blessed.

June 6, 1933. Canada was in the depths of an ongoing depression. On that day, the burden of a third child on struggling farmers must have been disheartening. I was that third child. My brother (six years my senior) and sister (five more beyond that) were bound to become needed helping hands around my parents' horse and hayrack farm. It kind of makes me suspect that I was not a planned addition. If that was indeed the case, it was never ever mentioned in my lifetime.

My parents fulfilled my needs and responded to my desires for attention, but I do not recall being held, cuddled, and cared for to any great extent. As I explored the world around the place of my birth, I did feel secure within the four walls of our old, whitewashed stone house.

My father, John Ritchie Geen, a lean, masculine man of medium stature showed a perpetual suntan on a face that seldom smiled. His faded bibbed overalls carried a Westclox watch that could be heard ticking all the way across the dinner table. He farmed at the foot of Gravel Pit Hill on the fourth concession road of Huntington Township in Ontario, Canada. The year was about 1921. He was a dairy farmer in a land where the cheese industry was the source of survival.

He did, in fact, become president of Moira Cheese in 1926 and eventually the president of Acme Cheese. This company united a patchwork of community cheese factories that permitted many farms to survive during the years of financial correction, the years when businessmen became beggars and beggars became numerous. Alas, these products have faded into history

At this tender age, the terms *poor* and *poverty* were unknown to me. I did not understand why people came to the door looking for work or for food, water, and sometimes shelter in the barn. Sometimes it was an entire family. I watched them approach the house with cautious reluctance, having much respect for the dog and knocking on the door gently, seemingly with reservations.

Mother would answer the door, speak with them, and tell them to wait outside while she prepared homemade-bread sandwiches slathered with homemade butter and thick-sliced chicken or salt pork. This she would place in a brown paper bag with a sealer of milk. Many walked away to consume it elsewhere; others would stop outside the front gate and consume it with gusto right there. When I asked why they did that, I was simply told they were homeless, hungry, and poor. Some faint recollection of those days probably conditioned me to never be homeless, hungry, or poor.

Lest I forget to mention it, before marriage Mother was, at different times, a local telephone operator and a clerk in Blakeley's Grocery, the only grocery store in the village of Thomasburg. Not sure of which order, but the subject did come up at different times during my life at home. It probably also explains why just about everyone I ever met from the Thomasburg vicinity knew her. She knew much about them—very much—and she was respected!

At what age does one begin to remember life's occurrences? Which ones are most often remembered? Do we tend to remember the times of glory and glee and reject the incidents of fear and frustration? Not really! Even during the preschool years, I remember the elation of getting candy from Santa Claus while walking behind a logging sleigh during a Christmas parade. I also remember the opening of Christmas presents that were few.

I have crystal clear memories of fright when being assaulted by a tyrant rooster while playing in the front yard. I still feel the terror of being surrounded by a herd of cows when I tried to cross the barnyard, and the calming relief when the collie dog came and they scattered. I even remember people chuckling in church because my father could blow his nose louder than anybody else.

When we left that farm in 1937, I was but four or five years old. Could such memories still be stored among the treasures of my mind? They are!

For instance, I remember the winter day I had somehow gotten myself into mischief, and Mother was about to do her duty in making me regret it. As she approached me with a flyswatter, which she kept handy even in the dead of winter, I reached for the seldom-used front-door latch and managed to manipulate the snow-encrusted door open. It was cold, and I was ill-dressed for a winter outing, but having no will to face certain discomfort, I jumped headfirst upon my little sled and scooted down the front-yard slope.

I aimed for the gateway to the road, which was, fortunately, open. But steering a sliding sled on icy snow was not a skill I had developed. I hit the gatepost face first. As a result, I lived most of my life with crooked front teeth. In fact, it was not until some sixty years later that I had a bridge with nice straight teeth fitted.

This is one of a multitude of early life lessons I have remembered. Did I learn from it? Naw, not really!

Let me relate a few more memories of life on that farm—and yes, I was still in my preschool years. In fact, that big red rooster occasionally still comes to mind even today when I am enjoying some reflective moments. He either considered me a threat or felt a need to establish a pecking order. If I stayed close to the back woodshed door, he left me alone. He kept his distance from that woodshed, since that is where the dog usually loitered while protecting me at play.

Occasionally, that rooster would spot me when I ventured into the front yard to play, and once, when the distance to the woodshed was too great to escape his wrath, I sought sanctuary in a nearby lilac bush. I was pulling branches in after me, which the rooster was in the process of penetrating, when the dog came to my rescue. I marveled at the influence the dog had on that rooster! I knew then that I would always need a friend, even if only a dog.

Oh yes, the memories are flooding back. For years, my mother had a wonderful time embarrassing my older brother and sister when she gleefully related a story about catching them bathing together in the rain barrel. I was playing nearby at the time and had noticed the structural difference between girls and boys, but at that tender age, I did not get the significance of the situation. But I do remember to this day my sister's embarrassment to the point of tears. New lesson: know what is right or wrong, and don't get caught doing the latter.

I have further memories, like the time my brother fell into the well. Now this was not very funny at the time, but it was one of those accidents waiting to happen. There was no pump on the well, so the household water was dipped from the well with a milk bucket on a rope. To maneuver water into the bucket, boards covering the top of the well were pushed aside.

Big brother Raymond was the appointed water boy, and it was truly just a matter of time. On this occasion, Dad was summoned by the screams of my mother, and together they extracted a very wet, scared, and bruised-up boy from that very cold, hand-dug, stone-walled well.

Apparently, I learned no lesson here. I have had many falls in my life, falls I could have avoided with the application of common sense—a commodity I never developed enough of.

If I may put aside my reminiscing for a moment, I will mention that the Geen name was familiar to the Huntington and Hungerford townships. In fact, on the brow of Gravel Pit Hill was the Geen homestead, the home of Grandfather Albert Geen. I really don't know much about him from my preschool days, since he was a prospector and went for long periods of time to wherever there was a potential for a get-rich-quick gold discovery. He never found any, but he did get to do a lot of traveling.

He was by nature an adventurer, a fortune hunter, and an entrepreneur. In the year 1934, he made one last prospecting trip to Telegraph Creek in British Columbia. He seemed quite sure that there, he would find a mother lode of coveted yellow gold. He never returned, and no one knows exactly when or where his trail ended. So I never really got to know Grandpa.

My father's brother, Uncle Cecil, took over the homestead. He proceeded to make it a going concern even in this serious Depression era. There he made a comfortable home with my Aunt Annie and his two sons: Bobby, my own age, and Stewart, more the age of my sister. I remember them very well.

In my preschool days, I ran away from home with monotonous regularity to play with Bobby and visit Aunt Annie in that huge rambling old house on the brow of Gravel Pit Hill. It even had the luxury of two three-hole outhouses, one of which could be reached from the attached woodshed so one would not have to wade through the deep snow of winter. That was a very welcome convenience. Many rural dwellings had a long path to their only outhouse, which probably accounted for those yellow holes in the snowbanks just outside of their back door.

Aunt Annie always had a good supply of oatmeal cookies and milk. It was at this tender age of innocence that I would climb upon the horse-drawn cheese-factory milk wagon during a summer morning pickup, and the driver would let me ride with him up Gravel Pit Hill to Uncle Cecil's milk stand. Once there, I would navigate my way through high goldenrod weeds in the laneway to the barnyard, toddle across it before the cows spotted me, then run to the house. Aunt Annie always made me welcome. I would spend the morning playing with Bobby, who never spoke a word to anyone except his mother. He and I seemed to communicate perfectly with just one-way dialog, though I am not sure how.

Anyway, I guess this is when I began to understand that to get to the better things of life, one may have to leave home, even if it was only a milk-wagon ride up Gravel Pit Hill. This philosophy I carried forward with me for the rest of my life—and perhaps there was a little bit of Grandpa in my genetic makeup. But let's visit that subject in a later chapter.

Instead, let me speak a bit more of that rambling old house on the brow of the hill. It had a number of sleeping areas, like bedroom suites, and one of them housed dear old Aunt Maud. Neither Bobby nor I was ever permitted to enter her suite. She never spoke, walked about without appearing to see anyone, and never seemed to blink. She could be heard playing the piano in her suite, but no one ever entered to listen. There were many theories as to her illness, but to most people, Aunt Maud was a mystery of which no one spoke.

The house sat on prime farmland and featured a beautiful, mature sugar bush. This stand of hard maple was another source of income for the family. My father and Uncle Cecil together would undertake to tap over a hundred maples.

Now, the making of maple syrup takes energy, much energy, and the energy available was wood. Before the tapping of the maples, my brother Raymond and cousin Stewart waded in the snow to locate and stack wood by the evaporator in preparation for the boiling down of maple sap. It takes about forty gallons of sap to make a gallon of maple syrup. The larger trees would accommodate up to three sap buckets.

In the late winter until spring of each year, they would make their high-quality maple syrup for consumption and sale. Bobby and I were often allowed to ride the sap-collecting sleighs or sit by the roaring fire of the evaporator but were forbidden to venture onto the snow trails. Wolves liked to follow those trails, and although I never saw one during the sugar season, there were precautions. At the end of a long winter, those wolves could be hungry.

Hence, in my primary youth, I understood there were things to fear, and precautions were to be taken. I sometimes didn't do well at grasping the need for caution in the years ahead, but I have been fortunate to survive—so far!

As spring approached and the snow melted, our rubber boots were filled with wet snow, our mittens were wet, our ears and nose got cold, and occasionally there were even some major discomforts—but it was all a part of growing up. Yes, these discomforts came about as we were at play, but make no mistake about it: life is not all cookies and milk. Many times during my life, I have looked back and remembered that truth.

That homestead farm also had a productive apple orchard. Each fall, there was a picking season when wooden bushel baskets and barrels were filled and sold or stored in the root cellar. There was a tree of huge Wolf River apples that would make one pie per apple.

Alas, the Wolf River apples are no more, and many other apple species that were in that orchard—like the Spy, the Snow, and the succulent Tolman Sweets—have also vanished. There have been many new and wonderful botanical developments during my four score and many more years of life, but the sweet fruits of that orchard are still with me. The taste of the apples, cookies, and maple syrup I enjoyed in those childhood years has never faded.

Now back to the foot of the hill! Each time I ran away to Aunt Annie's, I was eventually sent home to the little white house where we lived. The house is long gone, but there are certain things about it that are truly indelible in my mind. They are the black and white memories of things that were, that are not anymore and never will be again.

I want to remember those wide windowsills where I would stand and emulate the Reverend Beazer by shouting a random sermon with no point to anyone in earshot. I remember the bellows organ that sat, seldom played, in the parlor. No instrument today, electronic or otherwise, will ever sound as sweet to me as that wheezy old bellows organ. It was ours. It was a part of my home, part of my childhood.

I also want to always remember my battles with that old red

rooster, and the time I ventured into the barnyard and got surrounded by the giant sniffing and snorting beasts known as cows. The farm dog showed up by my side, and those huge monsters scattered to the far corners of the barnyard.

I am sure it was at this point in my life that I noticed that these great creatures had respect for something about my size. I am further sure that it influenced me to never again be frightened by something just because it was larger than me or outnumbered me.

One last tale of my lingering recollections—a mystery! On the last hay harvest at this farm, I was riding on the toolbox of the horse-drawn hay mower, facing back to where it had been. This was in the field across the road from the house, beyond which was an extensive swamp.

I had been told—nay, warned—many times to never go into that swamp. Now here I was on the back of this hay mower looking directly into this inner sanctum of vine-covered dead trees and moss-covered fallen logs. It did look creepy.

When a cockeye came off a Whipple tree, I had to give up my seat on the toolbox to give Dad access to tools. I could not help but stand and stare directly into that forbidden region. I imagined all kinds of things moving about; all kinds of groans and grunt noises came from those shadowed depths. My only comfort was the dog, who was lying there, tongue hanging out and panting in comfort, between me and that frightening netherworld.

It still sends shivers up my spine even four score and many more years later. What exactly was in that forbidden land? No one ever said!

I will end this chapter of our lives with a sinister tale I have never told. It was in this little white house that we—my older sister and brother and I—slept in the upstairs bedrooms. At the head of the stairs was the first, and turning left through a doorway was the other. Sister slept in the one at the top of the stairs, and Brother and I in the room to the left. My small bed was under the low end of the slanted ceiling. This was the setting of the story I am about to relate.

On an occasion during the last summer in that old white house, Cousin Barbra, about the age of my brother, and Cousin Stewart, about the age of my sister, came for a few days' visit. They were each to share those upstairs beds with an alike-gender cousin.

It didn't happen that way. Peeking from under a blanket and by the light of a coal oil lamp, I saw for the first time that the structural difference between girls and boys was functional.

CHAPTER 3

FAIRY TALES FADE

*Life is not a nursery rhyme. Everyone
will not live happily ever after.*

The year was 1937. Trans Canada Airlines was open for business.
Saskatchewan suffered scorching heat reaching 113°F, and the
rugged Mount Lucania was conquered by Bradford Bates.
Courts in Germany were forbidden to interfere with the activities of
the Gestapo, and 150 leaders of a Catholic youth organization were
arrested for treason. War was looming in Europe.

That year, our family moved from our peaceful little white
house at the base of Gravel Pit Hill to a larger farm with fewer rocks,
better fences, bigger buildings, and many squirrels. Furniture was
moved on a horse-drawn hayrack—two trips. Neighbors assisted in
a cattle drive that herded our stock along the concession roadways,
through the village of Thomasburg past Blakeley's Grocery onto an
unnamed road, then to a side road that led to the Old West Place,
our new home.

There were many more trips to haul farm machinery, a wagonload
of pigs, and several crates of chickens. With the wisdom of my five
years of life experiences, I noticed that I was now in a strange and
seemingly more remote location. The farm buildings faced a side
road—a road that connected two concession roads. There were no

neighbors in sight in any direction. Soon we settled into this big, cold, hollow-sounding and expressionless two-story red brick house.

I felt no remorse in leaving behind the place of my birth, my only known home. I had not developed that emotion. I felt no regrets in leaving the old dog that protected me from the rooster, shooed off those cows that terrorized me in the barnyard, and kept me warm when I went to sleep on the hayloft floor. I never asked why old Buddy didn't come with us and was later told he was dead. I did not comprehend the full meaning of *dead* and was given no further details.

Alas, it was at this Old West Place that a more diverse variety of people came into, and went from, my fledgling life. Some left worthy impressions; some left psychological scars. It was here, over a period of three years, that I took my first infant steps toward maturity, toward the realities of life. I learned to like and dislike. I experienced embarrassment and pain and began to develop emotions.

In this new location, there was, once again, no power, no telephone, no running water or indoor plumbing, and I still shared a room with my big brother, Raymond. Our upstairs room was furnished with a bed and vanity stand, on which sat an earthen washbowl and a water pitcher. There was a night-relief container under the bed we referred to as the "thunder mug."

Our room was positioned over the kitchen, so heat from the winter cookstove would make us comfortable in the cold winters to come. In summer, Mother cooked in the back kitchen, which was an unsecured area and was also the woodshed.

Sister Eva was in the next room upstairs with access to the balcony. I spent many nights in her bed. She liked to cuddle. Raymond did not.

I have previously mentioned my first painful injury when I ran into a gate post on a sled at the old white house. At our new home, I fell off a chicken coop and broke an arm. My father pulled one way to reposition the displacement, a doctor pulled the other. I loudly protested this excruciating pain, using cuss words only the hired man would have used. The doctor laughed; my father did not.

On a second occasion, I was turning a fanning mill without the benefit of the removable crank and ran my little finger between two gears. It was squashed. I carry that scar yet today.

I cried on both of those occasions, but enduring pain from time to time would always to be a part of my life. It was OK to cry, and I did so many times. I still do! Life is not without disappointments and pain.

I also experienced embarrassment. I once found a bottle of Milk of Magnesia. I tasted, I liked, I drank, and I soon experienced an embarrassment you cannot imagine. (Or maybe you can!) I ran to the kitchen and announced to my mother, "I shit my pants!" I need not elaborate on the rest of the story, which ended in a #3 washtub full of cold water in the backyard.

Soon a new pup named Gyppie became a constant friend and guardian. Many people would come and go in my life. Many left memorable impressions, some good, some not, but none more so than Gyppie. He was more than a pet—he was a companion.

Elmer, our hired man, stuttered and liked to playfully tease me. I learned to stutter just like him. When I now look back, I reflect on how Elmer would get his weekly pay after supper on Saturday and head down the side road hill to hitch a ride into Tweed, the nearest town with commerce and nightlife. I sometimes heard him return in the wee hours of the morning and sleep the rest of the night in the machine-shed attic. Sometimes he would be brought home in a car by someone on Sunday.

He once told my brother Raymond that if he sowed his wild oats on Saturday night, he needed go to church on Sunday and pray for a crop failure. I did not understand, but I felt that he must have been a good and thoughtful man.

Elmer sometimes spent Sunday afternoons hunting in the

second growth of woods that had been stripped of timber. One Sunday afternoon, Elmer's brother Bill came calling, and he, Elmer, and Raymond went for a hunt into those woods. In late afternoon, Raymond came running to the house in a panic to announce that Elmer had been shot.

Dad hooked a team to a utility wagon and galloped to the woods. There they found Elmer by an old horse stable left behind by a timber crew. He was weak from loss of blood and in pain and shock. Elmer was brought to the house in the wagon and carted off to the Belleville General Hospital in Dad's Model A Ford. I later learned he had been shot by his brother. I never saw Elmer again.

My father then acquired a new hired man, Gerome. He was on farm labor parole from the county jail and restricted from leaving the farm. I did not like or trust him. He cussed, beat and stoned livestock, and had deplorable table manners.

One time, I was leaning against an inside wall of the barn, fascinated by the huge noisy threshing machine. Wheat grains littered the floor and made it slippery. Gerome approached and kicked my feet out from under me. I fell, was hurt, and cried. Gerome laughed! I kept my distance from him ever after, and I am sure he enjoyed putting fear into me.

Shortly after the threshing incident, Gerome was harrowing a field near the house when the terrorizing scream of an injured horse rent the air. He had somehow made the team fall on the harrows. One horse was injured, while the other thrashed about trying to escape the harness. Dad rushed to the scene, and together they managed to free the uninjured horse. I was sent to the house but heard the gunshot that put the injured horse to sleep.

Gerome was informed that he would be returned to prison the next day, but during the night, he quietly left, taking with him Dad's .38-caliber service revolver. No one ever heard of Gerome again. No one ever cared to.

Time passed, and one day, I and the rest of the family went to Uncle Ed's house across the street from Blakeley's Grocery. Uncle Ed was propped up in bed and obviously not well. While others visited at some length, I bided my time, doing nothing.

Soon I was called to Uncle Ed's bedside and was lifted onto the bed. Uncle Ed hugged me and, with tears in his eyes, uttered words of encouragement that I never remembered. We left. I never saw Uncle Ed again.

More time passed. On September 1, 1939, Canada declared war on Germany. Mother was heavy with a child who would be born a few weeks later. They named him Dale Thomas.

We all gather around our battery-powered Marconi radio after supper and listened intently to progress reports on who would go to war, when, how many, and where. It began to dawn on me that there was life beyond Thomasburg—far beyond. There were trials, tribulations, and tragic events that brought tears and torment to those who understood it. For the first time, I felt saddened by the distress of others. I began to relate to their emotions. I was learning compassion.

On September 11, 1939, I walked to my first day of school with my older brother, Raymond, and sister, Eva. This two-way journey I would tread for the entire school year, through sun, rain, and snow.

When walking home after school, I was unable to keep pace with older students. They left me behind. A fellow classmate of my age, Douglas Fluke, lingered with me. We made it an adventure, walking on rail fences, shooshing sheep in the fields just to see them run, throwing stones at birds, and so forth, often getting home just in time for supper. Our folks never seemed to be concerned.

The school was a two-room red-brick structure with a rope-pull bell on the roof to summon students to class. The teachers, one for each room, were the unquestionable sovereign authorities. We were instructed to refer to my junior room teacher as Miss Huffman, nothing else.

The school had a divided playground, one side for girls, one for boys. Yes, these were the days of gender segregation. There was a water pump at the end of the school where boys and girls could gather and pump water to drink from a tin cup tethered by a chain. If there were too many gathering, Miss Huffman would come and shoo us back to our respective play areas.

Fraternal mingling was not permitted. Who knows what terrible things may have happened if precautions were not taken to keep us minor genders separated! Since we had not yet tasted the fruit of wisdom, what was feared?

Each side of the school had swings and a teeter-totter. The boy's side also had an assortment of fence rails from which the big boys built a range of log structures that were torn down and rebuilt many times over. They also had a soccer ball. Big boys ruled over that activity. My age group was relegated to the swings and teeter-totter, when and if the big boys so permitted. Otherwise, we played tag.

At this two-room school, I played with my cousin Bobby; another cousin, Clair; and many others. Some made it pleasant, some not so much. I could select who I wanted to play with, and they in turn could accept or reject me.

It became evident that I came from a poor, even impoverished home. We were about as poor as any family in the school. While I wore overalls and boots, others wore clothes without patches. They wore leather shoes and had haircuts. It reminded me of a *Grimm's Nursery Rhymes* poem that went something like:

Birds of a feather flock together.

So do pigs and swine.

Rats and mice would have their choice.

And so will I have mine.

At that point in life, I did not even begin to understand where I fit into the social scheme of things. As I matured, I would realize that many of *Grimm's Nursery Rymes* would be prophetic.

I was apparently never to become one of Miss Huffman's favorite students. I was shaken violently from time to time and had my ear painfully pulled on numerous occasions. Once I got the strap for calling her Miss Puffball! She apparently did not have a well-developed sense of humor, and I did little to contribute to it.

My father now bought a much larger farm in a more populated location. Once more we would move, so I never saw or heard of Miss Huffman again. I wonder if, in later years, she ever remembered the little boy who sat outside of the schoolroom door singing "The Bear Came Over the Mountain." (Yes, that was me!)

There were many who attended this quaint little school. Looking back, I remember only a few by name. I do remember the Flukes, Douglas and Lyle, who lived at the end of the unnamed road past the back lane to our house. There was Cousin Bobby, the silent one, who was my guardian on the playground. There was Cousin Clair, who lived near the old white house we previously moved from, and a pretty girl with beautiful brown ringlets called Betty Burley. Yes, I had a crush.

There were other faces I remember, but names no longer come to mind. I only hope they have lived a charmed life, as I have. I have been blessed!

<hr/>

The school year came to an end in the spring of 1940, and we were on our way to our last Sunday picnic at the Flat Rock area on the Moira River. Dad's Model A had unreliable brakes, and the approach to the picnic area was steep, rocky, rutted, and narrow, with thick-growth brush on either side. The descent ended at the base of Flat Rock Falls, the deepest part of the river.

Dad approached at a cautious low speed, but the car quickly sped out of control. He pulled on the emergency break, but it was ineffective, and our speed was increasing. Mother was holding baby Dale and did what only a mother would do. She opened the door and, with baby Dale in her arms, bailed out into the roadside brush.

The car, with the rest of us in it, finally came to rest against a stump by the water. All quickly jumped out to go get Mother, but there she was walking down the hill, carrying baby Dale. They were safe. She was crying.

What exactly did this chapter of my life at the Old West Place do to prepare me for the tempestuous years to come? For the first time, I was touched by emotion. I was exposed to death. I saw cruelty, experienced rejection, received painful punishment from an angry superior, and felt the loving warmth of a dying man.

There was still much to learn and many lessons needed to avoid dangers and to face the inevitable disappointments of life. I somehow sensed there would be victories and defeats in my future. By the grace of God, I was being prepared to accept either, and there have been plenty of both.

At this point of my life, I felt secure and protected by my parents. I had yet to learn that my future was really in the hands of God.

CHAPTER 4

MY EBBING CHILDHOOD

On the road to the land of milk and honey
you may get kicked by a few cows or stung by
a few bees, but the journey will be worth it.

It was 1940, and the J. R. Geen family relocated to its final farm—a farm referred to as the Old Malory Place by the local people. It is a location I still consider to be the launching pad of my life. Here I lived for nine years. Here there was further development of my emotions, my ambitions, my hopes, and my dreams.

Many things that would influence my future began on this farm. It was here that I got my grade-school education, here I became a contributor to family economics, here I learned many facts of life, and here I spent many Sunday afternoons sitting on the hillside in the back pasture watching foxes, woodchucks, squirrels, and chipmunks. This was where I contemplated my future: *Will my older brother, Raymond, inherit the farm? Will I explore the world in search of riches like Grandfather? Will I face a secure but uneventful career working in the Bata shoe factory? Will I be prepared to face whatever life will bring?*

Books I had yet to read would influence my future. Books would convince me that I would strive, and I would succeed. It was in the books!

Over the next eight years, I learned the facts of life by observation. My parents never had to explain about the birds and the bees. I saw reproductive activity in action as I witnessed the breeding of cows and swine, and I often spotted the spontaneous mating of dogs and cats. I was amused at roosters surprising the hens in the chicken yard and once sat on the steps of the milk stand and watched the much-supervised breeding of a mare.

It became evident that one single performance brought about a new life. Only the hired man gave me council on that. "With people," he said, "it is not so," and he gave me some insight on the subject.

On the breeding-of-the-mare episode, Mother had asked Dad, "Did John see that?"

Dad simply said, "Yes."

Mother turned to me and said, "I hope you don't think people do things like that!"

She was right—I already knew that people did it differently.

While I was growing up, the war in Europe was raging, and our troops were facing a well-equipped, well-trained, and highly mobile Nazi army. It had not been going well, and it had a significant cultural, political, and economic effect on our homeland. Our country had gone from the despair of a Depression to a deadly war. I did not understand why it was the responsibility of the British Empire countries to defend Poland, France, Czechoslovakia, and so forth.

On December 7, 1941, Pearl Harbor happened. The vicious Japanese attack on an American territory drew neutral America into war. Their military numbers and manufacturing capacity to produce war machinery, ships, and munitions would turn the tide. Dare we say, at last?

Lawncrest Farm was the most expansive in the immediate

neighborhood. There was a large livestock barn with five second-level haylofts, two machine sheds, a pigsty barn, a henhouse, and a brooder house. Other structures on the farm included a couple of smaller houses for hired help.

The one on the back acreage of the farm had a well and some of the prettiest lilac bushes and spring tulips I had ever seen, but it was going to wrack and ruin. It was never lived in again. The one up the knoll from the back of the barn was a two-story functional structure that was seldom vacant. Some nondescript families of hired hands came and went. The initial family to occupy it was the Escae family.

Obviously, my father needed workers, and there were few, since men were drafted as they came of age or were already on the front lines. Our expanded acreage could not be worked with a team of horses, so the seller left a Cockshut 80 tractor and some machinery behind to get my father started. There was a one-year limit.

Within that year, a used steel-lug Model C Case tractor was purchased, and sufficient machinery to plant and harvest crops. At an auction, Dad bought a huge manure spreader, needed to haul the ever-accumulating piles and spread them on the fields. Brother Raymond was Dad's only help when he was not in school.

We now had electricity and could leave the electric-powered Stewart-Warner radio on for hours at a time. After supper, we listened to the grim news of war, and on Sundays, to comedy programs like *The Charlie McCarthy Show,* Jack Benny, and scary mysteries like *The Inner Sanctum.* Electricity brightened our life—no pun intended—but there were few other comforts.

The huge brick house had thirteen rooms and no plumbing. The uppermost tower room was separated from the lower rooms by a four-foot space that contained mildewed books, mysterious gadgets, and mice. This space was open to the attic of a spooky wraparound veranda, which in turn was accessed from the bedroom next to mine. As I sorted through some stuff left there, I found religious books and others on subjects like how to contact the dead and how to conduct exorcisms. Could mysteries like those of *The Inner Sanctum* be haunting our very home?

———◆•◆•◆———

It was while living on this farm that the family unit began to change. Sister Eva left home to attend business school, went to work in Toronto for a time, then returned to Frankford to work as a teller in a bank. While she had occupied the room beyond the tower room for a period, essentially, that room and the tower room were now empty.

In the meantime, my brother Raymond found employment in Belleville with the Canadian National Railroad. He moved to a boardinghouse near his work, so now I was the sole inhabitant of the second floor. As you may have already surmised, the creaking, cracking, groaning, moaning, and things that go bump in the night made it spooky.

In the year 1944, not sure what month, I came home from school to find my parents not there. The hired man, Clarence Escae, came to the house and informed me they had gone to Belleville General Hospital. Raymond had been involved in a work-related accident. It was serious.

I had dinner with the Escae family that evening and was comforted by Evelyn and Marilyn. After dark, I went back to our spooky, empty house.

Dad came home late and told me of the extent of Ray's injuries. He had two broken legs from a fall. I went to bed and cried.

———◆•◆•◆———

Let me give you some background on a tale that gives me the creeps even today. In the bedroom next to mine was a doorway leading into that veranda attic and hence to that mysterious vacant space between the parlor ceiling and the tower room. A large earthen washbasin had been placed in the center to catch drips off a leaking roof.

Very late one night, I was awakened by the unmistakable sound of someone tripping over that washbasin. No one slept in that room, nor in the tower room beyond, or the room beyond that. In fact, I was the lone inhabitant of the second floor. In terror, I relocated downstairs to spend the rest of the night on the couch, shivering in fear. Next day, I told my parents about it, and they checked. There was no evidence that anything in that room was disturbed.

I knew better.

There were other niches, other attics, and a second-floor tack shop accessed from the woodshed, without a lockable door. A door from my bedroom closet led to that shop with but a simple bolt for security. I make no apologies for the fears the raced through my imagination.

In the parlor, the sellers had left a wall cupboard filled with books – many that I would eventually learn were classics. Those books spoke to me of hopes, dreams, endeavors, and accomplishments that would influence me in the years ahead. Yes, I was encouraged by such authors as Horatio Alger, Harold Bell Wright, Victor Hugo, and Zane Gray. Over the years, I would read them all with great gusto.

Growing up was not an idealistic process for which I had any passion. I did have time to frolic and play, but I also helped with the chores, carried household water from a distant hand-pump well, and fed the hens and pigs. There were ever-increasing responsibilities.

Over a period of eight years, I became strong enough to clean the dairy stables, horse stable, pigsties, and henhouse. I loaded and spread that very same animal waste on the land. There was also planting and harvesting work, which eventually made me a significant part of the family economic survival.

Now let me go back to September 1940, when I went to a new school to pursue my education. Today it would be hard to imagine a school with no football team, no gymnasium, no cafeteria, no assembly hall, no electricity, and no flush toilets. It was a one-room school with a woodshed in back on an acre of land.

The school's well was polluted, so water was carried by pail from a neighbor's well. We all drank from a dipper at the back of the room. A washbasin was available, and a slop bucket to dispose of wash water, but these were used sparingly. No one wanted to go for more water.

This was simply known as S.S. #10 Sidney County School and located on the lower fourth concession road in the Trent River Valley. It was to be a significant part of my childhood and probably was a noteworthy influence on the rest of my life. When I first attended, I was seven years old.

Thus, my journey to adulthood began. On the first day of school, the teacher, Miss Helen Wallis, assigned all students a desk, introduced herself, and distributed the Blue Readers and the spelling and arithmetic books. In this one-room school, grades one through eight were taught simultaneously, with about two to four students in each class.

I would spend six years under the humorless supervision of Miss Wallis. She was well-organized and a dedicated disciplinarian. I, having had no benefit of worthy social guidance, was a free spirit. We were a perfect mismatch from the onset. Obviously, fate had so willed!

Miss Wallis was a conscientious individual and seemed convinced that harsh discipline would correct me. I, on the other hand, never quite understood why I needed correction. This misunderstanding lasted the duration of her reign.

Looking back from where I am now, I truly do sympathize with her. Nobody likes to lose a battle, and I am sure she felt that with me, she did. If she were still with us today, I would be the first to assure her she did not.

Some of our misunderstandings were minor, some not so much so. For instance, there was no rooftop mounted bell with a pull rope here. She just rang a cowbell through an open window. Someone hid it; someone snitched; I was punished.

Once a profane word was written on a fence post in the schoolyard. Someone snitched; I was punished, this time with the strap.

Once I peed out of the gable window of the woodshed. Someone saw me; someone snitched; I was punished by detention.

Once I took all four of the blackboard erasers and arranged them under a stack of books on her desk. She looked for them in drawers, in the wastebasket, in vacant desks, and so forth, becoming more annoyed by the minute. Someone finally pointed to where they were, and she demanded to know who did it. I raised my hand; I was punished.

I could go on, but by now you may have an indication of my relationship with Miss Wallis.

By grade eight, we had a change of teachers. A youngish lady by the name of Wilma Burnt was now in charge. She was fresh from Normal School, and this was her first assignment. By now, I was a teenager, and Miss Burnt and I got along just fine. She did not speak to me as a subordinate but as a real person.

She boarded at a place about halfway between the school and our farm, and when I stayed after school for study or do some catch-up work, she walked with me to her boarding place. We talked about my family, our farm, our neighbors and her hopes and ambitions in life, and of books we had read. I credit her for giving me some form of social confidence. I have given Miss Wallis no credit for that.

Life on the farm was not always just work and school. Above and beyond the relationships with my neighbor friends, there were quiet warm summer Sundays in the back pasture and under the full foliage of the sugar bush. Just me, my .22-caliber Savage rifle, and the dog. At that time, it meant relief from something, I'm not sure what. I just liked to be alone.

I remember it now as being my field of dreams. Have you ever remembered the things that crossed your mind as you lay in a grassy spot and watched the reformation of drifting clouds? Weren't those moments precious?

Speaking of such memories, let me relate to you a story about an annual Christmas-tree hunt. My little brother and I, accompanied by the dog, were dispatched to the woods to find a suitable Christmas tree. On the fringe, we found a fledgling symmetric spruce with thick green healthy foliage. Perfect!

For a time, we stood and watched the chickadees flutter in and about its snowy branches. Snow tracks revealed that cottontails had sheltered under the low hanging ones. We discussed the many tall spruces that boarded our living complex. Would anyone miss a six- or seven-foot top? We left the woods without a tree.

Back at the house, we managed, undetected, to decapitate one of those stately spruces that bordered our lower garden plot and hauled it into the house. With much acclaim, it was erected in the parlor and decorated. We had our Christmas tree.

Some fourscore years have passed, and I still wonder if there now stands in that woodlot a majestic spruce that provides shade and shelter for partridges, chickadees, squirrels, raccoons, porcupines, and so on. I will always believe that God willed us to spare that tree.

Many hours I spent hypnotically steering a tractor back and forth across fields, pulling ground-preparation machinery. The serenity of daydreams overcame the offensive inhaling of exhaust fumes. There were brief refueling breaks, essential nature breaks, and drinking from a sealer of warm water—or a cool creek if nearby.

There was satisfaction in well-turned sod that would produce the next crop. The farm dog dutifully followed in the furrows of the plough, and gulls lined up after the dog passed to devour exposed grubs. Life has patterns. All have a purpose. I was still contemplating mine.

Church on Sunday was a regular duty in the first few years on Lawncrest Farm, but as I matured, I began to successfully resist the weekly ritual. I preferred to stay home and rest, hunt, weed the garden, or read. While my mother encouraged the reading of the Bible, I somehow preferred a Zane Gray book. My relationship with God was mutable, a fact that I kept to myself but shared with you previously.

On May 8, 1945, and thereafter, we would look upon life with a different attitude. The war in Europe ended. We could buy tires for the truck and car. Gasoline was no longer rationed, and food-rationing books were thrown away. In Frankford, car horns were blown incisively, and there was dancing in the streets. The heroic Johnnys would come marching home. Life would once again be good.

After those war years, Dad and some of his cronies took up fall hunting in the vast forests of the North Country—like north of Highway 7 near Marmora and Madoc, Ontario. This brought him much pleasure. He would buy a bottle or two of good rye whiskey, a new pack of playing cards, tobacco, and a pipe. Mother packed up a week's food and some warm bedding that pretty much filled the back of his 1933 straight-eight Pontiac, and off he went to the hunting camp. That was his reward for a hard summer of work. It was the happiest I had ever seen him.

At this point in time, Dad and I would occasionally spend an evening fishing in the nearby Trent River. It was a short drive and a short walk across someone's pasture to the river, where we caught northern pike, bass, and suckers aplenty, as well as a few lunges and channel catfish. The catch was not the highlight of the occasion but listening to Dad's life experiences.

He once related to me how he rode in a cattle car loaded with farm machinery when his family moved from Orillia Ontario to Tweed. It was the year his dad established the Geen homestead at Thomasburg. Apparently, he had barely taken enough food and water with him and faced hunger. He could not get out of that cattle car until someone opened it from the outside and was almost caught on one occasion when a railroad worker saw a suspicious leak from the cattle car, and there were no cattle on board. When you got to go, you got to go!

That reminds me of another of his stories. A few years back, when we still had the Model A Ford, he was taking a urine sample to the doctor in a whiskey bottle. It was left on the front seat while he went into a store. When he came out, the bottle was gone. We had some laughs speculating on the thief's probable experience.

As we sat by that wide quiet river, a part of the Trent Canal system, we would watch an occasional pleasure boat cruise past. On board were people of wealth, people who may have purchased the products of our farm. They often waved and watched us fish. Where they came from, we didn't know, or where they went to, but on they go!

Dad loved to fish and hunt. In the years far ahead, the opening of bass season became our weekend together on a remote lake near Brockville, Ontario. They were precious days. I will bring that subject up after a while.

The war was over. Dad's farm was prospering. My brother Raymond was now married and the owner of a pool hall in Oshawa, Ontario. My sister Eva was also now married and working at a bank in Frankford.

It was 1947, life was good, and my future remained in the hands of me and God.

CHAPTER 5

NEXT-DOOR NEIGHBORS

Home is where you live among friends and
neighbors are made welcome at your door.

When I was a child, I had the wisdom of a child, the reasoning of a child, and the confidence of a child. It did not occur to me that one day, I would cease to be a child.

After sharing much background on the places from whence I came, I will now share some of my experiences with people. School brought new faces into my life; some I embrace in memory to this day. I will introduce a few.

I didn't get to know our close-by neighbors prior to starting school. Soon after arriving at this farm, my mother, of Northern Irish descent, took me aside one day and, placing a hand by the side of her mouth as if to deflect her message from unwanted ears, whispered, "They are Catholic." With this information available, I made no effort to befriend them.

I wasn't quite sure what a Catholic was, and I was puzzled when I found they didn't seem any different. They lived just a couple of stone's throws down and across the road, and in the years ahead, I spent much time coming and going into and out of their house, like I was family.

The Melvihall's were dairy farmers. Jim, the head of household, was a short, stocky man of few words. His tall slim spouse, Elizabeth, spoke impeccable English and fluent French but could neither read nor write. I can still hear her musical voice telling me to "get in here and close that door" when I came to play. She had a cheerful smile for everyone.

I could easily relate to this family since they obviously were as poor as us. They had but a few toys and wore work boots and overalls like me. Their eldest son, Frances—my age and in my grade at school—became a friend. He was born with one short leg and wore an elevated sole boot to compensate. I pretended not to notice.

Frances considered himself a person of strength, one who played to win or didn't play at all. Frances could throw a baseball farther than me, hit that ball farther than I could, and perform other feats of strength greater than I. I learned to give him no reason to ever doubt it. If there were to come a time of conflict, I wanted him on my side.

Katherine was one grade behind me in school. Over the years, she developed from a pretty schoolgirl into a beautiful and curvaceous young lady with flowing dark hair.

Her younger brother, Tommy, at this time had yet to start school but would become a fringe-zone playmate. He was always around. He had flaming red hair like his dad, as did his brothers. Tommy was a quiet person and a brilliant scholar.

Walking to school with the Melvihall children became a seven-year routine. In the morning, I simply walked into their dimly lit kitchen like I lived there and waited while they donned their boots, jackets, book bags, and such. Their kitchen area was dark and cluttered. It featured a wood-burning cookstove, a sturdy family table, chairs, and a fold-down daybed couch. Over the years, this changed very little.

During that first winter the snow was deep, and Frances insisted on breaking a path through the banks. He was more macho than I, but he did permit me to be next, followed by Kate and, in later years, Tommy. A level of rank was established.

Once at school, we and other arrivals gathered in our respective boy/girl entry rooms, where boots were removed and snow dumped out. When our coats were hung, we entered the classroom to gather around the woodburning furnace. Eventually, as the room warmed up, Miss Wallis called "Class," and we made our way to our desks.

I clearly remember when the Melvihalls installed electricity in their house, barn, and drive shed. During the process, I followed the electricians at work and often was sent to fetch tools for them. I envied them their skills. It may even have influenced my future.

Years passed. I developed a mutual affection with Kate, and on some winter afternoons after class, we would stay behind to sleigh-ride down a hill by the school. I rode my little sled face down, and Kate would position herself face down on my back and hang on as we whizzed gleefully down that icy slope. A warmth came through her winter-clothed body and from her breath. I grew fond of her closeness.

As we walked home from school, Kate and I would often linger behind the others and discuss personal things. For instance, she thought it important that I know that during the cold winter, she wore those elastic-leg bloomers for warmth. In spring, she switched to more skimpy panties, and during the hot summer, there was no need for either.

This was common practice when girls wore mid-calf dresses, and I could have told her I already knew. In fact, I had pretended not to look as she sat on the kitchen couch pulling on snow pants and goulashes, tucking stocking tops into personal dainties, and buckling shoes. I think she pretended I wasn't watching.

One cool spring Saturday, I climbed the ladder to a half-empty hayloft in their barn and hollered to her, "Come on up and play." As she did so, I scaled the ladder at the back of the mow and stepped onto an outside support beam. She was looking around, puzzled, and could not see me against sunlight glaring through spaces between the boards behind me.

She called out, "Where are you?"

I uttered a sound but stood still. She could not locate the sound and was patrolling the edges of the mow, thinking I had covered myself with hay.

When she was close beneath me, I jumped, landing close behind her, grabbing her around the upper legs as we fell. She uttered a brief yelp in momentary panic, but when calmness prevailed, I was lying on her, our faces close.

For a fleeting moment, we locked eyes in a blank expressionless gaze. A curious feeling came over me. I rolled off and lay close beside her. We began to laugh.

Kate took this opportunity to tell me about entering the dairy stable one day as the hired man was relieving himself in the gutter. She laughed as she told me that he just said, "Don't look," finished, calmly tucked himself away, turned his back, and buttoned up his fly. She proceeded to graphically describe exactly what she had seen, and in surprising detail. We laughed.

She asked, "Have any girls ever seen your thing?"

I was embarrassed. We had touched on gender topics before, but not this personal. For once, I felt awkward.

———◆·◈·◆———

More years passed, and our relationship matured as we began to develop and further discuss life interests. Kate had been sheltered from the facts of life. I once explained to her in some detail how cows, swine, dogs, and even chickens mated, and why. She listened attentively to my account of the procedures and, with a shy sideways glance, said, "I would like to see that."

That opportunity did present itself one day when I spotted her dad's breed bull in the stockyard behind their barn. Together we sneaked unnoticed into a machine shed from where we watched Frances and his dad heard two cows into that yard and got bred.

We said little at the time, but in the days ahead, we speculated on people's positions, feelings, frequencies, and related theories and conjectures. We even exchanged stories on the squeaky bedsprings and giggles we heard from our parents' bedrooms in the dead of night and laughingly guessed what they were probably doing. I also told her what I had learned from older siblings, and together we snickered about our developing knowledge on the subject.

Adjoining our farm and across from, and a short distance beyond Jim Melvihall's place, was the Leo Melvihall farm. He and spouse Louella had but one child, Marilyn. Leo was younger than his brother Jim, and he was muscular and handsome. Louella was extensively overweight and a recluse. As we walked home from school, she could hardly hide her bulk while peeking at us around the corner of their two-story shoebox house.

Marilyn, a couple years younger than I, walked with our school group, but we seldom conversed. She was chubby. She sucked her thumb incessantly and was pestered mercilessly by many students at the school. She was ill-treated by the teacher, and her hygiene practices were questionable. She also had long, flowing, silk-like blond hair that fell carelessly over her face, and she could sing like an angel. A true anomaly. She was, in her own way, just one of us.

And more years passed. Marilyn was never much of a factor in my day-to-day life until early one morning when I was reinforcing a wire gate in the back pasture. It was breeding season, and the bull would be running with the cows. Our bull had a reputation of walking through fences to visit other pastures, so one cool morning I was sent to the back pasture to reinforce that gate. I wore a warm Mackinaw coat and carried tools and wire.

As I was finishing the task, I heard singing in the distance. It was Marilyn, perched on the stone fence at the back of her father's farm. I waved to get her attention, and she acknowledged. When I motioned for her to come on over, she walked along the armpit-deep wheat to join me. As I helped her to the top of the combination stone-and-rail fence, her silky dress floated in the breeze and exposed her well-developed inner thighs. I noticed!

I bade her sit on the top cedar rail, then nestled by those legs as I sat myself on a lower base. At my request, she sang "You Are My Sunshine" many times over. I eased my arm around her lower legs and stroked them as she was singing. She took no notice. A sensation I was not familiar with washed over me. I was emboldened.

One of the dairy cattle attracted by her singing was hesitantly approaching, followed by the bull. I encouraged her to keep singing, with assurance that the dog would not let them get close. They got very close! At this point, the dog gave a warning growl, and the cow took a step back and turned sideways to our position. The bull took this opportunity to perform.

Now, Marilyn had never witnessed the like before. She grabbed my arm and with concern in her voice asked, "Is the cow being hurt?"

I graphically explained that the two were meant to fit, and it was fun, not hurt. When the bull backed off, there followed a discussion of our own endowments and the significance of our pubic hair.

Soon we were climbing down the fence to the corner of her father's wheat field. I spread my Mackinaw jacket on the soft grass, and, after some appropriate removal of garments, we enjoyed a few delightful moments of amusing show and tell.

Marilyn had but a little peach-like fuzz to show but, with some coaxing, she lay back on my Mackinaw jacket and allowed me to make some clumsy fitting efforts. At first, it was kind of like trying to push a marshmallow into a piggy bank, but as I grew firm, she did some steering with her fingers, and a warm insertion happened.

With a few gliding shoves, I experienced an intense wave of

feelings, then a sudden thrill sensation like an electric current passing through a nerve. I had achieved my first ever coital success.

Along about 1942 or '43, a new Melvihall was born to the Jim Melvihall family. Kate now had a little brother named Robert. As Robert grew from baby to toddler, Kate would often babysit while the rest of the family went Saturday-night shopping. As soon as she lured Robert to sleep, she generated two short *dings* on the magneto party line to alert me to come visit and spend time with her. We experienced many warm and loving intimate moments on that kitchen daybed. We were growing up.

I have never heard from Kate since those days. Life went on, and I eventually left the farm to make my mark on the world.

I would see Frances only once more, at my father's funeral in Bellville, Ontario. That was 1993. The rest of the family I totally lost track of. They are a major part of my fond school-day memories.

Looking back, do I feel remorse for the childhood transgressions I have revealed? Should I feel guilty? Should I repent?

I did not unduly entice my young playmates to share in our carnal development. It was mutual enjoyment and driven by the God-given instinct of species survival. That instinct exists in every surviving species.

The Melvihalls left a lasting influence on my life. During the grade-school years, we grew from innocent infants to insightful adolescents. We prepared ourselves to be more than huers of wood and carriers of water. We were destined to be more than the proverbial fig tree in the vineyard. (Luke 13:7).

Who was to judge, except me and God?

CHAPTER 6

OUR OTHER NEIGHBORS

In life there are choices—options that,
good or bad, affect us only.

B ack to the war years. During this time, a couple of unsuitable farm-help families came and went from the house on the knoll. They were little more than drifters. The war was still in progress, and farm help was still scarce. Brother Raymond and some sporadic day laborers was all my dad had in those early years on Lawncrest Farm.

In the summer of 1944, Clarence Escae and family settled in and remained employed for a couple of years. Their family— Marilyn, a year younger than me, and Evelyn, a year older—became playfellows, while a younger brother, Douglas, tagged along.

These were not fragile or delicate little girls. We played rough and tumble in the barns and the stables, and we roamed the pasture hills and valleys of the farm. Evelyn and Marilyn liked to demonstrate how they could fearlessly make daring jumps from a hayloft beam into a well-packed hay mow. Their skirts bellowed outward on the downward trip, with dignity being timidly restored after impact, along with much laughter and a pretense of coyness. I took obvious delight in watching, and they never got tired of performing.

I somehow felt that there was much mutual enjoyment in this

play, and much mutual fascination. Once when we played hide and seek in that spacious barn, Evelyn and I hid in a hollow space that was formed under a beam between two mows of hay. It was a tight squeeze as we lay there together, breathing in synchronous silence.

Marilyn and Douglas finally grew frustrated in their futile search to find us and decided that we must have snuck away. They abandoned the search and left the barn. Evelyn and I had exchanged some touchy play under that beam, and we came out of our hiding hollow better acquainted.

On other occasions, we cavorted, tumbled, and huddled together in play on the stock-bedding wheat straw in the lower-level stables. During birthing season in late winter, when I was assigned to overnight care of newborn calves, either Evelyn or Marilyn, or sometimes both, would share a blanket with me as we lay on a heavy buffalo robe placed on this soft, comfortable wheat straw. We were just kids easing our way into maturity. Neither their parents nor mine ever questioned our activities during these nights.

Clarence Escae and family were the typical farm laborers of the time: poor, but living in hope that prosperity would materialize when God so willed. During their tenure on the Lawncrest Farm, they had a house to live in, were treated with respect, and lived in harmony with our family. They were happy to be there.

One day, Clarence approached my dad and sadly said he would have to leave. His brother had taken his own life, and Clarence felt obligated to take care of the widow's farm in the Oak Lake vicinity, about five miles away. It was 1946. I lost touch with his children ever after.

I have mentioned a few people who were a part of my life during the impressionable grade-school years—the ones who lived close by and were probably the most influential in these developing years. I will add one more to this group for the time being.

Further up the road lived another student of the S.S. #10 school, Bobby Burkett. His father, George, and mother, Bess, were thriving farmers. Their home was large, with a tastefully landscaped brick house, a painted red barn, and matching multicar garage. They projected the perfect picture of prosperity and boarded the schoolteacher, Miss Wallis.

Bobby was one grade behind me. He also was the best-dressed student in the school and had all the latest toys and sports paraphernalia. I sometimes played in his barn, rode his pony, visited his pup tent, skated on their farm pond, and envied his late-model lever-action .22-caliber rifle, but our friendship was not close.

I did attend a year of high school with Bobby in Belleville, Ontario, years 1948–49. We were in the same home classroom but did not share time together outside of class. I played pool and sometimes skipped afternoon class to attend a movie and such. He did not.

———◆◆◆◆———

There were other friends and other adventures that came and went while I was attending the S.S. #10 school. The last I will mention is the family of our hired man, Mr. Bill Tomkins. The Tompkins family moved into the house on the knoll in 1947. He had a family of two boys—Delbert, a year younger than I, and Keith, a year older—and a girl, Della, about three years my junior, slim, blond, and beautiful.

Della pretty much kept to herself, but I knocked about quite a bit with the boys, who introduced me to tobacco, to which I would become addicted, and beer, for which I developed an insalubrious liking. They had little other impact and left no further scars on my life.

Keith would eventually become a professional wrestler, and "Dub" faded into the vapor of time. I lost touch with the boys when I left the farm to live with my parents in Stirling.

After Dad's heart attack in 1947, my brother Raymond took care of the farm for a couple of crops while Dad went to Stirling, Ontario, to run Ray's failing taxi business. (All of Ray's businesses tended to fail.) I stayed on the farm with Ray, attended high school in Frankford for a year, and failed. Ray's farming skills were not up to survival, so the farm was sold and all machinery liquidated by auction in the fall of 1948.

I sadly watched the selling of the tractors and machinery I had worked with day-in and day-out. I watched the selling of horses I had ridden and cattle I had rounded up, milked, and fed. I marveled at the unreasonably high bidding on our commercial cider press and saw the tools and gadgets I had handled, cuddled, and cussed go away to the highest bidder, to be seen no more.

The numbing reality of no return dawned upon me. That night, in my little upstairs room in Stirling, I sobbed myself into a fitful sleep. I loved that farm. There comes a time when one can't go back from where you are to where you would like to be.

The Tompkins family continued to live in the house on the knoll for many years after the farm was sold. After leaving the farm, I often danced with Della at the Walbridge Saturday night barn dances, and would have liked to pursue a much closer relationship, but it never worked out. I would shortly leave home and leave my junior years behind. I will always wonder whatever became of the beautiful Della.

There were many others who attended this little school. All were good Christian people who came into my life when I came to the community and who were soon out of mind when I left. Some have become faces without names; some are names without faces. All probably left some impact on me in some way. Dare I wonder, did I leave any impact upon them?

In 1948, I elected to attend a two-year vocational course at the Belleville Collegiate Institute and Vocational School and did rather well in my first year. Going back for the second year, I exercised some very bad judgment and, after a few weeks, quit. My reasoning was that a person needs to work for a living, and a person does not need an education to work.

It is said, "By the sweat of thy brow shalt thou eat bread" (Genesis 3:19).

CHAPTER 7

MY TIME OF DECISION

*Home is where you go for asylum when
rejected by the rest of the world.*

It was 1949. I was now living in Stirling with my aging parents, and I spent the summer working at odd jobs. When September came, I commuted to the Belleville Collegiate Institute and Vocational School with a radio and television sales and repair shop owner named Harry Hutchinson. I was never very enthused about education. Most people I knew either worked on farms, in auto repair shops, or at the Bata shoe factory.

After class, I had the luxury of watching TV in Harry's shop until five o'clock closing time. The miracle of black and white pictures being transmitted by air to screens that measured up to twelve inches diagonally was a miracle that intrigued me. I had hopes of one day even owning one! His shop closed on Wednesday afternoons, so I simply hitchhiked home. I was picked up by the same people on multiple occasions.

Many courses I selected in the colligate institute were beneficial. There was motor mechanics, small engine repair, woodworking, and machine-shop training as well as agriculture economics and animal husbandry. These were skills one could use to make a living. Then there were mandatory classes where we learned to conjugate verbs and analyze Shakespeare plays and poems, for which I could see no practical need. I had to read and summarize books like *A Tale of Two Cities* by Charles Dickens. Not nearly as intriguing as *God's Little Acre* or *Tobacco Road* by Erskine Caldwell. What reading, writing, and arithmetic I already had I deemed sufficient.

One day, I bundled up my books and took them home. The rest of the winter, I had a job cleaning and repainting a fire-damaged auto-repair shop. In the spring, I worked for Earl Fox, doing farm work and delivering coal for his fuel-supply business. In the evenings and on weekends, I drove my father's taxi.

In the summer months, I spent whatever time I could relaxing at Sorrel's Beach or Bird's Beach on nearby Oak Lake. The Saturday barn dances at Wallbridge provided some additional recreation, and I spent other evenings at the Joe Whitehead Restaurant (Joe's) playing the nickelodeon, drinking Stubby Cola, reading unpaid-for comic books, and hanging out with the idle youth of the town. I was good at that!

Stirling seemed to be kind of a coming-home town, a place where many of my mother's kin lived. In past years, we had visited my grandparents there, as well as aunts, uncles, and so forth. For instance, Uncle Bill Bolete was a plumber, Uncle Harry Frances owned a haberdasher shop, Cousin Don Frances ran a Sunoco gas station/repair shop, and his sister Shirley lived with her parents in perpetual recovery from tuberculosis.

This beautiful town of old and elegant residences reflected past prosperity as it nestled at the foot of the Oak Hills range. Rodin Creek ambled into the center of town, where a dam created a picturesque mill pond. The base of the dam denied the spring migrating fish their upstream spawning benefits. Downstream from the dam, the river wound through fields behind Uncle Bill Bolete's house. Cousin Ann often came with me when I went there to fish and swim.

Stirling was the center of a thriving dairy community. I soon made new acquaintances and made myself at home in the upstairs bedroom of my parents' abode.

Dad's taxi service was conducted from the house, a few blocks from downtown on Main Street. On Saturday and Sunday afternoons, I would sit and listen to the car radio in front of the house, and boys and girls my own age would stop to talk. Young ladies often came in pairs and threesomes, piled into the taxi, and I took them for a drive up and down Main Street. They liked to go past Joe's, the favorite hangout for indolent youth, and they waved from the window with that *look at me* plea. Apparently, there was some sort of prestige in riding around town with the local taxi driver.

A young lady I took a liking to was the daughter of my boss, Earl Fox. Elinor was a petite, slim, trim beauty who I was fond of, but since she was Earl's daughter, I did not make my feelings known. Before long, that slim, trim waistline began to grow, and soon Elinor left school to "help a relative in Toronto." She never returned home while I was in Stirling.

I also took a shine to party girl Muriel Devolan. I even took her to a picture show once. Then she paired up with some guy from Frankford. I lost again.

Another young lady, Marie Montgomery, caught my fancy. Marie was fun, but noncommittal. She dated whom she pleased, and there were many whom she pleased.

Another young lady named Mable Scenea took a shine to me and made it quite apparent. But alas, she was the chosen interest of a good buddy of mine. I guess you get the picture. My romantic endeavors were meeting with little success.

------◆•◆◆◆•◆------

Speaking of romantic endeavors, my mother's sister, Aunt Helen, lived on the knoll on the street behind us overlooking our garden. She often visited with Mother along with her daughter, Ann. Now, Cousin Ann had a childish beauty beyond her years. She had long flaxen blond hair, and her body was in the early stages of curvaceous development. Ann made her attraction to me apparent.

Ann and I were often encouraged to make ourselves scarce while our mothers talked of family affairs, and a couple of times, I took her to a movie. She held my hand and walked close on the way to the theater, and she held my hand during the show and on the way home. I hoped none of my friends noticed.

One evening, we were simply told to go upstairs and play. Now by *play*, they probably meant board games or cards. Once upstairs, however, Ann did not have board games or cards in mind. She became very close. She hugged me, pressed herself against me, and eventually led me to the bed and lay down.

I sat on the edge of that bed, placed my hand on her midsection, and could not help but admire her every feature. She placed her hands over my hand and laughed as she began a gentle massage on her body. She pulled her knees up and let her silky dress expose her entire upper legs.

Nothing good could come from this. Ann was three years my junior, she was my cousin, she was extremely vulnerable, she was fourteen years old, and our mothers were just downstairs talking. I reluctantly exercised some conscionable common sense.

"Ann," I said. "We can't do this."

She simply said "Why?"

I just replied, "We can't," and pulled away.

Let me digress. We are all born with the God-given instinct to obey Geneses 1:28: *be fruitful, go forth, and multiply.* God put no age parameters on that message. Let us not forget that the mother of Jesus gave birth at the age of fourteen. Parents often seem oblivious to the bloom of early maturity.

Paul Wannamaker came to live with his grandparents in Stirling. He was apparently being sheltered from a shotgun threat by some young lady's father in Alberta. I met Paul at Joe's, and we became friends. He was a couple years older than me, personable and handsome. I had access to a car; he didn't. He had an ability to attract the admiration of girls; I didn't. It was apparent that we had mutual needs.

Paul soon was dating the most beautiful girl in town, Sharleen Eaton. While he was in the back seat romancing with her, I was privileged to share the front seat with Sharleen's friend Betty Cook, who was not amongst the town trophies. We attended dances, drove the back roads, parked in the picturesque Oak Hills, swam at the Oak Lake beaches, and waded by moonlight in the shallow waters on the flat rocks of the Moira River. We had a summer of fun.

A few years later, I heard that Paul had joined the Royal Canadian Mounted Police and was shot and killed in a highway incident in Alberta.

Driving nighttime taxi exposed me to the covert lives of some of our townsfolk. In many cases, I saw and heard things I kept between me and God. I could have written a book that rivaled *Peyton Place* (by Grace Metalious—it sold 60,000 copies). From time to time, I listened to confessions of successful lovers, and those of the discarded loved. I absolved them of their sins. I was the psychological consultant who soothed their troubled minds and was myself subjected to investigative questioning by suspicious parents and spouses.

A taxicab can also take on a romantic aura, like in the movie *The Yellow Rolls-Royce*, although I never benefited from that. The townsfolk who subscribed to our services trusted in my discretion, and on a few occasions, demanded it. Thus, at this impressionable age, I was introduced to community realities.

Stirling is where my parents, sister, brother, and some nieces and nephews would eventually be buried. I kept in touch with Eva, who lived out her life in nearby Frankford. She kept me posted on who became what and went where. Many of my friends never made their escape from Stirling.

There was a world somewhere beyond the horizons of Stirling that called to me. I had illusions of doing things I had read about in books like *Toby Tyler*, by James O. Kaler, and *Never Love a Stranger*, by Harold Robbins. I also craved to prosper like the characters of Horatio Alger's *Strive and Succeed* books.

I had not yet been farther from home than Belleville.

At this point, I felt I was owed a life of some significance, and some choices about my future were due to be made. Would I go seek the fortunes of life or go to work in the Bata shoe factory?

When a choice is made, it becomes a decision. Decisions exclude further options. Only I would experience the results.

My affectionate, if somewhat chaste, relations with the folks of Stirling were about to end. I would soon leave this episode of my life behind forever to seek opportunity and prosperity.

So, I have come down to rescue them from the
hand of their captors and to bring them up out of
that land into a good and spacious land, a land
flowing with milk and honey - Exodus 3:8

CHAPTER 8

THE HARVEST EXCURSION

Grow where you are planted vs.
Go where you can grow!

I t was the late summer of 1950. I signed on to a harvest excursion to western Canada to reap and thrash the record wheat crop. Harvesting was something I could do. Somewhere out there in the yet unknown, there was the presumed promise of prosperity.

I had neither career plans nor thoughts of future needs or challenges. At the age of seventeen, with the hesitant blessing of my parents, I boarded a train in Stirling, Ontario, with twenty dollars in my pocket, a lunch, and an abundance of confidence. Thus, the uncharted path of my career was launched.

There was a train change in Toronto. The enormity of Union Station was awe-inspiring, and I was mesmerized by the streaming crowds who seemed to know exactly where they were going. I didn't! I lugged my old and well-worn suitcase packed with work clothes and a lunch and carried my coat into the terminal to find ticket wicket number seven, the CPR connection that was to carry me away.

After a cold and drafty hour of waiting, I trudged back to the boarding platforms and was herded into a passenger car packed full of other harvest excursionists. Many were in groups, and all were obviously more adult than me. I found a seat with two cheerful strangers, Carl and Jim, both a few years my senior. They regarded my slim and youthful stature and asked, "Why are you going on this excursion? Are you finished with school?"

I began to feel out of place but told them a bit about myself as the coal-burning locomotive blew two fierce blasts on the steam whistle, lunged a couple of times, then settled down to a steady chug-chug pull, and the journey to an uncertain future began. I would never again return to live in the quiet little town of Stirling, Ontario, Canada.

During the two-day trip, Carl and Jim sensed my lack of worldly knowledge and gave me valuable guidance. They had been here before and related as to how they were made welcome in some great houses with modern conveniences and comforts, while some were primitive structures with outhouses and few modern conveniences beyond electricity. The farmers paid in cash, fed the harvesters well, and were grateful for the much-needed help. I felt reassured.

For many, this would be a two-day party. For me, it was an experience of declining confidence. I ate little, drank little, and slept little. The train passed through cities, towns, graveyards, and junkyards. There were backyard clotheslines of humble homes and a scattering of rural farmhouses. Soon we were leaving industrial Canada behind.

As evening approached and the train moved on, the coach cars of harvesters came more and more to life. The three-person-wide passenger seats were on swivels and could be turned to face the seats behind. There was much swiveling as social cliques developed.

Someone discovered a closet of portable tables to secure between these facing seats, and a pandemonium rush to secure what there was erupted. There were tussles, cussing, pushing, and a few slaps as the strong laid claim to what tables there were. Card games broke out, harmonicas wailed, there was off-key singing, laughter, and the sound of long-neck beer bottles being popped open. This went on into the night.

Across the aisle from me, a four-player poker game was in progress. Cards were dealt and money exchanged hands, with some occasional hoots of joy as a pot was claimed. Late into the night, one very disconsolate soul had lost his pocket money. Every penny! As he slumped up against the far window, hand on his forehead, looking down at nothing and sobbing, I felt a little more secure with twenty dollars still in my pocket.

By moonlight, we could see swamps and sloughs and forests where deer, elk, moose, and carnivorous creatures watched the train go by. It was the vast living muskeg and wilderness of Northern Ontario.

Soon, we emerged from wooded rock-lands and remote lakes and started crossing the flatlands of wheat country. Tall castle-like grain elevators rose from the black earth. A skinny power line crossed our path from time to time and followed a narrow line to infinity. There were fewer deciduous trees and more coniferous clusters surrounding dwellings. (The patriotic song "The Maple Leaf Forever" was not written about Manitoba.)

I gazed in amazement at the expansive fields of grain. Some were being swathed, some were being bindered and sheaved, and others were already stooked and awaiting the threshing machine. I pictured myself out there loading a hayrack, pitching sheaves onto a thrashing feeder, and earning money. I felt confident that a life of independent living was at hand. Manitoba is where I would launch my future. Life was good.

———

Upon arrival in Winnipeg there was evidence of the devastating spring flood. As I gazed from my window, scars from the damage were evident. Flooded houses and commercial buildings had been bulldozed and awaited disposal. Flooded vehicles were packed and stacked on vacant lots, and new street and road construction was still in progress.

With grinding brakes and puffs of steam, the train eased into the CPR station, where we disembarked, were documented, and were ushered onto buses. The excursion director was the last on board as we began moving to farm communities in the immense southern plains of Manitoba. Never had I seen land so flat and extending so far. Here on these vast black loam prairies, we would be paid to harvest that bumper crop of wheat. My search for fortune was at hand. Confidence was easing back into my persona.

There were many stops, and at each, an agriculture representative awaited. As we piled off the bus, we were regarded as commodities. Selections were made and documented. The remainder of us returned to the bus and moved on.

Eventually, in the fading light of late afternoon, we arrived at the last stop: Piolet Mound. I noted that the sunset occurred late here. Yes, we were now north of the 49th parallel where long summer days and short nights are the constant.

The evening chill of late summer had already set in as the last of the group lined up for selection. An individual named Chester Wheeler and I were the last to be chosen. We were hauled to a spacious homestead dwelling, introduced to the family, fed a hot meal, and herded into the bedroom we would be sharing.

Piolet Mound was an unincorporated village situated on a featureless, flat, windblown prairie of black earth in Southern Manitoba. It was a land of wheat. The town was so named from a mound of land that broke the monotony of a straight-line horizon, assuming you were not far away from it. Grain trains ran nearby to carry their products, almost exclusively wheat, to the markets of the world.

The population was but a few hundred, and legend had it that every time someone was born in Piolet Mound, someone else left town. The rainy season was typically September, so our objective was to get the crops off with all expedience. Time was of the essence.

Regrettably, I do not remember the names of this employer/host. They were a middle-aged couple with a daughter, Rose, who was a high school senior. They were of stout Mennonite stock—tough and determined people who had experienced years of poor to miserable crops. This was the one they had prayed for. This was the one that would clear their debts. Chester and I, two high school dropouts, were their God-sent help. (Sometimes faith in God is difficult to explain.)

————————◆•◈•◆————————

It was daybreak Tuesday morning when Chester and I and a couple of local persons were assigned to be hayrack drivers. That meant we were the ones who harnessed the horses and hooked them to the hayracks while the threshing crew aligned the tractor drive belt to the thrashing machine. Shaft bearings were greased, wheels blocked, driving chains and V-belt pulleys checked and adjusted, fan openings set, loading augers positioned, and grain carrier wagons maneuvered into place, and soon the whirling, shaking, clicking, and clanking machine responded to the grumble of the powering tractor. We were harvesting!

It was quite clear that when a hayrack was unloaded, the next one was to be ready and waiting. Production was crucial. At first, the sheaves misted us with morning dew, but as the sun grew warmer—much warmer—the sheaves were light and gave up a dry choking dust.

After a few days, the granaries were full, and the overflow had been bagged and stored in an outbuilding. The harvest was bountiful, and soon it was over. Our hosts were delighted and overjoyed at the yield. That evening's supper had a festive air about it.

After breakfast, we were given a fat envelope of pay, and the agriculture assignment agent was waiting to drive us to the next farm on the list for harvest help.

I shall always remember the gratitude my first hosts expressed for our efforts. *By the sweat of my brow and aching muscles, I shall eat bread.* During the night, the threshing crew had moved on, leaving a massive stack of wheat straw to rot and return to the earth from which it came.

> *All living things return to the ground—because*
> *from the ground it was taken. For dust you are,*
> *and to dust you shall return.—Genesis 3-19*

CHAPTER 9

BREAKING THE CHAIN
OF INEVITABILITY

*Without the element of uncertainty, the
road of life would be about as exciting
as a casual walk to the mailbox.*

From Piolet Mound, we moved on to other nearby towns and villages with names like Crystal City, Mowbray, and Mather. At each one, the threshing process was repeated. We worked on large, prosperous, section-size operations and some struggling drudgeries on a small pocket of land. All were totally dependent on the wheat harvest, and some were desperate for a rapid and successful harvest. The cold rainy season was near, and time was running out.

At a Crystal City farm, the same threshing crew showed up for the harvest. They were fast, capable, and efficient. They were also among a fading generation of threshers. Soon, combines would crawl across fields, eliminating the need for swathing, sheaving, stooking, loading hayracks, feeding sheaves to the stationary thrasher, and leaving a mountain of decaying straw behind. The end of harvest excursions was near.

In later years, I would fly over these very fields and view the results of how the Diefenbaker Progressive Conservative (Tory) government, over a four-year period, had eliminated the federal subsidy on wheat. Many of these amber fields of grain would be replaced with rows of sugar beets, yellow rapeseed, and blue flax. In some communities, golden sunflowers stand proudly facing the sun, and hemp, canola, and rye have replaced Durham wheat. A new economy emerged, new industries were established, and the total dependence on wheat came to an end. But I digress.

In Crystal City, we worked a large farm owned by a delightful Ukrainian couple with a last name something like Bauska. Their preteen son, Mike, became my friend. He sat beside me at the dinner table and played cards with me in the evenings when I should have been sleeping.

He never tired of asking about my home in Ontario. I told him tales of forested hills, great lakes one could not see all the way across, and life in a community where you could see and hear your neighbors. He was pretty sure that one day he would come and visit. He had never been to a city, did not know what a streetcar was, and wondered why anyone would ever need to hire a taxi.

His sister, Olga, was in her late teens and a great help around the house. She cooked before going to school and served the threshing crew breakfast. In the evenings, she helped serve dinner (they called it supper). She seemed to be perpetually doing dishes and laundry as well as some barn chores.

Later in the evening, she spent time in her room doing homework and playing a radio. She wore a babushka most of the time, but when she took it off and shook loose her beautiful long hair, she was a sight to behold.

It was at this farm that I encountered my first badger. Now, I knew nothing about badgers and had no idea of their reputation for fierce combat. When a thresher told me to go kick it, I made a move to do so. A very forceful shout from someone stopped me in my tracks. That badger was already viewing me with an evil eye and front paws raised in readiness.

I backed off and was told to never ever mess with a badger. We watched as the badger burrowed into the soft pliable earth and pulled the hole in behind it.

We spent many days at the Bauska farm, and chill winds were moving in. The final day of threshing was a Saturday, and I was awaiting my turn to unload the last load of sheaves. Olga climbed up onto my load, sat close against me, and asked when I would be going home. Now, I thought she was just idly visiting, so I told her I was not going home; I would find a room in Winnipeg and work in the Fort Whyte sugar factory.

I was shocked when she put her hand on my arm and said in a half-whisper, "I want to come with you. I need to get out of this hole of a town and live."

I am not often speechless, but I came close to it at this point. Fortunately, I am also a bit of a quick thinker when it comes to handling such situations. I told her to give me her mailing address, and I would send her bus money when I was settled in a room and working at the sugar factory job. For some reason, I had no doubt that I would get such a job, so after some further exchange of hopes and expectations, she climbed down from my load of sheaves and left.

That evening, I found her mailing address written on school notepaper in my suitcase. I could relate to her feelings. I had been there once myself.

Manley and I moved on to the next assignment in Mowbray, Manitoba, a farm on the US border, so marked by a set of tracks through wheat fields. There was nothing to be seen on the American side except the top of a distant grain elevator breaking above the horizon.

This was a small tract owned by an elderly couple named Mac and Ann Gordon. They both had heavy Scottish accents and were obviously in financial desolation. The house was small and dark, with no electricity and no obvious amenities whatsoever. Manley and I moved into their upstairs room, under a slanted ceiling with barely room to stand up. Sharing a bed was not something I was fond of doing.

This was not to be an enjoyable assignment, but we were here to do a job, make what money we could, and move on. The good news was that it was but a quarter-section operation. It would not take long.

On Sunday afternoon, the threshing crew moved in, made the threshing machine ready for use, and left. Harvesting would start the next day.

There was a cool breeze blowing, and the sky was dark. The Manitoba fall weather was threatening, and during the night, the threat turned into an assault. It was a forceful cold hard driving rain.

The thresher and drive-tractor had been weather-covered for protection against the elements. During the next few days, our hosts fed us sausage and eggs for breakfast, tater soup for lunch, and a stew-meat supper, every day.

Manley and I helped with barn chores during the rain, cleaning horse stables and the two-cow dairy barn. We spent afternoons and evenings exchanging life experiences and listening to fascinating stories of our hosts' life. They came from a Scottish island where they grew barley, which was sold to distilleries to make fine Scotch whisky. The demand was great, and their land was small. The lure of extensive tracts of land in Manitoba appealed to them.

They received Canadian government assistance to move here and homestead the land. Their vision of a prosperous farm operation and leaving a legacy for their children was motivation to endure the struggle and stay the course. Now their children had matured and left Mowbray to live and work in Winnipeg and Regina, respectively.

Mac and Ann were left to fend for themselves with no heirs to their land.

Finally, the weather cleared, the sheaves dried, the threshing crew made the wheels turn, and we threshed until Saturday afternoon. The weather-beaten crop was adequate to justify the harvest, and for Manley and me, it was time to move on.

Since the Gordons had no phone, Mac drove us to town to contact the excursion agent. There were no further assignments. Our 1950 harvest endeavors were over. Mac took us back to his home to spend one last night in the tiny upstairs bedroom in the lumpy bed tucked under the slanting ceiling of an unheated room.

On Monday morning, the excursion agent came to the Gordon farm, drove us to Piolet Mound, issued us return tickets by bus to Winnipeg, and gave us a voucher for train transportation home. He bade us a fond adieu and left us at the Piolet Mound bus depot.

My old suitcase was stowed in the baggage compartment. I climbed onto the bus, threw my coat on the overhead hat rack, and plunked down in the seat beside Manley. In my jacket pocket was an envelope full of the most cash I had ever seen, and I had more aching muscles than I had ever known.

During the past weeks, I had worked for farmers who were winners in life, and they were happy. Sadly, the Gordons labored in vain to leave their children a heritage of land the children did not want. They would be confined to live there, far from their native Scotland, for the rest of their days.

I had come on this excursion with hope and to prove something. I came because I craved an adventure. I had already chosen to not spend the rest of my life with the uncertainty of a farm. Neither did I wish to spend my life eking out a living driving a taxi. At this moment, there was a conflict between uncertainty and hope. The fear of failure would drive me safely home to Sterling. The feeling of hope would send me looking for a job at that sugar factory. Which would win?

We arrived in Winnipeg in the late afternoon, checked our bags in a bus-station locker, ate a sandwich at the coffee bar, and milled about the depot for a while contemplating our next move. Manley came to his decision: He recovered his suitcase from the locker and, in the misty afternoon, we said our good-byes, and he walked off toward the CPR station. He was going home. I never saw Manley again.

I bought a *Winnipeg Free Press* newspaper, opened it to "Rooms to Let," and with a handful of nickels, began calling. After a few calls, I found an interested response. "Eddie" would come to the depot; we would talk and decide.

Upon arrival at my new home at 333 Fleet Avenue, Winnipeg, Manitoba, I was ushered into a comfortable room, unpacked all the belongings I owned, took a warm bath, and, returning to my room, counted my money. Never had I imagined I would possess that much money.

I relaxed on a comfortable bed and looked toward the future with renewed confidence and hope. I felt sure I had just broken the chain of inevitability.

When our path forward requires it, we will have choices. From these choices we decide. My decision would eventually alter the course of many lives.

CHAPTER 10

WINNIPEG—MY HOME-TO-BE

*Hope and faith will nourish the soul, but does not
put a roof over our head, put food on our table, or
make us happy, wealthy, and wise. It takes effort!*

F all came to Winnipeg with a vengeance in 1950. The cold was
beyond that which I had ever endured. I was now sheltered in
a comfortable home and had a job in the Fort Whyte sugar
factory. I opened my first bank account at a Toronto Dominion Bank
and was living a self-directed life of hitherto unknown freedom. The
shackles of dependence were being shed, and it was good.

Winnipeg was the largest city I had experienced to date. There
was more than one movie theater, a museum, dance halls, and many
men-only pubs. The professional football season had ended with the
Winnipeg Blue Bombers defeated by the Toronto Argonauts 13–0
in the Varsity Field "mud bowl" in Toronto. There was professional
hockey and even a commercial airport within the city limits.

I was captivated by the large department stores and wandered
through the Hudson's Bay and T. Eaton Co. stores for hours, seeing
and touching lavish items I had only previously viewed in catalogs.
Streetcars and electric trolley buses were crowded with working
commuters going to and coming from their daily employment. The
city was vibrant with life.

The fact that my sugar-factory job was seasonal brought no concerns. When it came to an end, I would just go find another job. Yes, I was truly that naïve.

My boardinghouse hosts were Eddie and Joyce Wilcock. He made a living driving a Northwest Laundry delivery truck; she was a stay-at-home mother of two beautiful preschool girls. They kind of adopted me, and we spent evenings listening to their complete collection of Hank Snow records and drinking beer. Eddie was a very determined beer drinker. I felt comfortable with them and their Doberman pinscher dog.

My career at the sugar factory was uneventful. I worked on the second floor in the most remote corner of the building, the end of the digestive process in making sugar. Here the bran wastes poured from noisy driers, we sacked it, and it was shipped away to be used for livestock feed.

Most of my workmates in this cool corner of the factory were transplants to Canada from the war-torn continent of Europe. They came as prisoners of war and exercised the option to stay. One I remember, Heinz Friesen, probably in his thirties, was taken prisoner by the Canadian First Army during the battle of Antwerp. He lost all his possessions and family when the Russians entered Berlin, and he spoke of it sadly but sparingly.

Another displaced person on the bagging crew was a young, mid-twenties lad I remember only as Hans. He was not outwardly friendly and spoke little. I was never sure if he was bitter or heartbroken. He hid himself behind a shield of silence.

There were others, mostly of Ukrainian descent, who were second-generation immigrants. When we discussed my origin and background, they would ask, "What are you doing here?" There were times when I wondered too.

———————◆◆◆◆◆———————

December 15 passed, and my home excursion ticket voucher expired. Any possibility of returning evaporated. I don't believe I ever considered doing so, but now the dye was cast. The choice was no more.

I became more acquainted with the family of Eddie and Joyce Wilcock. Her family, the Atkinsons, lived a street or two over on Mulvey Avenue. He was a career butcher, and I knew her only as Ma or "Mother Atkinson." Their son Allen, about my own age, became my friend.

I spent Christmas at the Atkinsons'. We feasted, we sang, we played cards and drank beer. We gossiped, traded stories of life experiences, and approached a state of inebriation. They were British by birth and had emigrated to Canada after the war, their home and butcher business in London having been destroyed by V1 Buzz Bombs.

Ma Atkinson was a kind soul. She gave me a warm overcoat that Allen no longer used because I had none. She gave me wool-lined gloves for commuting during the Manitoba winter weather. She prodded me relentlessly to tell her why I really left home without finishing school. (Apparently, I never gave her a satisfactory answer. I never really had a good one to give.)

New Year's came and went. The sugar factory warehouse was getting empty, and workers were speculating on when the plant would close. It was something I had not given a lot of thought to.

A couple more weeks passed, and the word came on a Monday that this was cleanup week. I accepted my final paycheck on Friday and took one last homeward ride on the work bus. I was now unemployed.

Monday, I started looking for a job. The *Free Press* had many listings for which I did not meet the educational requirements. The unemployment office had plentiful openings for jobseekers who could endure outdoor Manitoba winter exposure. I felt that I could not. As a week or two passed, my hopes dimmed. The search was beginning to look fruitless.

At an age when I should have been looking forward to graduating from high school, I was in urgent need of employment. Was I being deprived the privileges of a normal misspent youth? Was I a victim of overconfidence? Would I finally be forced to pay my own way home? I could still do so.

One day, Ma Atkinson sat me down and, in a stern tone, made it clear she had a plan. She said, "A friend owes me a favor, a big favor, and it's time to collect. On Monday, we will get you a job!" She continued, "It's in the telephone exchanges."

We traveled by trolley bus into the bowels of the Winnipeg industrial district, to the assembly plant of Siemens Bros. Ltd. The company was a branch of a British-based telephone switching manufacturer located at 419 Notre Dame Avenue. This day would launch my lifetime career.

I met with Alan Bradly, a British bloke who hired the installation-department personnel. On one hand, he made it clear I was not qualified for the job. On the other, there was much cable to run and lace in the St. John's telephone exchange, and no one needed a high school education to do that. That would carry me through the winter. I was hired, and Alan Bradly's debt to Ma Atkinson was paid.

For he will command his angels concerning you
to guard you in all your ways.—Psalm 91:11

CHAPTER 11

THE DAWN OF MY CAREER
AND MY FUTURE

*Home is something you miss when you are
not comfortable with where you are!*

I t was January 15, 1951, and I found my way to the St. John's telephone exchange in north-end Winnipeg. The foreman, Jack Shepley, was quite British, and expecting me. The two-story building was jam-packed with busy rattling and chattering mechanical apparatuses driven by an unseen power source.

At this point in my life, my electrical knowledge did not go far beyond changing a battery in a flashlight, but that didn't faze me. There were frames of endless terminal blocks, all having miles of fine wires soldered neatly onto each terminal and running … somewhere. This all appeared to be a befuddling nightmarish mess, but I was committed. I would survive, I would conquer! It would be a part of my life, my career.

When Alan Bradly hired me, he made it quite clear that I did not qualify for permanent employment, and when the ironwork was assembled and the cable was run and laced, I would be laid off. That would be but a few months, but in the meantime, I was comfortable at the Wilcocks' boarding house, had a job, and worked with a great bunch of guys. They didn't know I was a temporary. Life, for the moment, was good.

I was never very good at thinking ahead. I think that is called worrying. I had not learned to do that yet.

———————◆◆◆————————

One evening, my landlord Eddie approached me and said, "I need help on the Saturday hotel deliveries." The word *help* translated into doing all the heavy lifting for him. He paid me a few dollars for hauling baskets of bedding up and down flights of stairs. It meant a little more income, which I pretty much spent in the beer parlor after work. I was not of legal drinking age, but anyone who went to the Empire Hotel beer parlor with Eddie, no questions were asked.

He was also making small loans to many people for big profits. The beer parlor was his after-work office of operations. It became clear no one messed with Eddie. He collected, one way or another.

Eddie's arrival at the Empire beer parlor on Saturday afternoons was a ritual. "His" table was always available for him upon arrival, and his "customers" were numerous and became familiar to me. Some who did not need a loan did crave feminine companionship for the night. Eddie would go make a phone call, return to the table, hand the "customer" a handwritten note, and accept some money, then the "customer" would go away.

My job seemed to be to keep the table occupied during any of his brief absences. After his "business hours," we would go home to a delightful dinner, after which we listened to soothing Hank Snow records and Eddie counted his money.

I was also enlisted to help in another of Eddie's enterprises. When hauling the soiled bedding from hotels, he would take a few "uncounted" sheets, pillowcases, and what-have-you from their shelves and throw them in with the laundry. I was allotted the job of removing the embroidered hotel name from that bedding for resale. I did note that the sheets in my room had evidence of embroidery removal.

71

From time to time, I would attend dance halls and movies with friends from work. One Saturday, a friend from work, Lloyd "Fingers" Harris, invited me to an evening of roller-skating. I had never roller-skated, but Fingers assured me lots of girls were looking for skating partners. Yes, there is a little species survival instinct in all normal people, and I am blessed to be somewhat normal.

I went roller-skating to check on the availability of feminine companionship. This evening would eventually be an influence on the rest of my life.

After a wobbly start, I managed to make the oval circuit with some poise. Many, if not most, skaters traveled in pairs, and I noted a couple of apparent sisters skating alone. After a while, Fingers and I approached and offered to accompany them on a pairs skate.

They were indeed sisters. Bertha skated with Fingers, and her younger sister, Nora, skated with me. I was shy, I was clumsy, and I had to concentrate on my skating more than making a personal impression. I did learn that she was a file clerk at the T. Eaton Catalog Company building right near the bus stop. At the end of the evening, they declined to go for a coffee with us. We said good night and went our ways.

Fingers and I made our way to the roller rink the following Saturday evening. The sisters were not there, but I did polish up my skating skills to the point to where I could weave gracefully around the oval with an air of self-assurance. It was not that different from ice-skating and less strenuous than hockey.

March winds were still blowing as I made a lone pilgrimage to that roller rink once again, this time by myself. I rented roller skates and hit the rink with hopeful anticipation. There they were: the sisters, skating alone. I approached Nora, and we skated together for the remainder of the evening.

As we skated, I learned that Nora was my age; was Mennonite; came from Altona, Manitoba; and was working to send money home to her widowed mother. At that time, I wasn't sure if *Mennonite* was a nationality or a religion, and I did not want to show my ignorance by asking.

When I mentioned I was from Ontario, she told me of how she had lived a summer in the Niagara district. Her family had motored there to work in the fruit harvests in 1946. She would later tell me of her father meeting with a tragic traffic death and his remains being returned to Altona for burial. At that time, she was thirteen years old.

As the evening ended, Nora and Bertha rode the trolley with me to a coffee shop on Osborn Avenue, after which I walked with them to their rooming house on River Street. Not wanting to spend for another trolley ticket, I walked all the way home on that cold March night. Having obtained the number of the hallway phone at Nora's rooming house and a promise of possible future dates, I felt warm.

> *The Lord God said, "It is not good for*
> *the man to be alone. I will make a helper*
> *suitable for him."—Genesis 2:18*

CHAPTER 12

THE COURTSHIP OF NORA PENNER

Who can find a virtuous woman? for her price is far above rubies. She will do him good and not evil all the days of her life.—*Proverbs 10 and 12*

The approach of spring in Winnipeg was a slow process. Snowplows created compacted roadside banks that resisted sun penetration. That and applied road salt caused ponds of slush to accumulate between them. Lumps of heat-resisting material accumulated on the snowy surfaces of fields and lawns, creating grotesque sculptures as the melting snow around them settled.

Sidewalks were a ribbon of slop during the day and a frozen hazard during cold nights. In the northern climes of North America, spring was a three-month transition from long cold dark nights of winter to long hot days of summers.

During this blustery early spring weather, Nora and I enjoyed Friday evenings at the roller rink, dance clubs, movies, and occasional private parties and gatherings with an ever-expanding circle of friends. After each occasion, we found our way by transit and on foot to the sanctity of her rooming house. At first, we shared warm embraces and a fond good-night in the hallway, but one evening when Bertha was not home, she said, "Let's go in." This was my first time ever alone with her in her room, her home.

Nora and Bertha lived together in one room. They cooked on a two-burner hot plate, had an aged refrigerator, and dined on a small table. On a shelf, they had a radio for entertainment, a one-bulb light fixture to illuminate the room, and a headboard reading lamp on the bed. Water was brought to their room in a metal pail from an upstairs bathroom, and a second pail was used for wastewater.

Their economic status was evident, but monetary plight was no stranger to me. I felt that I had at last met someone who could relate to my own convenience-deprived background.

I learned to treasure the walk from her door to my boardinghouse, a one-mile path during which I savored a warm affectionate relationship I had never experienced before. We were both refugees of economic deprivation and were developing a social co-dependence on each other. We were birds of a feather.

My roller-skating skills were somewhat choppy, if not downright clumsy, but repetition quickly improved us both. Soon, with typical cross-over hand holds, we could glide to the music from the organ loft with skill and dignity. I was developing a very warm feeling for this girl from Altona.

Nora's religion forbade dancing, but I enticed her into local dance halls which, at this point in time, neither served nor permitted alcoholic drinks. I could lead her in the two-step and waltzes as we nestled closer and learned to move in melodic unison. Neither of us was attracted to jive, country and western, or other showy forms of attention-attracting dance. We were shameless snuggle dancers.

My meager wage did not provide for an abundance of social dating, so now and again, Nora and I would spend a Saturday night babysitting the Wilcock girls. During these evenings, we stacked Hank Snow records on the record changer and lay together on the living room couch. We felt much warmth that filled a need in both of us. Our fond affection became mutual, a bond developed, and the promise of an intimate future was evident.

In Winnipeg, trolley service ceases at one o'clock, and single young ladies did not ride alone at night. A couple of times after babysitting, Eddie drove us to Nora's home, but his excessive beer consumption was a concern. I soon persuaded Nora to spend the remainder of these nights at the Wilcocks'. We folded the couch down into a comfortable daybed, and Joyce provided us with bedding. We slept in fond embrace and somehow kept the relationship platonic.

In early summer, Winnipeg becomes a beautiful city, The legislative building grounds and city parks were well-manicured expanses of green lawns with flower beds of glorious color. We spent many Sunday afternoons there lounging on a blanket on the grounds, visiting coffee shops, and dining at the local Salisbury House café. Life was a joy for us both. Our lives had become meaningful and happy.

Another of our summer activities was taking a weekend party train to Winnipeg Beach. The first one left on Fridays around 6:30 p.m., and the last return trip boarded at midnight on Sunday. It was popular with both the young and the mature. A couple of times, we were accompanied by friends.

At the beach, we rode the shaky wooden-framed roller coaster and other more stable midway thrill rides. We visited soda fountains, coffee shops, and restaurants, and enjoyed great swimming in the chilly lake waters. This was the first time Nora had ever worn a bathing suit. She did it justice. She was beautiful!

These trips were refreshing and added a dimension of variety to our activities. Other summer activities were Sunday walks in the spacious Assiniboine Park, where we feasted on hot dogs and soft drinks; visiting the zoo; and picnicking on the legislative grounds or in the backyard of her rooming house.

Summer passed, and once again, the chill of fall was upon us. Over the next couple of months, the skeletal limbs of deciduous trees replaced the lush leaves of summer, the football season played out, vehicles were winterized, coal bins in the basements were filled, and bulky winter clothing was purchased.

Winter was finally in evidence when the city police donned to-the-ground-length buffalo coats and aviator-style buffalo hats. They literally disappeared into a mound of brown fur. This was an unneeded assurance that the long winter had come to Winnipeg.

It was Thanksgiving weekend in Canada. The two-blocks walk from the trolley stop to Nora's place had left me cold and damp. She was not anxious to go to the movies as planned, so she said, "Let's just stay in and listen to music."

Sister Bertha was out and about with a boyfriend who had a car, which gave us a welcome opportunity to be alone. The ceiling light was turned off and a towel draped over the headboard light on the bed, leaving a soft shadowy glow in the room. We cuddled, listened to music, and were enjoying the warmth of endearing contact when, late at night, the hall phone rang. Nora answered it to learn that Bertha would not be coming home. She was detained "somewhere."

Without a word being spoken on the subject, we both knew we would spend the night together. When I said, "Let's go to bed," she, hesitantly at first, began to remove clothing. I slid out of my trousers and shed my shirt, underwear, and socks in haste.

As I slipped under the sheets, she was removing the last of her garments: her panties, garter belt, and stockings. The shaded headboard lamp was left aglow, and the radio serenaded us with soft music as our warm bodies came together.

This was not to be a clumsy fitting on a Mackinaw jacket by a wheat field, some child's play in a hayloft, or a moment of stolen pleasures on a kitchen couch. We alternately pressed our upper bodies together, then our lower pelvises, and knew we were about to answer the call of God's instinctive act of species survival.

Adjusting to the traditional missionary position, penetration took place. Let there be no question, a lasting bond was being established. We were mating.

This, then, was the romance of Nora Penner. Here we were, two young people, born in paucity, raised by poor but well-meaning parents, and with no experience in cosmopolitan living, finding a common interest in the pursuit of a life still to come.

Nora was to be the angel who gave love and affection to me and to our family-to-be for the remainder of her life.

CHAPTER 13

MY CAREER HAS BEGUN

*The path of life is often chosen for us, not by us. A
guardian angel placed me onto the road of my career.*

T he St. John's telephone work had progressed well into the
summer of 1951. After iron frames were installed, shelves of
equipment secured, and cables run and laced, I was given
training that qualified me as a wireman. The month of May had
come and gone, and the termination notice of my ninety-day
probationary time passed. It never came.

It seems that Alan Bradly had returned to England, and a
replacement plant manager—another British bloke, Ron Conway—
had succeeded him. Ron apparently did not know or was possibly
not notified of my provisional employment, and the subject was
never brought up. Was the guardian angel who had brought me to
this job still hovering over me? I cared not whether my blessings
came from good luck or bad management. I was still employed!

Throughout the summer, I worked as a wireman, and frankly,
I was good at it. My foreman, Jack Shirker, took an interest in me
and seemed pleased with the speed and accuracy of my work. He
said, "John you're a natural." (Come to think of it, he never said a
natural what!)

Eventually, the wiring, grading, and jumpering was complete, and placing it into service was the jurisdiction of switch adjusters and testers. It was time for us peons of labor to be moved on.

I was reassigned to the main exchange in downtown Winnipeg, located on the corner of Portage and Main, the windiest corner of any streets of any city in any province or state in North America. It was in fact walking distance to most major stores, to the Northwest Laundry where I worked on Saturdays, and to Nora's place.

Across the street was the Grain Exchange, where the most beautiful women in Winnipeg worked. At quitting time, that windy intersection presented an attractive show of blowing skirts. We were also next door to the Corona Hotel, a convenience that contributed to my beer drinking habits, which would rapidly become a problem.

Here I worked for Reginal "Reg" Sterns, and I soon became a drinking companion of him and many others. To name a few: George Rutland, John Lechow, Ben Litwinowich, John Phiffer, Mel Phiffer, Jack Ings, Peter Sterne, and John Holroyd. I would travel the country from job to job with these people in the years ahead. Their influence was not always to my benefit. With some I did excessive drinking and with some I gambled, but I blame them not. Only I was responsible for me.

The main exchange was large and complex. There was a perpetual crew of equipment construction workers on hand, and many envied me the assignment. The main floor was a business-offices complex where people with suits and ties came and went. I worked on the second floor, where switching equipment served the business district. On the third floor were, at one time, switchboards that provided pre-dial local service. Now it was mostly storage of paper records, and one corner was used by a radio broadcast station.

When the switchboards were retired, many operators became jobless. Most found other employment, but those who chose to remain were offered alternate switch-room jobs, such as cleaning selector switches and wiper banks or taking traffic counts. One such person was Ilene, a good-living lady of mature years. When the language of the switch-room workers got bit crude, she scolded at length. No one wanted to bring the wrath of Ilene upon them.

There was no women's washroom, so Ilene hung an "in use" sign on the door to indicate her occupancy. We were aware of what it meant. On one occasion, a switch mechanic did not notice the sign. Dick Webb pushed through the door and unzipped on his way to the urinal. As he walked, he was hauling luggage, and upon arrival, there was flow. He then noticed Ilene emerging from a stall.

Since it was too late to alter the activity, he simply said "Sorry" and finished. Dick was soon transferred to another location.

———————◆◆◆◆———————

Months passed. Another winter descended upon us, and Reg gave me more and more responsibility. I rose to the challenges, and there developed between us a mutual confidence and trust. Work became increasingly enjoyable as we fraternized more and more on and off the job.

Workday routines formed: work eight hours, drink a couple beers after, go home, eat dinner, read in my room, and drift off to a hazy sleep. Nora did comment on my beer breath from time to time but accepted me for what I was. We were not yet of legal drinking age, but that was of little concern to anyone.

I must tell you of an amusing event that happened on a streetcar ride home from work one winter evening. I was wearing my full-length overcoat and, in the pocket, had placed a partial spool of lacing twine. As I was swinging and swaying from overhead grab bars, a middle-aged lady standing in front of me bounced against that spool of twine. She turned, looked me straight in the face, and with absolutely no expression, pushed her way to another location. I will always wonder exactly what it was she thought she had encountered!

Time would pass, and my tenure with Siemens Bros. would take me to towns, cities, and territories from the province of Manitoba to British Columbia and all lands in between. My profession not only expanded and upgraded services for grateful residents in these locations but took me into the bowels of business activities that many people will never see. I saw hardships, courage, and miracle achievements that convinced me that man will do what man must do to earn his daily bread. One must believe.

I was also exposed to the idle opulence of a fortunate few who held positions, not jobs. Frankly, some made me uncomfortable, but envious.

In my wildest dreams, I could not have visualized a more appropriate career. I was to work in cities I had only heard and read about during the sheltered years of my youth—cities of history and mystique. In the years ahead, I met some of the most delightfully wholesome persons one could ever imagine, as well as some of the evilest persons one could envision. In some instances, it took me a while to perceive the difference.

I thank God daily for every one of those journeys down this path of life—a path onto which a guardian angel had placed me. I will now divulge some of my many life's adventures and the people that shared them with me.

I will work in silence and let the results speak for me!

CHAPTER 14

THE ROAD TO A UTOPIAN LIFE, MILE ONE

T ime passed. Life went on. On Valentine Day, 1952, I proposed to Nora Penner. On April 1, we were married in the St. Michael's and All Saints Church on Mulvey Avenue (now a preserved historical site by the City of Winnipeg).

The Reverend W. C. Turney officiated. Allen Atkinson was best man, Bertha Penner maid of honor, and the services were attended by Nora's mother, Mary Heinrick, as well as her sister Martha Zacharias and Martha's husband David. I was honored by the attendance of the now-widowed Ma Atkinson. There was no reception.

Prior to our wedding, we had located an upstairs apartment in a private home on River Avenue; yes, it was but a few doors down from Nora's previous rooming house. We had made a down payment for a three-room furniture package at the Hudson's Bay department store and spent a couple of nights in the Empire Hotel awaiting delivery.

Nora awaited the delivery in the vacant apartment until the afternoon of April 3, and we finished setting it up after my day at work. Late in the evening, she prepared our first dinner. We dined on the first kitchen table we had ever owned and retired late in the evening in the first place we were ever to call "our" home.

In my mind, I had ceased to be just some guy from Ontario, and she was no longer the girl from Altona. We were an entity. We were the John and Nora Geen family.

We were eighteen years of age.

Summer came to Winnipeg, and we settled into the routines of a married couple. She quit work when we married, as was the custom of the day. I had a few blocks' walk to work each morning and dutifully arrived home for dinner when the day's work was done. We had little need for anything more than what we had. Life was good.

I developed a true fascination with telephone switching technology. Many of the magneto switchboards my mother had once operated were still in use, but the generation of dial technology was rapidly replacing them. One could now spin a dial that generated a select number of pulses, which in turn selected the person to whom you wished to speak.

I felt it an honor to be a part of this industry. I asked many pertinent questions and was given much information, encouragement, and technical literature by my supervisor, Reg Sterns.

It was during this summer of 1952 that Reg received a call informing him that technicians were needed on a toll switching job in Edmonton, Alberta. All foremen were asked to submit names of men they would recommend and release. My name was submitted.

In my one and a half years on the job, I had become aware that when assigned to a new location, one must quietly go. That was the nature of the job, and a person's value could be influenced by willingness to relocate when and where needed, even if it was to Edmonton, Alberta.

On the brighter side, there would be a per diem allowance while away, and my transportation was paid, with no allowance for spousal accompaniment. My assignment was to leave for Edmonton on July 7, the week after the Canada Day holiday. We had three weeks to prepare.

Our transfer preparations reflected the assumption that one day we would return to Winnipeg, so our new and not fully paid-for furniture was packed and placed into Security Storage. I was given the option to travel by rail or accept equivalent funds for alternate travel and given a three-day travel and resettlement time frame. This, then, was our introduction to the mobile life of telephone-equipment installers—a life that many marriages would not survive.

As luck would have it, a work buddy had the same transfer schedule and was driving. Nora and I were invited to share the fuel cost and the ride.

Babe Backhouse was kind of a unique person in his own right. Aside from being a capable switching technician, he was a one-of-a-kind human being. I do not remember his first name; everyone only knew him as Babe. (Yes, that last name is real.) He was a tall, skinny, underdressed individual who would make you think he had just finished a day's work herding cows. His wife, Rose, was a tall wispy lady who looked delicate, but she was not.

Thus it was that Nora and I jammed our two old suitcases and a box of kitchenware into the back seat of Babe's car on a journey to a new chapter in our lives. We were going to Edmonton!

In 1952, there was no direct road from here to there, and what roads there were, were not the finest. The distance from Winnipeg to Edmonton as the crow flies is but 820 or so miles, but if that crow was driving a 1949 Pontiac, it was a good two-day drive.

On Saturday morning, we embarked on our journey. Babe swung south and hooked up with the old US Highway 5 at Dunseith, North Dakota. As we drove through vast flatlands of unharvested wheat, my thoughts drifted back a mere two years to when I helped harvest that wheat. Farms were owned by those who loved the land and felt a need to feed a hungry world. It was in farming communities such as these in which Nora had been conceived and raised.

Night was spent in some town along the way, and on Sunday, we swung north at Shelby, Montana, to Lethbridge, Alberta. There we spent our last night on the road and arrived in Edmonton before noon Monday.

Two years earlier, I had left Stirling, an unsophisticated farm kid with only pocket money and more hope than expectations. Far from the sanctity of home, I had worked on threshing gangs and at a dead-end sugar factory job, with nothing to look forward to except perhaps another dead-end job. To that point in my life, there was nothing to lose except that which I had gained. If I screwed up, no one would have suffered but me, I could have at any time pulled the plug on my adventures and gone home to my parents in Stirling.

Now, things were different. It was not just me anymore. Close beside me in this back seat was Nora. Her whole future swung on my rope.

On those lonely roads of North Dakota and Montana, a realization came to mind. Others had an investment in my abilities. Others could suffer from my mistakes. Others had a faith I didn't even have in myself. Motivation is often encouraged by necessity. In the back seat of Babe's 1949 Pontiac, it dawned upon me that I now had those necessities.

By the grace of God, I had employment that offered me a secure future in the communications industry. I was married and embarking on an adventurous career. Was this not exactly what I had been seeking when I left Stirling? Had not my hopes and prayers been answered?

Little did I suspect that my career would span the remaining life of the Strowger switching system.

CHAPTER 15

LIFE AND FAMILY IN EDMONTON

*Choices made from necessity often differ
from those made from emotion.*

E dmonton, the utopian complex of the north, was probably chosen as the capital of Alberta because it is somewhere near the center of the province and a railway hub of the north. At this point, I considered it in the middle of nowhere, but we would come to feel at home in Edmonton.

It is the farthest north of any major city in Canada—about 350 miles north of the US border. In early July, the dawn came at about five in the morning—or is that still nighttime?—and it fully sets about seventeen hours later. This makes drive-in movie exposure pretty late.

In December, the equation was somewhat balanced, as we went to work in the morning in total darkness and got home after work when it is already back to total darkness. At some point during the day, there was a brief period of daylight.

Edmonton was a bustling metropolis of business endeavors, including oil and natural gas production, mining of precious metals, and a plethora of natural resources, including lumber, coal, and the nearby bituminous sands that secured one of the great oil reserves of the world. The surrounding territories offered some of the greatest fishing and hunting any man could hope for. The majestic Rocky Mountains to the west were truly monuments to nature's might and beauty.

We would come to Edmonton on several future occasions. I would fish the lakes, hunt the forests and fields, and grow to love this region. We would make everlasting friends and, eventually, from time to time, call it home.

Upon arrival, we found our way to the toll switching office, where we met with Percy Briggs, our boss-to-be. Percy gave us a lot of information on how and where to look for living accommodations, and he had a few addresses to check into. Since it was a boom economy, Percy advised us to "take whatever you can find—and good luck!"

Monday night was spent in a motel, and the next morning, the search for a place to live ensued. Babe and Rose were also in this search, so together we went through the *Edmonton Journal* ads, looking for furnished accommodations. There were few, but Nora and I decided on an affordable upstairs apartment one block from a transit stop, at 2224 Stony Plain Road. It was owned by a German immigrant, Irving Wichard, and his wife, Blossom.

We moved in with our minimal household goods: sheets, a blanket, two pillows, a quilt, a kettle, a frying pan, a couple of cooking pots, and enough tableware for the two of us. Once again, we had a home, a job, and a future. The good news was, our weekly per diem just about doubled my salary, and—oh yes—we had a family on the way. The gods were smiling upon us!

On Wednesday, we cased the neighborhood to locate nearby services within walking distance, like food stores, laundry locations, and domestic supplies. On Thursday, I went to work.

Our landlords lived on the lower floor of the house. They were charming people. Irving worked for the railroad, and Blossom was a model homemaker. She and Nora struck up an instant friendship. She was the mother Nora didn't have.

Irving and Blossom liked to drink beer and play dealer's choice poker for small stakes. They enjoyed our company, and we were often joined by a previous tenant, David, and Shirley Jones.

Blossom noticed Nora's "condition" soon after we moved in, if not before. She began enthusiastically giving Nora family advice and otherwise spoiling her. Blossom was the blessed support-person a teenage mother-to-be really needs. She advised Nora on the purchasing of baby clothes and supplies and other prenatal preparations.

Our life was maturing. The tragic family tribulations of Nora's youth were becoming an unhappy memory. She now had a noble purpose.

One day, Blossom was helping Nora upholster a large basket to accommodate the upcoming birth. As I watched, Blossom stuck a safety pin into her breast and went on about what she was doing. I almost dropped my beer. Seeing me squirm, she quickly explained it was a prosthetic, not to worry. She chuckled away to herself, and I had a feeling she enjoyed the joke.

Irving had been displaced by the war, was brought to Canada as a POW, and had chosen to remain. His only remaining family member, Helmut, had emigrated to Canada later and created a prosperous timber business. Helmut bought stumpage rights to large tracts of land and at any given time would run two or three mills. He was not a chubby cheerful person like brother Irving. Helmut was all business, and it showed!

On Thursday, Babe and I were put to work at the toll exchange—which was, to us, a new technology. No more rattling Strowger switches reacting to dial pulses. Now it was a buzzing, fast-spinning, two-hundred-outlet motor-driven rotary switch, and numerous test racks to monitor long-distance networks from about everywhere.

Upstairs there were cordless switchboards with push-button dials operated by a multitude of the best-dressed young women in the city. Pneumatic tubes delivered toll-tickets to a billing office, where there was security monitoring of who came and went and when. It was a whole new ballgame.

As the months went by, the daylight hours grew shorter, and chill winds blew in from the north. Nora's gestation time was closing in, and "the day" was becoming guesswork, as well as a concern. Nora had access to a phone to call me at work if need be, and more days passed. We had no car, but the phone number of a taxi company was by the phone. We awaited the inevitable.

Then, one day, it happened! While at work, I received a phone message that Nora was on the way to the hospital. A friend drove me there, and I was ushered into a waiting room, where I waited and waited. Finally, late in the evening of October 2, we became parents of a baby girl. Nora named her Gail Ellen.

In a couple of days, Gail Ellen was placed in the upholstered baby basket that had been lovingly assembled by Nora and Blossom; covered with warm, soft, recently purchased baby blankets; and taken home. At the age of nineteen, Nora's life of devotion to family was underway.

During the fall of 1952, we endured the coldest weather we had ever experienced. Edmonton people were prewired to accept it; we were not. I spent the winter riding the transit buses to work and playing cards with the Wichards and the Joneses. Nora threw herself into parenting. We were now living for the future of us, and of our family.

In the spring, we would return to Winnipeg in a compartment

of a railway Pullman coach. Over the next five years, we would return to Edmonton many times.

A firstborn will naturally be raised with a mixture of instinct and trial and error.

CHAPTER 16

WINNIPEG: "I'D LIKE TO STAY HERE"

*Concentrate on counting your blessings
and you'll have little time to count
anything else.—Woodrow M. Kroll.*

April 1953: We were back in Winnipeg, have located an upstairs apartment in a private dwelling on Hargrave Street, retrieved our furniture from Security Storage, and settled back into a routine. We even had a refrigerator on loan from one of Nora's relatives—the first time we had enjoyed such a luxury.

I was counting my blessings. In the past fifteen months, I had found a career, gotten married, worked an out-of-town assignment, and became a parent. It seemed a long way from plowing fields on the farm just a few short years earlier. We would remain at this assignment longer than any other while I worked with Siemens— long enough for me to become the father of a boy child, John Ritchie Geen, born March 15, 1954.

The snowmelt had already begun, but I did get to do some ice fishing on the Assiniboine and Red Rivers. Winnipeg felt more familiar this time around, a little bit like home. Nora once said, "I think I would like to stay here."

I just replied, "We'll see." Life had not yet become peripatetic.

I was assigned to the Fort Rouge exchange, adding modern Strowger switching equipment to old plunger-generation "type 13" switching. It was a challenge of a different nature but one that would add to my résumé of accomplishments. Our foreman, Carl, was a good assembly person and accepted the technical benefits I could provide.

Carl once asked, "How do you know all about this old stuff?"

I just said, "Experience, Carl!"

The fact was, I had never worked on this antiquated equipment before. My understanding came from studying the schematics in the evening on the dining room table at home. We made it work.

For morning and afternoon breaks, we all tossed a dollar into a pot every so often, and an aging cleanup man made coffee and took donut orders for the morning break. Break periods were kind of an event.

A jovial English bloke named John Holroyd introduced us to the card game Red Dog. John had many undesirable behaviors that, though not unique, were pervasive. He was a drunk, a gambler, and addicted to the pursuit of women. His favorite expression of achievement was a drawn-out, expressive "*Wicked!*"

His game fit in with our limited break time. It was simple, it was fast, and it could get addictive. A dealer (the bank) simply put a sum of money into a pot and dealt all players three cards. Players would, in turn, voluntarily bet a chosen amount that any one of their cards would be of a greater number than the one in the suit the dealer would turn over from the top card in his deck. All discarded cards were face-down, and there was no minimum bet. If the bank went broke, the deal passed to the next player.

The Red Dog game became widespread throughout the

company. It was played during breaks, we played it in pubs and had Red Dog parties in homes and hotel rooms. Wherever a crew of Siemens workers went, there was a game of Red Dog during which someone would let out an expressive "*Wicked!*"

During this period, I worked at the Fort Rouge exchange, the West exchange, and the Main exchange. Nora and I were becoming settled and comfortable—and then came another out-of-town assignment notice. We would return to Edmonton in June.

Nora's first remark was, "Oh no, not again."

Oh yes. There were to be many *again's*.

We placed our furniture back in Security Storage, and in late June, Nora, Gail, baby Ritchie, and I took a compartment in a Pullman coach to our destination, during which the two children got a lot of attention from the servers. One of the Pullman attendants even brought us extra blankets and cushions for their comfort.

On arrival, with the help of some local acquaintances, we found a furnished house for rent. It was our first stand-alone housekeeping experience. It was a summer-only lease in the developing south side McKiernan Lake area of Edmonton. It had all the comforts and conveniences we could not afford. It was a dream.

Alas, a few weeks into our stay, there was a cloudburst. The unmerciful rain flooded the street, then the lawn, then crept up the basement windows—and came in. We spent the night rescuing much of the owner's material from the basement, and still the rain continued.

Nora began lamenting, "What are we going to do when it starts to come into the house?"

The phone was out, and I had no answer to her question. I put my faith in the fortunes of fate. The water was icy cold, and now we knew why it was called the McKiernan Lake district!

In the morning, a rescue boat came and asked us if we needed supplies, milk for the baby, medications, and what-have-you. We didn't. It took four days for the water to recede. I missed a couple days of work and waded to the bus stop for a couple more. Then the owners wanted their house back—for obvious reasons.

We had been in touch with our old friends Irving and Blossom, and as luck would have it, they had a tenant in their upstairs apartment who was about to be evicted. Would we like to move back to their place? We accepted their offer.

A few days later, back at work, I was greeted rather coldly by my usually cheerful friends. At the coffee break, I learned that Irving and Blossom were evicting Mel, a fellow worker, and it was mutually assumed it was to make the place available for Nora and me. While some understood the situation, others apparently did not.

My fellow worker Mel was more than just a drunk. He was an evil person. While he was carousing, a fellow worker was in his apartment romancing his wife. There were also some all-night sleepovers that the Wichards found offensive. Mel was not a good tenant.

I was soon reassigned to a new installation site in southeast Edmonton, a region called Idyllwild, and was put on emergency power-plant installation with a barrel-chested man by the name of Al Dudard. Al was a displaced Lithuanian who had elected to remain in Canada after WWII. He was a gentle giant with the patience of Job and the strength of Goliath.

Al's wife owned a beauty salon and had fallen upon poor health. Her medical bills and shop obligations imposed a heavy debt upon them, and he decided to sell his 1948 Chevrolet. Asking price: $1,600.

Al solicited buyers from his fellow workers. He ran ads in the *Edmonton Journal* and tried peddling it to used-car dealers. He was getting desperate.

One day, Al was lamenting his situation during a break period when I offhandedly said, "Al, I'll give you $1,200 for your car if that will help." It was an impulse—I have no idea why I said that. Perhaps I was just looking for some attention, or some respect. In any case, I said it! He didn't seem to take me seriously.

A couple of days later, Al approached me in the basement power room and, in an almost suppliant tone of voice, said, "John, I'll have to take your offer. I can't wait any longer."

Now, Nora and I were, by nature, frugal. We came from poverty-stricken backgrounds and understood the psychological burden of Al's financial deficiencies. But we did not have $1,200. Surprisingly, Nora said, "You know, we really need a car."

We cashed in $700 of Canada Savings Bonds and borrowed enough to buy Al's car. Our first car ever!

Now, when word got around about our purchase, you would think our fellow workers would have respected my facilitation of Al's circumstances. No! I had clearly taken advantage of Al's desperate situation.

> *But whoso hath this world's goods, and*
> *seeth his brother having need. And shutteth*
> *up his compassion for him, how dwelleth*
> *the love of God in him?—1 John 3:17*

━━━━━◆◦◆◦◆━━━━━

Now back at Stony Plain Road. Life went on. I spent many weekends during the summer and fall doing what I loved: fishing and hunting just about every weekend. We fished perch at Alberta Beach, pike in Lake Wabamum and Isle Lake. At Sundance Creek, near Edson, we landed the plentiful Arctic char, and at Beaverhill Lake, there were trout. In the fall, we hunted duck at Sandy Point and pheasants in nearby farmlands. I was living a dream.

Edmonton was a second home to us, although it was evident that we had no home anywhere. Our furniture had spent more time in Security Storage than with us. They say home is where the heart is, and Nora's heart was still in Manitoba, her birth home being Plumb Coulee, near Altona, where her father lay buried. One sister lived there, and two others, Bertha and Jessie, now lived in Winnipeg. Nora wanted to go home.

In October, she would get her wish.

CHAPTER 17

THE ROAD HOME

*If he that is married cares only for the
things that are of the world, how may he
please his wife.—Corinthians 7:33*

I n October of 1954, the Geen family embarked on our journey
to Winnipeg in our 1948 Chevrolet. It was loaded with every
possession we owned.

We crossed the harvested Canadian prairies on a variety of roads
that were not designed for the convenience of through traffic. Road
maps were only as good as the often-absent road signs they referred
to. We were not sure where we were, or were not. Gas stations were
where you could find them and not placed for the convenience of
travelers.

We did eventually make it to our destination—to Winnipeg.
Nora felt good! She was back in her beloved Manitoba among
relatives and friends.

During the trip, she had asked, "How long can we expect to live
this way? We have a family." She added, rather hopefully, "When can
you get off the road and just work?" I assured her my time would
come.

With two dependents, our nomadic way of life was inappropriate.
Yes, the money was good, but the peripatetic existence was not. Nora

wished for a place to settle, to nestle into a warm little house with a white picket fence.

A friend at work, Ben Litwinowich, knew of a place to rent close by his home near the village of St. Adolph, an eighteen-mile commute from Winnipeg. We found it to be primitive, with outside plumbing, no running water, and phone service not yet available.

It was situated on one acre of great gardening soil; it backed up to the Red River; and it was private. The rent was extremely inexpensive, and I sensed an opportunity to build some reserves for a future purchase. Yes, we were reverting to the lifestyle of our youth.

The community was French, but we reasoned that the low cost of rent would compensate for the difference in community culture. Thoughts of that coveted cozy little house in town were discarded in the name of economics. We moved into that bucolic little house on the prairie.

Was I making decisions based on my needs only? Was my wife obligated to abide by my decisions? My background in life led me to assume that wives submit themselves unto their husbands (Ephesians 5:22). I knew no different.

My work assignment started in the Fort Rouge exchange. One day, on my drive home, I spotted a 1949 DeSoto on a nearby car lot. I liked, I test drove, I bought. We now had a big comfortable car with a fluid drive transmission that Nora could drive.

Our nearby neighbors Ben and Gloria had bought a fourteen-inch TV, and we often spent an evening watching TV with them while I drank beer with Ben. We were living in relative comfort.

Winter came. We celebrated Christmas in St. Adolph, and soon the inevitable came: a notice to return to Edmonton in February. We discussed our alternatives and decided to keep the house. The rent was just a few dollars more than placing the furniture back in storage.

In mid-February, we loaded some essential household goods and two children in the DeSoto and, in the dead of winter, headed back to Edmonton. One night, while we were still in Saskatchewan, it was so cold we could not keep the car warm enough for the children. We stopped for the night in the town of Plunkett.

As far as I could determine, we were the only guests in that little hotel, and in the morning, we were fed breakfast and advised by the owners not to continue. Cold snaps like this came and went, and being on the road was unsafe. The car engine circulation heater had been plugged in for the night, and miraculously, when it was time to leave, it started. In the frigid Saskatchewan cold, we once more headed for Edmonton.

Upon arrival in Edmonton, we soon found a furnished house near the city park, the zoo, the racetrack, and the hockey rink. It was but a few blocks from the Edmonton Eskimo football stadium and next door to a corner grocery. Perfect! Once more we set up housekeeping, and I went to work.

The Edmonton assignment proved to be longer than anticipated, so we spent a glorious summer there, paying two rents but getting by. It was May when Nora revealed she was once again with child. We were preparing to have another child born in Edmonton, but the company had other needs. In mid-October, I was transferred to Saskatoon, Saskatchewan.

In Saskatoon, we lived in a furnished cottage near the Saskatchewan River. I worked on an addition to the main exchange in this city of bridges. There, on January 1, during one of the most severe blizzards in history, Nora gave birth to son number two. She named him Ronald Wayne Geen. In late March we left our rented cottage with now a family of three to reclaim our home in St Adolph.

<hr />

That spring, the Red River once again came over its banks, and access to our house was flooded. I put Nora and the three children on a Pullman car and sent them to the safety of my parents' home in Stirling, Ontario. They stayed about six weeks.

During this period, I could get to the house with high rubber boots on, so in my spare time, I built a little ten-foot rowboat in the living room. By the time the flooding receded, the paint was drying. Time for Nora to come home.

The trip for Nora was a hardship, but she had now met my parents and had an insight as to where I had come from. She left all the warmth, comforts, and conveniences of my parents' home and returned to St. Adolph.

We planted a garden and were enjoying a beautiful summer, but once again, the call to go elsewhere came. There were several small equipment additions needed in the Okanogan Valley of British Columbia.

The Okanogan Telephone Company was using an advanced "type seventeen" motor-driven rotary switching system, and my experiences in the Edmonton toll office would be an asset in the Okanogan Valley.

This time, Nora stood her ground and stayed behind to raise the family. She simply said, "I can't do this anymore, and I won't stay here forever."

I left the DeSoto with Nora and left for the city of Kalona in late July, accepting a ride with a work friend, Jack Ings. We traveled the same American route I had experienced with Babe and his wife, Rose, years before. This time, we went through the Glacier Park in Montana and reentered Canada at Osoyoos, B.C.

The breathtaking beauty of this valley has been a postcard memory in my life to this day.

CHAPTER 18

THE OKANOGAN EXPERIENCE

Should I be led into temptation,
deliver me from evil.

If Canada were to ever have had a Garden of Eden, it would have been the Okanogan Valley. This two-hundred-mile-long valley between two mountain ranges had deep colorful lakes, green valleys, and snow-topped hills, which hosted a population that typically were the offspring of the previous generation that were, in turn, offspring of a previous generation, and so on back to infinitudes. It was a typical socially sequestered neighborhood where everyone was, in one way or another, related to everyone else.

The fertile foothills were blanketed with irrigated vineyards of grapes and hops and orchards of cherries, peaches, and apples. The Okanogan Lake stretches for one hundred and thirty-five miles between these mountains and offers endless sandy beaches that quickly drop off into untold greater depths than had ever been confirmed. It was said that creatures never seen by man lurked in these depths. One, known as Ogopogo, had been sighted from time to time but never photographed. It appeared to be a cross between a serpent and a dragon.

The quaint towns scattered along this lake were connected by a single highway with views that included the multicolored Kalamalka Lake of many colors.

I was to spend the next five months in this valley.

———❖———

Our first assignment was Kalona, where we, as a group, stayed in an older midtown hotel with a beer parlor and bar. It was but a few blocks one way to the telephone exchange and a few blocks in the other to a sandy, uncrowded beach. Our site supervisor was known to me: Percy Briggs from Edmonton.

Percy took me aside and, for reasons I was not sure of, said, "John, I've been here before. Be careful!" He advised me there would be enticements and emphasized that "Many local men leave the valley to work in Vancouver. Many young ladies are left hungry for romantic adventure." With a very sincere air of concern, he repeated, "John, be careful!"

I opened a bank account with five dollars to establish check-cashing assurance. On Fridays, I would cash my pay and per diem checks, purchase a money order, and get money off to Nora in the Saturday mail. The letter from home would come next Thursday or Friday to confirm its arrival at destination. That would be our routine for some time to come.

As we went about our job of expanding the capacity of the exchange, many telephone operators, their lady friends, restaurant and coffee shop waitresses, and others became curious about our presence in town. Newcomers do not go unnoticed. A code of moral hush developed among the crew: *Don't tell on anyone who is married.*

Romances developed. I made no secret of my own marital status but, shamefully, kept the secrets of those who did. I will not comment on the activities of others, but there was plenty of it. The gene pool of Kalona would be expanded. It was not just the weather that was hot and healthy, and pleased libidos do make happy humans.

One little moment of drama involved my boss, Percy. He did

not swim, and while backing away from shore, he stepped off that sudden incline from beach sand to the great depths of Okanogan Lake. He went under. Now, I am not much of a swimmer, but I did get ahold of him, and we somehow flailed our way back to good footing. I think he was more embarrassed than grateful. He never brought the subject up at any time after.

Temperatures were warm and humid in Kalona, and I spent much non-working time either on the beach or in the beer parlor. One evening, when returning to my room, I saw a bat fly into the second-floor fire-alarm bell. Well, why not have a little fun? I dinged the bell with something, and it flew. I and a couple of others harassed the creature to exhaustion, and it fell to the floor.

I hung this poor fatigued little bat on my trousers and casually walked down to the lobby. Well, it was spotted, and panic broke out. What few there were in that lobby quickly left with screams, hollers, and curses. Neither the management nor the bat was pleased. The bat recovered and flew back to its fire bell. The desk clerk flew off the proverbial handle.

I was moved to the city of Penticton, located at the boot-end of Okanogan Lake. While working on toll positions, I did strike up an acquaintance with a supervising operator by the name of Clara. She told me of her absent spouse who, like me, was working on an out-of-town job assignment.

I later ran across her at the beach one evening and she hailed me with, "Hey, sir, come meet my daughter." I approached, we talked, her pre-school-age daughter took to me right away, and we splashed and talked until dusk descended.

The following Sunday she shared a picnic lunch with me at the beach, and I remember having a couple of late-night phone discussions about a book she was reading: *Elmer Gantry*. I had read it. Elmer Gantry was a preacher and, among other things, a lecher and a scoundrel. We had some laughs comparing him to people we knew.

We kept our relationship guarded and wholesome. She was a delightful person, but I never was at her home, nor did she ever visit me. We both just needed some assurance of being desired. Our fleeting friendship is a little secret we both kept.

The summer days became shorter, and beaches were being abandoned. Letters from Nora informed me that the garden crop was plentiful. It provided much for the table all summer and a good potato, cabbage, and pumpkin crop was evident. The children were in good health and had even befriended some of our French neighbors.

Nora was getting along on the money I sent, and I still had payroll withholdings to purchase Canada Savings Bonds. We were making the best of what we could, with an understood promise of escape from St. Adolph.

I was relocated to the extreme other end of the lake, to a town called Vernon. Here I would work on a technology more familiar to me: Strowger step-by-step switching. Percy had stayed behind in Penticton and appointed me installer-in-charge to get the job underway. I was given a little bonus pay for the responsibility.

Vernon was not quite a tourist town like Kalona or Penticton. There were no miles of sandy beaches to attract the Vancouver weekenders. There was a modest beach in a quiet secluded valley where local families spent a weekend afternoon. Nobody seemed to be in a hurry. Wherever you needed to go, you could walk. There were only two hotels, and each had a beer parlor for men and a ladies-and-escorts tavern.

The Vernon job was quite extensive. I moved into the Allison Hotel, along with other crew members, and settled into this new environment. I visited a local bank to establish a presence for routine financial transfers. At the mention of Winnipeg, the teller's ears perked up, and she seemed eager to discuss her connection to it. Her name was Mavis.

From her eye contact and mannerisms, I sensed she was reaching out for attention. Did she have romantic longings? Was she seeking a carnal connection, or just being nice?

I did not intend to make any approach. Percy had warned me!

On about my third paycheck-cashing trip to the bank, my favorite teller once again greeted me with enthused attention. As she counted out my cash, she mentioned that she and her roommate were planning to drop into the Allison for an after-dinner drink. She said, "There is not much else to do on a Friday night."

I did not take the bait but was flattered that she had at least cast the line. I had no desire to fall into the deceitful life that some of my working buddies had fallen into. No—it couldn't happen to me!

That Friday evening, I did not go for the usual evening beers. Instead, I sat in the Allison lobby and worked on the ever-present coffee-table jigsaw puzzle with Linda, the evening desk clerk. This we did several times a week.

At about eight o'clock, Mavis and her friend passed through to enter the ladies-and-escorts tavern. We acknowledged each other with a brief wave as they passed. I had never seen her outside of her teller cubicle before and did notice that her slim curvaceous figure was contained in a fitted sheath dress.

Linda asked, in an officious tone, like I owed her an answer, "Who is she?"

I had never mentioned my marital status to either of them. Neither had asked. Did I have some subconscious reason for this? Was my will to sow the seeds of life yielding to a women's resolve to stalk and entice? Both are intrinsic instincts possessed by every living thing. I was a living thing.

Linda was a tall slim model of a woman and often joined me at the jigsaw table during idle moments. She was native to Vernon, seemed to know everyone, and was the daughter of an influential businessman. Why was she an evening clerk at a hotel? Her background indicated she need not be here. There was no logic!

I was to learn that she did not live at home and enjoyed a good party. In fact, she invited me to join her for Thanksgiving at her parents' house the very next week. I declined.

In a later week, I did accept an invitation to be her escort to a house party. It was an evening of music, dance, and heavy drinking. There I danced with a cute, chubby little girl named Jamie Hewit. We were compatible dance partners, but later in the evening, I walked home alone, to the Allison.

It was on the following Sunday afternoon that I went to the drugstore for Sportsman cigarettes. I was smoking a flatpack of twenty-five cigarettes every couple of days. While scanning the material on the newsstand, I looked up to find Mavis standing and looking at me.

She said, "You look deep in thought. Want to tell me about it?" She laughed, and we chatted for a few minutes, and I walked with her to her home.

Once there, she invited me in, made a cup of tea, put a dash of rum in it, and we discussed her memories of Winnipeg. Yes, it would be cold fall days back there by now. We spoke of the pros and cons of the city and decided we liked it just fine where we were.

Why did she leave Winnipeg? How did she get here? She was not yet prepared to tell me. As I left, there was a brief embrace, and we decided that we must have a drink sometime. She gave me her phone number to arrange a time.

Later in the month, a game-fest banquet was held in the grand ballroom of the Allison, and I was asked by the owners, Owen and Bella, to help with the setting-up and other preparations. On the evening of the banquet, I and other volunteers assisted in welcoming guests, keeping the serving platters filled and the beer cooler stocked, and so forth. Another volunteer was assigned to work with me. It was cute, chubby little Jamie.

When the evening was over, we gathered plates, cups, glasses, and other dishes, rinsed them, and stacked the dishwasher. We cleared paper covers from tables and so forth. Eventually, our duties were done.

It was in the wee hours of the morning when Jamie came with me to my room for a nightcap and rest. For the first time, I permitted the inevitable. I, like Onan, son of Judah, who had entered his brother's wife, "withdrew in compunction, and wasted his seed upon the ground" (Geneses 38:1-10).

In the future, I vowed I would come prepared.

There were several future trysts in room 202 of the Allison Hotel. Jamie had needs. I fulfilled them. I had now fallen to the level of some of my disreputable work buddies.

I did contact Mavis again. We did go for drinks, and we did attend room parties with my working buddies in the hotel. I spent a couple of weekends at her home when her roommate was away, and a relationship was established. My rationale was that the job was ending, and soon I would go home. What harm could come of it?

A couple of weeks before Christmas, the work was done, and acceptance was underway. The crew was released to go home for Christmas, but Percy informed me that until the acceptance was complete, someone would stay. That would be me.

I wrote that difficult letter to Nora that I would not return until after New Year's. I spent Christmas with a local family who sympathized with my situation. On New Year's Eve, I attended a party in the Allison ballroom with Mavis. We spent the remainder of the night in my room.

As it is written and long understood: "Man does not live by bread alone" (Deuteronomy 8:2–3).

On January 15, 1957, I embarked on my journey home—first by bus to Revelstoke, where I boarded a train to Winnipeg. As I gazed from the windows during this journey through towering mountains, through dark oppressing tunnels and onto wide expansive snow-blowing prairies, I reflected, with mixed emotions, on the past months in the Okanogan Valley.

I had worked hard, drank hard, and yielded to the God-given creature acts of species perpetuation. Had my sins relegated me to the level of a creature?

Had I, from weakness, dishonored the wedding vow I made in the presence of God to forsake all others?

Had I, from weakness, violated the ninth commandment?

The Bible denies this. "The desire of the flesh is not from God, but from the world" (1 John 2:16).

Had the world led me astray or was it just that "the spirit be willing, but the flesh be weak" (Mathew 26:41).

Anyway, I was going home.

CHAPTER 19

MY RETURN TO ST. ADOLPH

Dark betrayals enter our marriage.

By prearrangement, my working buddy and St. Adolph neighbor Ben Litwinowich picked me up at the station in Winnipeg and delivered me home. Nora had not expected me until the following week and was surprised at my arrival. I anticipated a warm embracing welcome but somehow sensed a lack of enthusiasm.

The kids were delighted to see me as I told them of the train ride through the Rocky Mountains and shared stories of blowing snow from mountaintops and of herds of elk and deer by the railway tracks. I followed this with tales of endless miles of blowing snow across flat prairies and the sighting of an occasional coyote. They perceived such a travel experience as an adventure.

After a wonderful home-cooked meal, I wished nothing more than to relax and rest, and looked forward to bedtime. Once more, I sensed Nora's apprehension. It had, after all, been almost six months since we had slept together.

Shortly after dinner, a car pulled into the driveway. Nora looked out the window and said, "I wonder who that could be." I detected concern. She acted like someone anticipating bad news.

Our—or rather, her—guests came to the door and entered without the customary knock. It was her sister, Bertha, and two men, carrying a case of beer. My presence was obviously unanticipated. Greetings were muted. Explanations were required. Who would speak first?

Bertha put her hand to face, drew a breath, and said, "We were just passing through." Turning to Nora, she said, "We wondered if you needed anything."

Nora responded, "No, everything's fine. John just came home today."

Bertha replied, "We need to be on our way."

A hasty departure followed, and an embarrassing moment was over.

A beautiful woman alone without affection will radiate an aura of desire. Instinct will encourage men to approach and prevail. The need to discard a chaste existence has been embedded in women since Eve ate of the apple. When libido peaks, there are no moral boundaries.

What I understood from this incident was evident and obvious. Nora never offered an explanation, and I never asked for one. Neither of us spoke of this occurrence ever again.

I worked on a toll switchboard addition in the Fort Rouge exchange for the next few months. A few personnel changes had happened since my last assignment at this location. We had a new cleanup and gofer person, an aged and cheerful gentleman with many life experiences. His name was Howard Bell.

When I was not playing Red Dog during breaks in the coffee room, I visited with him. Howard spoke of the early days, of clearing the prairies of stirrup-high grasses using fire. He also spoke of a plant root system under the surface of the ground that challenged the passing of a plow, and of numerous underground creatures like badgers, prairie dogs, and gophers.

He further spoke of the buffalo herds that once stood and watched as settlers cut sod to build shelters, and of flocks of prairie chickens that scattered when approached. Howard was speaking of wheat farms like the ones I had worked on seven years ago. He had been one of the hardy souls who helped create this breadbasket of the world.

Things done in the name of practical jokes were often not practical. One of our technicians, John Lechow, had a metal toolbox of personal hand tools. One day, he left it unlocked and located on an area with a wooden floor. A couple of my prankster colleagues drilled two little holes in the bottom of it and screwed it to the floor. At quitting time, John placed his tools in it and closed it, and when he went to pick it up with a jerk, he got only the handle. While he concealed his anger very well, he must have been royally perturbed.

I admired his ability to control his anger. It takes a great deal of character to do so.

Another of my colleagues on this job was a chap named Lorne Day. Lorne was an amiable and reliable person, but he had a weakness: Lorne was an alcoholic. At afternoon break time, Lorne would show up in the break room with a refreshed odor of rye whiskey on his breath. The mystery was, where did he stash it? In my three months on this job, no one ever found out. One might say he was refreshingly resourceful.

Another of my work buddies, John Holroyd, the one who promoted the Red Dog game, was also an alcoholic. Much time had passed since I had worked on a crew with John, but obviously, his habit was progressing. His work production and wiring accuracy suffered. It would ultimately come to no good and cost him his job. More about that when the time comes.

Yes, we were a company of a widely varied personalities. One was Jack, a former British commando. He had been involved in brutal action during the war, and it had carried over into public life. A trained killer is always a trained killer. He would get drunk and pick fights. He left a couple of severely injured victims that I know of. I was never sure how he was still walking the streets.

Ben Litwinowich, our St. Adolph neighbor, was also on this crew. We took turns carpooling to work, which took us across the frozen Red River to Highway 75. This avoided the ill-kept secondary road east of the river.

Ben and Gloria were social people and held many impromptu events at their house. He was a beer drinker, and many evenings, Nora and I would hire the landlord's daughter, Grace, to babysit while we walked to their house to watch Ed Sullivan, Red Skelton, and the ten o'clock news on their fourteen-inch TV.

Together, Ben and I would spend the occasional weekend wolf hunting on the plains near Portage la Prairie, or chop a hole in the river ice behind my house and fish. I once visited his birth home near Lake Winnipegosis. It was a small cabin where I was made welcome. He too had come from humble beginnings.

One cold winter's night visit to the Litwinowich house still haunts me. They had brought some supplies for us from Winnipeg, and I chose to drive the short distance to pick these up. The children were asleep, and the heater was stoked with coal. What harm could come from a few minutes' absence? Nora and I both made the visit to Ben and Gloria's.

As we visited, something on TV caught our attention, and our stay lasted over an hour.

Upon arrival back at the house, we found the place to be very very hot. The stovepipes were still burning red, and upstairs, Gail had collapsed into a grotesque sleeping position on top of her blankets. She had evidently been screaming in terror. This episode could have had a tragic ending.

Nora spent a restless night in tears. As I tried to comfort her, she said, through sobs of regret, "We could have killed them, every one of them. We need to get out of this place."

I will forever give thanks to God that our family was spared.

My guardian angel had once more prevailed, but that was of little comfort to Nora.

———————◆◆◆———————

Time passed, daylight became longer, and roads grew slushy during the day. Ice on the Red River was sinking and covered with water. Traffic crossings were halted, so now Ben and I drove the east bank road to work through St. Boniface. The toll switching addition in Fort Rouge was nearing completion.

Ronald Conway, head of Canadian Siemens operations, visited the Fort Rouge work site and took me aside to mention a contract to establish initial dial service in Ericson, Manitoba, to start in a few weeks. He offered me the in-charge position on the entire job. Would I accept the responsibility to supervise that installation?

I heard myself say "Yes!"

The job was scheduled to start in two weeks' time. I asked, "Can I select my crew?"

He smiled and said, "No! That's still my job."

I announced this development to Nora that evening, and she did not share my enthusiasm at all. She simply said, "How long will you be gone this time?"

I explained it was but 150 miles away, and I would be home most weekends.

Her immediate concern was, "Who gets the car, you or me?"

I told her of my intent to drive to Ericson and come home weekends. Ben and Gloria were close by and could always be called upon for any pressing supply needs. I sensed that she was not happy about this. Not at all!

As I have previously stated, when one turned down a promotion or a notice of relocation, one's career could forever be stunted. I did not want to be left behind with the company peons.

Throughout my career, I made choices based on my own perceived needs and desires. Nora was facing a decision of her own:

abide by me or leave me. Three children denied her a clear-cut choice. To leave, she would need someone to assume support for her and the children. Philandering men were not looking for commitments; they sought only trophies of conquest.

◆◇◆◇◆

Word of my appointment to the Ericson dial conversion spread, and a Friday night bash was planned by a group of coworkers. A party room was rented and stocked with booze and refreshment snacks.

There was liberal drinking to the point of intoxication, and a near-midnight decision was made to go have some "Chinese." Nora and I accepted an invitation to ride with George Rutland, himself a dedicated beer drinker. We made it only a few blocks on the night frozen streets before George ran off the road.

The impact threw us forward in the backseat, and Nora suffered a head injury. Another of our group who had been following transported us to the St. Boniface Hospital, where Nora was retained for observation. I was taken back to my car and drove home.

For that evening, we had employed the landlord's daughter, Grace, to babysit. She came wearing a wraparound kilt-length plaid skirt held closed with a large ornamental safety-pin fastener. The skirt was notably shorter than was traditional at this point in history, and I noticed.

When I arrived home, Grace was sitting on the living room couch with our oldest, Gail, who had removed and was playing with that ornamental safety pin. Grace's wraparound skirt was sufficiently unwrapped to allow a peekaboo display that included personal underthings. Now, alcohol removes inhibitions, and I had a pretty good snoot full. Yes, booze drives a man's Christian morals to regress from that of a civilized being to the erotic drives of farm animals.

After explaining why Nora was not here, I asked her to spend the night, since I would have to go back to St. Boniface in the morning. She said, "No problem," and went about putting Gail to bed.

With inebriated reasoning, I said to her, "It's cold and uncomfortable down here on the couch. Come up and share my bed."

She did! Grace was but fifteen years of age!

She came to bed with her personal dainties in place, but through a mist of alcohol-fueled fumbling about, I managed to remove them and attempted to assume the missionary position. She protested, and I promised I just wanted a corporeal touch.

She said "OK" and spread her legs.

To be true to my word, I did just that. I allowed myself a touch, but the laws of nature are strong. Soon I gently pushed, experienced entry, and ever-so-slowly permitted an inward glide. At some point, she stiffened up and said, "No! Don't do it, John!"

I stopped, felt her rigidness, and very slowly began a withdrawal. On completion of the withdrawal, we remained relaxed in the missionary position for a period, then I once again, slowly, very slowly, began a reinsertion. She let me pass the previous point of travel but once more stiffened and said, "No, John, please don't do it!"

Once again, I slowly withdrew, slid downward until my face was about breast level, and spread my seed upon the bed.

The Mother of Jesus gave birth at the age of fourteen. Therefore, by Canada law, the Immaculate Conception would have violated age-of-consent legislation. The father of Jesus could therefore have been proclaimed a pedophile.

While I carry the guilt of this evil, reprehensible act with me forever, I feel I have been in good company.

CHAPTER 20

THE ERICKSON MANITOBA STORY

*Do we not all have moments when we
just know we will glow tomorrow?*

It was Sunday. I would leave for the Erickson installation the next day and looked upon it as an adventure with more responsibility, more prestige, more pay, and a test of my management capabilities. It was a new and hopeful step on the critical path of my career.

In a fleeting five years, my progression from farm ploughboy to telephone office switching technician with management capabilities was beyond expectations. I was beginning to feel that I could be somebody.

On the other hand, Nora perceived this as only more sequester with three children in a primitive little house located in a neighborhood of less-than-caring people. She was now being asked to do so without a car.

After dinner, while still at the table, Nora turned to me, looked me square in the face, and asked, "Do you really intend to ever get us out of here?" Frustration was evident. She continued, "Can't we find a place in Winnipeg?" With a shallow sob, she continued, "We can afford it!" She obviously felt her life sliding from intense anxiety to downright sensory deprivation.

The "for better or for worse" vows were losing their balance.

—◆—◆—◆—

Nora should not be left so alone. What to do? A change in our living situation was essential. Could I justify more sacrifice on her behalf to accommodate my perceived career successes?

We were without debt and financially capable of moving to a home with more modern conveniences, like an electric cookstove and a refrigerator. I concede that no one in this day and age should have to wash cloths in a zinc wash tub with water heated over a coal burning cookstove.

I assured Nora, "We will look for a place in Winnipeg when the Erickson installation is complete." For some reason, I added, "The kids need a better place to grow up."

I did have high hopes that a good showing on this Erickson assignment would lead to an elevated salary or even a staff appointment with the company. Yes, I was riding on a cloud of optimism, but confidence is often a feeling one gets before one fully understands the situation.

My employer was the primary supplier of switching equipment for the Manitoba Telephone System. Since its primary market was Winnipeg, many employees seldom, if ever, left the city. Those were the more senior, but not of necessity the most capable, technicians. In the meantime, there was still my worth to prove. Every day gave me an opportunity, and I wouldn't want to waste a one.

—◆—◆—◆—

On Monday, I drove to Erickson with a soul full of hope and a will to achieve and thus justify my family's domestic inconveniences. Upon arriving, I found a village of perhaps five hundred souls. I met with the Manitoba Telephone System people and was given a key to the new switching building. A telephone had been installed, much equipment was already located on site, and I was given a list of equipment stored in a warehouse. Tomorrow, we started work!

Checking into the only hotel, I was assigned the room next

to the second-floor emergency exit. This would later prove to be convenient for letting in crew members when they outlasted the main door lock-up curfew at midnight. The accommodations included a communal hallway toilet and a separate bath and shower.

On checking the arrival of the crew, I found all present and accounted for. I rounded them up, took them for a beer in the hotel pub, then dined next door at Gunderson's Café. The crew consisted of Ozzie Culbertson, James Scott, Mathew McClure, and John Holroyd. All were known to me. It was a small installation with a seven-week schedule that included a two-week period for acceptance and cut-over to dial service.

On week one, we marked the floor plan; assembled equipment racks and terminal frames; and placed cable. During week two, we hung selector shelves and trunk relay units; mounted terminal blocks; and placed the emergency batteries and backup generator. An electrician was contracted to provide lighting and convenience outlets in the aisles, and then power up the battery-charging converters.

The next three weeks would have us placing, stripping, and terminating cable onto equipment and distribution frames; running jumper assignments; and then powering up the whole assembly. Week six would be testing of the entire unit and preparing for cut-over that would place dial phones in service and retire old magneto phones and manual switchboards. Week seven was customer acceptance, ending with an early Sunday morning cut-over to dial.

Everything did go well, but let me relate to you some of our experiences along the way.

The hotel was a typical small-town hotel, with a beer parlor for men only. There we went for a beer after work and then for dinner at Gunderson's Café. Ivar Gunderson and his wife were down-to-earth locals. His father had a farm a few miles up Highway 10 near the Riding Mountain Park entrance.

After dinner, I would often return to the worksite to plan the next day's activities, write reports, then go for a beer or to the café, where I'd visit with Ivar at the coffee counter. As a native resident, he had many colorful stories to relate.

His café had obviously been a grocery store at some time, and when I asked about it, he simply admitted failure in keeping it profitable after his children graduated high school and went to Winnipeg for employment. There was another restaurant in town that, as Ivar said, was "beating my ass off!" He and wife Brenda were struggling. I understood!

During the installation, my authority was being tested. I was a stickler for promptness and attendance, and one of my men was not. John Holroyd was an alcoholic and, in Erickson, there was no place to get anything but beer. John liked rye whiskey, and without it, his attitude suffered.

He stayed in town over the weekends, and James would bring him a mickey of rye when he returned on Sunday. John might or might not show up on time for work Monday mornings. His mickey (a twelve-ounce flat bottle) was gone by Tuesday. By Wednesday he was ornery, and his work attentiveness suffered.

I had always regarded John as a friend, a beer-drinking buddy, and had played Red Dog at many of his card parties. I tried to counsel John from day one, but he just waved me off. He was, after all, a middle-aged man with over ten years with the company. Who in hell did I think I was?

After three weeks, I made a painful but necessary decision. I sent him back to Winnipeg by bus. He was fired!

John was a well-known and well-liked member of the company, and as the word of his dismissal spread, I became an unloved in-charge company boss. It separated me forever from the productive employees' pool and placed me into the autocratic management class. I would carry this stigma for the remainder of my Siemens Brothers career.

On week five, a test engineer was sent to assess the quality of our work and prepare it for acceptance by the customer. He was an English bloke name of Bill Barr, loaded with British humor that, frankly, went way over my head, but he always had a good laugh at his own jokes.

For example: "The queen offered to give Canada back to the Indians, but they had reservations!" OK, you get the picture. That is pure and unadulterated British humor. Here's another. "A British man ran his hand through a friend's thinning hair and said, 'It feels just like my wife's pussy.' 'Yes,' said his friend, 'I noticed that!'" (We can take a brief break now while you have a good laugh.)

At an evening beer break, Bill confided in me that there was talk back at the office of sending another hand to the Halifax Nova Scotia sales office. He said confidentially, "John, your name has come up. Has anyone approached you?"

No one had, but I told him that although I would like to go back east, Halifax was a bit *too* far east. We laughed about it, and the subject was dropped.

A new face had appeared in Ivar's café. It was his sister Hazel, who had arrived from Winnipeg to spend a week with him and her parents in Onanole, near the Riding Mountain Park entrance. Hazel was probably a few years my senior and worked at a bank in Winnipeg. A couple of evenings, we chatted at the coffee counter about her job, her life in Winnipeg, and her apartment in a home on the bank of the mighty Red River.

She had big brown haunting eyes that were hard to avoid. Her flowing flaxen hair fell to her shoulders in ringlets, and her laugh was like that of a songbird. This indelible image would be imbedded into my memory.

As Hazel was serving us Thursday dinner, she asked, "Can I catch a ride back to Winnipeg with you tomorrow?" She added, "I could take the Saturday bus—just thought I would ask."

I was pleased at the thought of having her accompany me. Of course, the crew members kidded me about not getting caught driving home with a strange woman, but what the heck, what harm could come of it?

On Thursday, Ozzie and Mathew had been released to serve elsewhere. Bill and I would remain for the week's customer acceptance and cut-over procedure. On Friday, after work, I headed home, with Hazel on board. The job was ending, and I had not yet been given a reassignment. Rumor had it that it was in Saskatchewan. I thought, *Dear God, no! Not back to Saskatoon!*

Arriving in Winnipeg that evening, I dropped Hazel off at her place, wished her well, and headed home to St. Adolph. I never expected to ever see or hear from her again. The kids were glad to see me. Nora filled me in on her week's activities, and we turned in for a good night's rest. Life was good.

Saturday morning, we had breakfast, and Grace came to look after the children as we headed to Winnipeg to shop for next week's groceries. Just barely out of the driveway, Nora suddenly reached to the front dash shelf and pulled out an eyeglass case. The name inside was Hazel Gunderson! Her mind locked onto the obvious.

Her first exclamation was predictable: "Who is Hazel?" I explained as best I could and said, "We better drop her glasses case off on the way to Safeway."

It was a frosty ride to Hazel's place on Tod Road. I remembered that big classic house on the banks of the lazy, peaceful Red River. I left Hazel's glasses case with the pleasant, middle-aged lady who answered the door.

In the car I faced further harsh questions. Nora seemed to be lost in unpleasant thought, perhaps even hostile, or dejected, and that was not her nature. I was facing atonement, but it was Nora who was hurt, not me. I had this abysmal feeling of guilt.

I returned to Erickson Sunday afternoon for the final week of testing and preparation. The conversion to dial telephone service took place at two o'clock the following Sunday morning and went without a flaw. There was a ceremony with local persons of prominence present and much rejoicing and expressing of satisfaction with the result.

This, my first exchange conversion as an in-charge supervisor, should have been the high spot of my budding career, but my heart was heavy.

Could we continue to handle this means of living? I was beginning to harbor some doubts.

"A slack hand causes poverty" (Proverb 10:4.1), and I did not wish to always be poor.

"Love of money is the root of all kinds of evil" (Timothy 6:10), but I was willing to risk it.

CHAPTER 21

LOSS OF AN OPPORTUNITY

Success cannot be achieved by prolonged indecision.

T he Erickson experience was an achievement that reflected
well on my résumé. The cut-over went well, the customer was
happy, and I had demonstrated an ability to organize and
handle personnel situations. The Monday after the Erickson cut-
over, I reported to the main Winnipeg office for further assignment.
There I met with Ron Conway, our Winnipeg manager, and a
gentleman named Al Stevens, the sales representative from Halifax,
Nova Scotia.

After some chitchat about my background and future aspirations
I was offered a position in the Halifax sales office. I remember Al's
offer almost word-for-word. He said: "It is more of a customer service
position than a sales position, one that could benefit from your
problem-solving background. We can use that."

He went on to say that the job would be a salaried staff position
with on-call obligations. The territory would be the Maritime
Provinces, Newfoundland, and eastern Quebec, and I would enjoy
expense-account travel.

This offer seemed like everything I could have ever hoped for.
A salaried staff position—no more time clocks to punch, no more
hourly pay, a substantial advancement in income, a company car

for business trips, a desk of my very own in an office … what was there to think about? My mind did question why I was being offered this position when there were, in my opinion, many who were more qualified. What was the catch?

My inclination was to never turn down a position or promotion when offered. Such offers demonstrated management confidence, and refusal did damage one's company-loyalty image, but I did not want to go to Nova Scotia. It would take me far away from the very heartbeat of this company, which was right here in Winnipeg. This was the Promised Land.

I was then assigned to work in the Winnipeg West Exchange while I contemplated my response, and I reported there on Tuesday.

Nora was quite receptive to the Halifax proposal—partly, I am sure, because it would be an escape from St. Adolph, and our moving costs would be paid. I also believe she wished it because it would end long-term assignments away from home and family. Some pressure here: I really didn't feel comfortable venturing into this undertaking, but this was not just about me. It was, do the right thing for the good of the family, or do what best pleased me. I was wrestling with my conscience.

Be it a matter of record: whenever I wrestle with my conscience, I win!

———————

On Thursday morning, I declined the Halifax, Nova Scotia, position.

Nora was not as disappointed as expected. Her family and friends and her roots were here in Manitoba, and her number-one priority was to get out of St. Adolph and into a home with modern conveniences. To this end, I would pick up a copy of the *Winnipeg Free Press* after work almost daily, and together we would review the rentals. On Saturday mornings, we made our way to a public phone in Winnipeg, made appointments, and viewed what was available.

The month of May was ending, and June rentals that would have suited our needs and budget were scarce to nonexistent. Private-home leasers did not want three young children in their house, and most apartments just simply said "no children." It wasn't very encouraging. It would be easier to find a place if we had a dog and two cats than three preschool-age children.

By now, our June rent was near due in St. Adolph, and we had given no notice. Obviously, we would spend June in St. Adolph and hope to find a suitable vacancy by July. In the meantime, I continued to work in the Winnipeg West Exchange.

For the past couple of years, I had been studying circuit schematics and becoming conversant with their functions. This piqued more interest in my chosen technology, which led me to enroll in an evening electromagnetic circuit comprehension course in the Northwest Collegiate Institute of Manitoba. Further, I had purchased a book on fundamental electric theory, and between the two, was becoming familiar with our switching system, the how and why it worked. Some of this knowledge I had already applied in our day-to-day power-up difficulties, but it became obvious to me that the more I learned, the more I didn't know.

One of the classes I attended was taught by Ron Conway, our company general manager. This pleased me. It was surely an opportunity to show off my circuit skills and my desire to learn. It backfired one evening when I questioned one of his explanations. After I outlined my point of view, he simply sloughed off my opinion. Who could question the information he had right there in a book, written by experts who clearly explained the reason some feature in a circuit operated in the way it did?

I took this home, studied it, and dissected every conceivable alternative possibility that one might imagine. I was not wrong, and I intended to bring it up at the next class.

Mr. Conway beat me to it. He started the next class addressing the subject I had questioned. He simply said he was misled by the explanation and went on with the lesson. I sensed that one did not question Mr. Conway in class. I was never sure if this encounter was to my credit or consequence.

———————————

Spring came, and summer dawned on our lives in St. Adolph. We told our longtime landlord about looking for accommodations in Winnipeg but put nothing in an official writing of notice. He allowed as how he was considering turning the little house over to an aging relative anyway.

I had already spoken to one of my work friends about a small house he owned and would rent to us when they moved into their new home, now under construction. It was small but in a neighborhood that I was familiar with, near my old boardinghouse on Fleet Street. There was a kitchen, dining room, and living area downstairs, and a two-room bedroom suite and bath upstairs. A central coal furnace in the basement propelled heat through a large round register in the downstairs hall, which in turn heated the upstairs through a ceiling grate.

He more or less promised it to me when he was ready to move. There was nothing in writing, but we felt our pursuit of living accommodations was at an end. All was going to be well. Time and patience could heal all anxieties.

———————————

One day in late July, my foreman called me to his desk. Upon approaching, I saw waiting there Mr. Ron Conway.

Mr. Conway greeted me with a cheerful message that he had been impressed by my analytic approach to electromechanical circuitry at the collegiate, and my Erickson assignment had been exemplary. The result of this meeting was a job assignment. I would once again be promoted to in-charge status and undertake a switching and toll board addition, this time in Indian Head, Saskatchewan. I had three weeks' notice to be there.

Was this a triumph with a tragic result? Indian Head, Saskatchewan? Really?

Really!

Now about that promise of a Winnipeg apartment …

Moving to a house in the city would mean the purchase of a washing machine, refrigerator, stove, and additional bedroom furniture. None of this would come with the house we expected to rent, and which was not yet available.

A solution must be found. We had three weeks!

CHAPTER 22

THE INDIAN HEAD FAMILY EXPERIENCE

*To take away the outcomes of personal choice is
to destroy the opportunity of providing for love.*

When I revealed the Indian Head assignment, Nora had but one comment: "I'm not going to stay here!" There was a shaky note of sad finality in her voice, or was it frustration ... or determination? There could be no question: she was disheartened, almost fearful. I took a deep breath and considered the situation. Alas, it was my turn to make a sacrifice.

Finding a rental house in our income range within the time we had was unlikely. The house we were counting on would not be available for at least two, perhaps three months. Apartments that would accept three preschool age children were all but nonexistent, and the clock was ticking.

One alternative was for me to renege on my Indian Head assignment, which would still leave us living here in St. Adolph and most assuredly diminish my growing employee value. My job was our only security. I felt like a tube of toothpaste that was being squeezed in the middle. Something had to give at one end or the other.

I fully sympathized with Nora. Our decision to live in this place, void of modern conveniences, had been one of economics. Yes, we both had come from underprivileged backgrounds, but we had now seen and experienced modern amenities. We no longer belonged here. Our children did not belong here. We had modest financial reserves because of inconveniences and sacrifices made by her. Enough was enough. It was my turn.

One week prior to the commencement of the Indian Head installation, I proposed two choices: "Stay here until the job is completed or bring the children and come with me." I added, "Think of it as an adventure. Think of it as an escape. Think of how good it will be to come home in a couple of months and move into that promised house in Winnipeg."

She smiled. I knew we were on the right course. She would escape St. Adolph, Manitoba! We would be together as a family! It would be an adventure. Life would be better.

When she said "OK," a sense of relief washed over me. We would get to experience some life together.

We had no way of knowing what accommodations might be available in Indian Head. There was just mutual determination to do something without knowing how to do it. Blinded by, or motivated by, some strange lack of reason, we made plans.

Our landlord, Mike, was informed that we would pay the rent and leave the furniture in the house. I also told him that on our return, we would soon be moving to Winnipeg and give notice at that time. He understood and told me, "I'll keep an eye on your things and wish you the best." It was settled.

On a hazy morning in early June 1957, we headed down the two-lane hardtop Highway 1 for Indian Head, Saskatchewan—me, Nora, the three children, and what essentials we could cram into a 1949 DeSoto. The 315-mile drive took us through small towns and villages and endless flatlands of fresh sprouting wheat.

Our trunk was packed with household items and wardrobes. The back seat held cardboard boxes of travel needs on which sat the upholstered baby basinet Nora and Blossom had put together in Edmonton. It now held baby Ronald. Gail rode in the front with us, and during that entire trip embraced a round-faced, round-eyed fabric doll with great affection.

We had brought along sandwiches and Kool-Aid for the road, so only gas stops and pit stops for natural relief and diaper changes were necessary. Baby Ronald reluctantly drank unheated milk from a bottle, and Gail became quite fascinated with radio buttons to provide us with a variety of entertainment that kept us content.

We were together, we were a family, we were sharing an adventure. And by the end of the journey, we would also vow to never do this again.

The all-day drive landed us at Indian Head in late afternoon. A helpful attendant at the Highway 1 turnoff gas station advised us that the most probable and practical place to find living accommodations was a cabin rental place just down the road. We found it!

Good fortune prevailed. The owner's largest two-bedroom cabin, with a cooking and dining area, was available. The negotiated rent would take over half of my per-diem allowance, but it would work. It was a long-term rate with no provision for bedding or housekeeping services. There were cooking utensils, an electric stove, and indoor washroom facilities. We even had a laundry service close by. Indian Head didn't look so bad after all.

We spent the rest of the afternoon and evening grocery shopping, getting beds made, getting the children to bed, and eating the last of our sandwiches. We finally settled into a good night's sleep.

Indian Head was surrounded by extensive nondescript flatlands of wheat. Located about a half mile north of Highway 1, it straddled the Canadian Pacific Railway mainline. The skyline was interposed with countless grain elevators and streets that were dusty and rough. There were general stores; farm machinery sales and service businesses; a restaurant; a couple of hotels with beer parlors; a hospital; and a curling rink. This town of roughly a thousand souls was a pleasant surprise. We were not going to miss St. Adolph.

<hr />

Next day at the telephone exchange, I met the local phone company representative, arranged for delivery of our tools and switching equipment, got permission to use their break room (but we had to buy our own coffee percolator and supplies), and had a telephone installed. Tomorrow we would go to work.

My crew was staying in the nearest hotel and reported at eight o'clock the next morning. We were in business. The crew consisted of Ozzie Culbertson, James Scott, Frank Ward, Willie Leib, Mathew Martin, and an English bloke named Eric Robertson. The only new face to me was Eric, and all were experienced installers.

It was at this time I was to learn that Bill Barr, one of my Erickson installation crew, had been awarded the Halifax position. I was happy for him. It was a good choice for both him and the company.

Time passed, and installation progressed according to schedule. We settled into life in our little cabin, enduring the sweltering daytime breezes and cool chilly nights. I often drank beer with the crew on Friday evenings at the local pub, and on Saturdays and Sundays fished the Qu'Appelle River. Nora made regular meals, and the children gleefully played with the landlord's dog. Life was good.

One evening near bedtime, there was a knock on our door. No one was expected. Upon opening the door, I saw a couple of Royal Canadian Mounted Police constables. Their first question: "Do you know Frank Ward?"

I informed them that he was one of my employees and instinctively knew this was not good. The constable replied, "He's in the jail at the firehouse. He asked us to bring you."

Frank had been arrested over nonpayment for a case of beer. He claimed he did pay; the pub attendant claimed he did not. In any case, what Frank needed right now was $50 for bail—in cash. I did not have $50 in cash. The local bailiff lamented that if we could not raise bail, he would have to spend the whole night in the firehouse, because prisoners could not be left unattended. He wanted me to raise that $50 bail money. He wanted to go home!

I went to the hotel, rounded up the crew, and they came up with $50. James took on the chore to deliver it to the firehouse, where the bailiff took the cash, gave him a receipt, opened the cell door, let Frank out, and went home.

Next morning, Frank showed up to work his usual grumpy self and informed me there would be a hearing next week. It would mean a day off. This was not his first brush with adversity. In fact, just the day before, I had received a complaint from the Alberta Government Telephone management about his conduct and was debating with myself about getting him off the crew. Frankly, he gave me the creeps.

I called the personnel department next day and apprised them of the situation. It was decided that we would do nothing until his hearing.

The summer was passing. The job proceeded. Harvesting of the wheat in the surrounding fields had begun, and the installation was ending. A testing technician I now remember only as Moose came to prepare for the in-service cut. I retained James Scott and Ozzie Culbertson and released Mathew and Eric. Frank was now long gone. He had been fired.

As the job ended in Indian Head, our marriage had become somewhat affable. Over the past three months, I had been home for dinner every day, and we slept together every night. Together with the children, we had made weekend sightseeing drives to view the fruited plains of Saskatchewan. I fished the Qu'Appelle River with the family, and Nora and I had driven to a Regina Rough Riders football game. Nora cooked the prairie chickens I bagged, and together we hosted beer parties for the staff.

The children now expected Dad home every day and climbed over me as I reclined on the squeaky couch in the draughty cabin.

Life had evolved into something one might think of as normal. *So this is what it feels like to be a family. It is good.*

Now it was August 24, 1957. Tonight, at midnight, the major addition to the Indian Head telephone system would be placed into service. All verifications were completed, and all was in readiness. There was a small amount of post-cut-over activity to complete, and on the Labor Day weekend, we would bid adieu to Indian Head, Saskatchewan. We would journey back to St. Adolph, Manitoba, back to a house without modern-day conveniences, back to a neighborhood that cared not for our welfare.

However, a new development in my career was about to take place. Ronald Conway had come to observe the cut-over and brought tidings of good news. At a morning coffee break, he announced my appointment to the position of staff installer, effective September 1. I would be a salaried employee in a position that included many improved benefits, a much-improved salary, and a level of prestige I had only dreamed of.

At the age of twenty-four, I was the youngest person ever to have been awarded a staff position, for which I had worked so assiduously. I'd spent long hours studying circuit schematics on the job and in my room and created grading procedures that were now adapted as standards by the company. Nora and the children had sacrificed much for me to attain this triumph. At last, we might now harvest the fruits of these endeavors. I was elated.

My next assignment was to be one of the largest dial conversions currently on the books: Salmon Arm, British Columbia. The Salmon Arm job had a five-month schedule that would take us into next year, and we did cringe at the thought of returning to Manitoba in February—but we would cross that bridge when we got to it.

In the meantime, I had heard nothing from my friend Mike, my work associate in Winnipeg, regarding the availability of his house. One Saturday morning, I called him from a pay phone, hoping all would soon be in readiness. Mike regretted to tell me that he had sold his house a month earlier, saying he'd had no idea as to when, or if, Nora and I would return. He was sorry.

This would change the dynamics of our life.

CHAPTER 23

THE COMING EXODUS FROM ST. ADOLPH

*When facing adversity, one may view
only the potential for greatness and
forget that a pool of darkness lurks.*

We returned to St. Adolph, gave our rental notice, arranged to have the furniture transported to Security Storage at our beck and call, and obtained containers for Nora to bundle up those personal and household goods to be shipped later. The company gave me airfare and two days of travel to get to Salmon Arm. To drive twelve hundred miles across barren plains and treacherous mountain passes with family would be stressful. We agreed that I would drive, and the family would follow by train.

I drove the American route through North Dakota, Idaho, and Montana, and turned north in Washington State to Osoyoos. I once again drove through those lofty blue hills of the Okanagan Valley. How well I remembered having seen them for the first time. How good to hear once again the constant *swish swish swish* of irrigation sprinklers. How beautiful was the tranquil Kalamalka Lake of many colors that I gazed upon as I drove north through this peaceful valley. I had a new feeling of self-worth. Life was good.

Eventually, in late evening, I arrived at Salmon Arm, a city of perhaps four thousand located at the southernmost tip of Shuswap Lake, British Columbia. I checked into an Okanogan Street hotel for a much-needed night's rest. It was September 9, 1957.

My arrival ahead of the crew was an opportunity to meet customer engineering and construction staff and arrange storage and deliveries of equipment, the majority of which had been shipped from England in heavy weatherproof lumber containers that were hard to open and difficult to dispose of. Our construction tools were already on-site, along with much iron framework and support steel already stored along one side of the new exchange area.

The chief engineer of the Okanagan Telephone Company, Clifford Blain, was English. He was well known in the communications industry and a former employee of Siemens whom I had met on a previous assignment. He brought plant and equipment maintenance supervisors to confer with me.

As we sat at a folding table on folding chairs in the new equipment room, a plant supervisor drew attention to floor furrows—depressions like forklift tracks. There were other grooves and indentations that were out of place. A subsequent investigation revealed an unfortunate fact: the floor material was a soft, chalky, unacceptable grade of some material that was not concrete. Our meeting was called off, to be resumed the next day.

It was determined that remedial action by the contractor was needed, and commencement of installation would be delayed three weeks. This information was communicated to the head office. The crew would be delayed, and I was to go to Edmonton for a holdover assignment.

A message was relayed to Nora to stay put for the time being, and I was off to Edmonton by way of the treacherous Rogers Pass highway. I wrote her a heartfelt letter to make her aware of the reason for the delay and promised to keep her informed. Yes, our escape from St. Adolph, Manitoba, was delayed, but life would get better.

Now in Edmonton, as a staff employee, I did not do union

employee work. My stay in Edmonton was to keep busy and keep informed on the Salmon Arm building progress.

The cut-over date in Salmon Arm was not being extended so I took the time available to compile a detailed and critical path installation schedule. Using the specifications and the equipment layouts, I prepared a detailed time-graph and submitted it to my management and to the Okanogan engineering staff. It was scrutinized, questioned, and passed all critiques. It was acclaimed as one of the most detailed schedules ever presented.

All agreed we go for it. No cut-over extension. Salmon Arm would have dial telephone service in January 1958. Salmon Arm was the last city in the Okanagan Telephone System to still have operators for local service.

———————

On September 30, 1957, I would return to Salmon Arm, facing a compressed installation schedule. My mettle was about to be tested.

Meanwhile, back in St. Adolph. Nora was still awaiting her escape plan. Time was passing, and her mettle was also being tested. She had no car, was imposing on neighbors Ben and Gloria Litwinowich for shopping and water supply and such, and winter was coming on. In a telephone conversation, she pleaded, "What exactly is going on in Salmon Arm? What is happening to our family? I can't spend another winter here!"

She further stated, or threatened, "If worse comes to worse, I will move myself to Winnipeg!"

I worried. A youthful woman alone with three children in an urban community by nature becomes a targeted entity. I had learned from my travels that our marriage background could lead to Nora's vulnerability. God-given instincts will guide a married woman to secure social partners and engage in selective sexual affairs if her needs are not otherwise met. The desire for extramarital sex does not mean that women are not monogamous; it just is because it is.

I realize that an exodus from St. Adolph must occur, one way or another.

CHAPTER 24

MY SALMON ARM STORIES

By the sweat of thy brow shalt thou
eat bread ...—Geneses 3:19

L eaving Edmonton, I once more I navigated the rugged beauty of
the nerve-wracking highway to Salmon Arm. It was a winding
road along intimidating cliffs overlooking picturesque gorges,
canyons, and regal mountains as it wended its way through the
remote settlement of Rogers Pass, British Columbia. I experienced
breathtaking curves on the cliffs of Glacier Park, where the snow line
remained close and personal all year round.

Some drive this trail for vacation adventure, the thrill of danger,
to witness the beauty of unspoiled nature and the privilege of seeing
receding glaciers. Here, in the forested mountains, I heard the silence
of nature. No droning aircraft, no whining tires, no angry chainsaws
or screaming sawmills, just the call of birds, soft breezes straining
through coniferous foliage, and the occasional call of big game. A
sporadic sighting of mountain goats was an additional reminder that
this land was created by the hand of God and was, as yet, unspoiled
by human development.

Having arrived in Salmon Arm, and after the customary client
consultations and on-site arrangements, I began to seek appropriate
accommodations for the crew. Often the best people to ask are the

local telephone operators, and here I hit pay dirt. The chief operator knew a widow who was interested in accommodating boarders. She also had kin who owned a nearby motel and would negotiate family rates. Bingo. The crew would start arriving the next day, so my first approach was to the widow Brown.

Amelia Brown had been recently widowed by a tragic sawmill accident and was thrilled to accommodate up to four of the crew. Her home was located about a half mile from town in a modern house at the base of Mount Ida. A cold mountain stream ran through her large and neatly manicured yard. Perfect. I would refer crew members to her for accommodations.

I, on the other hand, settled for the Palomino Motel, about halfway between the widow Brown's boarding house and town. That evening, I wrote Nora and told her I was ready and waiting, and to have Security Storage come pick up the furniture, give final notice to Landlord Mike, board the train, and leave St. Adolph for the last time. I was waiting.

During the remainder of the week, my crew showed up, floor locations were marked, iron racks were assembled and secured, cable runway was placed, and the work area was a buzzing hive of activity. The progress schedule was posted week by week, and the staff consulted it, taking pride in meeting or exceeding the provisions of the plan. Salmon Arm was on its way to having dial telephone service.

On a cloudy Friday morning, Nora arrived with Gail, Ritchie, and baby Ronald. The Pullman trip had been long and stressful. Our family was now settled in the cramped quarters of unit one of the Palomino Motel. There was a countertop stove, a refrigerator, a table, chairs, cupboards, a double bed, and a fold-down couch. This was now home for the duration of the installation. We were a family—let no one put us asunder!

In the weeks ahead, I and members of the crew found time to drink beer at the local pub, fish in a nearby stream, do target practice at the widow Brown's country estate, and enjoy the approaching fall season. Let me tell you about some adventures outside of work that have blessed me with some memories I wish to share.

I was always intrigued by a little crystal-clear stream that originated in Mount Ida and flowed through the widow Brown's property. There was a constant flow year round; where did it come from? What was its source? It had become a topic of conversation that prompted me to go find an answer.

One Sunday morning, Nora made me a packsack of food, and I took my old .303 British Lee-Enfield rifle in hand and decided to ascend to that source. The early going was without incident, but soon foliage became thick and the slope was much steeper. Here and there, the creek bed was nestled in a deep depression I could not follow, and the stream was difficult to relocate when detours were necessary.

At times, the creek side rocks were too slippery with moss and slime to walk in or near it. This meant more forays into dense forest and even more difficulty in relocating the creek when elevation progress was made. This was not quite what I had expected, but what the heck, it was an adventure.

When the sun was high, I scooped up some of the clear sweet water in my telescoping cup and ate some lunch. During this lunch break, I could see Shuswap Lake in the distance, surrounded by misty mountains with a corona of wispy white clouds. I felt nowhere near the source of the creek, but the widow Brown and her boarders were awaiting a report on its birthplace. I felt a challenge to proceed.

The terrain became even steeper, with more vertical rocky slopes and fewer trees. The little stream source was still far up, and daylight shadows were getting long.

At one point, while approaching the creek ravine, I smelled an unpleasant odor—a strong, pungent odor. I was somewhat familiar with wild things and somewhat aware of which animals generated such an odor. I loaded a shell into the chamber of the rifle but did not feel all that comfortable in my safety.

I made not a sound for several minutes—a thing called fear had crept into my whole body. There was no fight or flight option here. I had never dealt with this level of fear before. These several minutes seemed eternal, as the rustle of footsteps beyond the creek gully moved away.

I decided that now was the time to return to the base of Mount Ida.

Moving downhill is as difficult as uphill on steep mountain slopes, and it is possible to lose one's way. Seems like there are more directions than just up or down. I lost sight of the creek and began to have hopes of emerging from the bush somewhere near where I started. Dusk was gathering. I never thought I was lost; I just wasn't sure where I was.

Near the bottom, I sighted the top of a ski lift and knew it to be on the widow Brown's property. My guide to the point of entry! As I entered the backyard by the little stream, the widow Brown and her boarders welcomed me and awaited my report. I told them, "I just lost interest and came home."

I still wonder if anyone has ever found the source of that stream. I wonder if it still provides water to the home of the widow Brown. I wonder if that thick forest of great fir trees has ever been harvested by man. Somehow, I do not want to know. May I forever live with memories of the intact beauty of Mount Ida.

Lengthy, sprawling Shuswap Lake was laced amongst mountain ranges. It was shaped like a modified K or crooked H. There were but two population centers of any consequence on the entire lake: Salmon Arm and Sicamous. The 120-square-mile surface was said to be more than five hundred feet deep in places and home to Shagamu, a serpent-like monster some twenty feet in length.

I had a chance encounter with an elderly man in a local pub who related some folklore about the northeastern Seymour Arm. He spoke knowingly of a ghostly settlement long abandoned by prospectors of placer gold. The tales were fascinating. Were these just ramblings offered in exchange for beer? Did such a place really exist? Other locals said he was for real.

He told me how prospectors once swarmed to the Seymour Arm to pan for placer gold. He also spoke of supply rafts that carried goods and mail from Sicamous to the camps and spoke of transporting mining tools and equipment by raft. He spoke of men dredging sand from the lake bottom and panning the gold on floating platforms. He spoke of claim disputes that ended in death, and bodies buried beyond the tree line above sandy beaches.

One remark that really caught my attention was when he said that an old "hermit of the hills" still lived in the forests of the Seymour Arm. Could he be making this up?

Further conversation revealed that he had spent his working life maintaining track in the mountain wilderness for the railroad. He spoke of long labor camp sequesters, and a departed wife and family who felt abandoned by his long absence on the job. (He began to remind me of me! I took notice.)

I and a couple of my staff decided to go on an excursion to the Seymour Arm. On a cool Sunday morning, "Mac" McNulty, John Nastiase, and I left Sicamous in a rented boat bound for the Seymour Arm. It was a full four-hour ride, and we saw not another boat on the lake.

As we approached the northernmost end, there was sparkling yellow sand in the shallow waters sheltered by mountains and tall timber. As we drew closer, we saw the shaky remains of an old hotel and, hold on now—a beautiful, partitioned pond of water lilies? Yes, just beyond that, nestled on a wooded slope, was a neat, well-maintained log bungalow. As we pulled up on the sandy beach, an elderly man came to greet us. Was this, then, the hermit of the hills?

He made us welcome, took us on a tour of the old boardinghouse, and showed us letters he had kept dry and preserved over the years. I read a couple of faded letters from home, written by a loved one with a fountain pen. Another was a Dear John letter that must have broken someone's heart. We were invited to his cabin and enjoyed a meal of preserved moose meat and baked potatoes.

We listened to tales of his life at the Seymour Arm—tales of the gold rush, tales that confirmed the stories of the old man in the pub, and more. He had remained behind when the rush was over, having no family and a full poke reflecting a successful endeavor. He needed little more than he had.

We visited an unmarked burial location in the wooded area. There were no names on the wooden crosses, and the scratching's on stone slabs were no longer decipherable. We drank from the stream that flowed down from the hills, filled our water bottles, and took a sample of the beach sand in a metal can. (Although we never did get it assayed for gold content, our host said there was gold in every shovel full.)

The sun was sinking as we left that old man on the shore waving us good-bye. I do not remember his name.

Winter came to Salmon Arm, the snow came, and our equipment installation progressed. We celebrated Christmas, then New Year's, and our cozy motel accommodations became home. Nora and I partied with the staff members and played Red Dog with them. We became a social block.

One day, a couple of visitors dropped into our work location and introduced themselves as telephone workers with the British Columbia Telephone Company. They had heard about this English Strowger switching equipment and wanted to see it for themselves. I proudly gave them a tour and demonstrated the operational features.

Being somewhat familiar with their Automatic Electric Co. switching equipment, I said that "comparing our equipment to yours is like comparing a fine Swiss movement watch to a Big Ben alarm clock, but your equipment has a reputation of reliability." Yes, there was mutual admiration of our rival products.

During the conversation, it was mentioned that the Canadian B.C. Installations Company was hiring. My mind latched onto those words. That company installed exclusively for the British Columbia Telephone Company, a company confined to the southwestern region of British Columbia with headquarters in Vancouver. Had my guardian angel just delivered a potentially life-changing message?

I obtained from them the name and phone number of the personnel manager of the Canadian B.C. Telephone Company. Opportunity knocks only so often. One must be alert.

In January of 1958, the little town of Salmon Arm, British Columbia, converted to dial service. The manager of Siemens was on hand, as was the chief engineer of the Okanagan Telephone Company. There was press representation and a proliferation of unfamiliar faces in white shirts, ties, and business suits milling about awaiting the "pulling of pics" that set the newly installed telephones into service.

Photographing of technicians pretending to make last-minute adjustments to electromechanical selectors or trunk circuits had taken place. At a few minutes before two in the morning, the telephone operators' switchboards were glowing with call lights from people staying up until this hour to make the last call on the manual board. Too bad—that had already happened! They would soon be making calls on the new dial exchange.

The clock was ticking. Silence was called. The countdown was in progress: 10-9-8-7-6-5-4-3-2-*cut*! Okanagan employees at the mainframe, in unison, pulled bundles of lacing cord attached to blocking pics. The pics fell to the floor in rustling piles, and rotary-line switches spun into action. First selectors were seized.

Late-night customers heard the sound of a dial tone for the first time. Then dials were spun, and Salmon Arm joined the modern world of automatic dial.

At 2:01a.m., there is much handshaking, back-slapping and insincere compliments as the new equipment rattled through the onslaught of first-time callers. Little by little, things quieted down, and I went home to the Palomino Motel.

My obligation to Siemens was over. It was good.

CHAPTER 25

NEW HORIZONS

Change may intrude into our comfort zone,
but risk is the only path to progress.

During the second week of January 1958, I phoned the personnel manager of the Canadian B.C. Telephone Company, and a man's voice confirmed they were hiring and invited me to apply. I hung up the phone with much elation about making a change in my career path. The new job would be confined to a single province, not the vast scattered populations of all Canada. I was ecstatic with anticipation.

While awaiting the arrival of that application by mail, I made the impulsive decision to submit my resignation to Siemens Bros. Yes—I was that sure.

On February 1, I drove the long snow-obstructed Hope-Princeton route and checked into the Hotel Vancouver. On Monday, an interview with the personal director of the Canadian B. C. Telephone Company was arranged for next morning.

My application had been received, but as the interviewer glanced over it, I sensed some sudden apprehension. As he glanced away and seemingly spoke to no one in particular, he said, "Does seven years of experience on similar equipment compensate for no high school diploma?"

For the first time, a feeling of panic crept into my mind and body. Good God, what had I done? After some discussion regarding my experience, and my family and marital background, the interviewer excused himself and left me stewing in the interview room.

Soon a young lady brought me a cup of coffee, placed it by me, and said, in a reassuring voice, "Everything will be OK." I will always wonder: did she already know something I didn't? Apparently so. I was hired!

Yes, my lifelong guardian angel was still with me. Once more, I had been blessed.

I obtained a crisp new paper map of city streets and spent two days hunting a home. A rental was located at 793 21st Avenue, just around the corner from the Royal Canadian Legion on Frazer Street. From time to time, that would prove to be a bit too convenient.

The house was the typical drafty old two-story frame structure. Its partially in-ground basement harbored a coal-burning furnace that fed heat upward to the first floor through a large hallway register. I paid a deposit from my rapidly diminishing cash, and on Friday began the long, lonely return trip back through those mountain passes to Salmon Arm.

Just north of Penticton, drowsiness and perhaps a bit of hunger got the best of me. I ran the car over a steep rocky cliff for about a twenty-foot drop. I suffered a few cuts and contusions but spent the night in a Penticton Hotel. Next day, I arranged for the disposal of the totaled car and arrived home by bus on Sunday.

———◆•◆•◆———

Back in Salmon Arm, I described for Nora the beautiful downtown Vancouver region, the constant daily rains, and the splendor of its many parks. She was cheerful and optimistic. She was envisioning a future she deeply coveted, had earned, and was about to achieve.

On Monday and Tuesday, we arranged for furniture delivery from Winnipeg, packed what household goods we could, and shipped them with my tools to our new home. On Wednesday, we bade Salmon Arm adieu and boarded a train as a complete family. I gazed from the train at the rugged beauty of these mountains in a land I was growing to love.

Among the rocky shale of crumbling hills, valleys, and streams is a land that has long defied man. Hunters, prospectors, surveyors, and adventurers have penetrated much of this hostile terrain, but only the railroads have left much evidence of their trespassing.

To the click of steel wheels on iron rails, the puffing of a steam engine, the occasional angry wheeze of a steam whistle, and a tracer of black coal smoke, I left my life with Siemens behind forever. My seven years there had been a building point in my life. The company took me from an unknowing backwoods farm kid with no social graces to a respected electromechanical technician. It set me on the first step to a prosperous life—but for my wife and family, it had been a life of deprivation and neglect.

Upon our arrival in Vancouver, we took possession of the unfurnished rental house equipped with a fridge and stove and little else. No furniture! Our bedding and kitchenware arrived from Salmon Arm, and that was our survival kit until the furniture arrived from Winnipeg.

Ten days of sleeping on the floor has its discomforts, but more importantly, on Monday, I had started work at the Trinity Telephone exchange and fit in like a part in a jigsaw puzzle. I was extending my career in the telephone equipment installation business and was now even more confident about our future. Life was good.

Having finally arrived by Canadian Pacific Express, our furniture was placed in the proper rooms. Nora arranged clothes, towels, and bedding into appropriate closets and furniture drawers. Dishes were placed in cupboards, and life took on a sense of normalcy. We occupied a complete standalone house with relatively modern conveniences. We even splurged and bought our first-ever television set. By unspoken word, we vowed that nothing would ever place us back into a place like St. Adolph. We felt good.

It was now that Nora decided to inform me that she was pregnant.

I found a comfort level amongst the technical staff of the new company and was made to feel at home. Trinity Exchange was large, and expansions and rearrangements were constant. Occasionally there were staff changes and personnel selections strictly at management discretion.

One day, I was advised that my services were needed at the main exchange in Victoria, B.C., a major city at the southern tip of Vancouver Island. Nora was but a few weeks away from delivery of our fourth child. This was a situation I had not contemplated. Why me? Well, it seemed as though to placate the union, employees of lesser seniority were first considered in decisions of such transfers. I had but six months seniority.

My first-ever flight was to Vancouver Island. The DC-4, perhaps better-known as the Douglas North Star, was a four-engine machine that vibrated and was noisy. I enjoyed looking down upon the broad expanses of the Strait of Georgia with its scattered islands, at the majestic snowcapped Mount Seymour, and at Tolmie Mountain, among others. Automobiles on roadways and ships at sea looked like toys. Another memorable moment for future fond recollection.

Once again, I was working remote from the family. The per diem pay made it less painful. It was an assignment, not a transfer, but my role of husband and father was bound to come into review. Where exactly did I stand in my domestic obligations?

> *Oh wad some power the giftie gie us*
> *To see ourselves as ithers see us!*
> *—Robert Burns*

CHAPTER 26

OUR VANCOUVER EXPERIENCES

Overconfidence has not driven me to accomplish
what I have. The fear of failure has motivated me.

The installation in the main exchange of Victoria introduced me to a new-to-me segment of telephony: toll transmission equipment, phantom circuits, and E&M signaling devises. This lifted my spirits, since multiple voice transmissions and data on single-pair small-gauge wire was the upcoming technology. I welcomed this opportunity to get involved.

Time passed. One evening, a phone call from Nora brought news of a depressing diagnosis. Her condition indicated that our son would soon need to be taken by cesarean section.

I did not take this news well. My room became a cage as I envisioned all kinds of dark and unknown consequences. Nora, a strong, healthy, indomitable woman, now seemed vulnerable and delicate. She needed me home, and I was not there!

The next day, I called the installation manager and explained why I was needed at home. My request was granted. I would report to the Vancouver main exchange on Monday.

It was evident that Nora would need some help and care. While I was at work, a sixteen- year-old neighbor girl was employed to do housework, laundry, and be the proverbial girl Friday.

Time passed. The delivery date was set, and then a phone call came. Our sixteen-year-old neighbor girl had been arrested and placed in juvenile detention. I'm not sure of the details, but an American aircraft carrier had arrived in port, and she was picked up for soliciting on the sailor-saturated downtown streets. (Yes, she was just sixteen!)

Number-three son, Gary Steven Geen, was delivered July 27, 1958.

Our life in Vancouver was relatively uneventful, and the nature of my current job made us a normal working family. Summer passed, baby Gary grew strong, our little backyard garden was productive, and I had developed quite an impressive workbench in the basement where I dismantled old radios and rebuilt them into stereo amplifiers.

We spent our leisure time enjoying the available attractions of the community, often taking the kids to Stanley Park and taking pictures at the famous Totem Pole by Lions Gate Bridge and of Nora and the kids standing in the hollowed stump of the giant redwood tree. We rode the Grouse Mountain cable car and strolled along the Spanish Bank beach. On occasion, we wandered through the colorful Queen Elizabeth Arboretum.

Nora and I attended many Vancouver Lions football games, patrolled the Lulu Island water's edge for driftwood, and attended many house parties with our telephone-company friends. What a delightful contrast this was from the prairie provinces.

One fall day, we got word that Nora's aunt Kay had moved to town for the winter. Aunt Kay was a product of the undereducated generation from the flatlands of southern Manitoba. She had never married and worked at the great hotels of the Canadian Pacific Railway cities of Toronto, Winnipeg, Calgary, and Banff, Alberta. She worked during the summers and took a three-month sabbatical each winter. This year, she had chosen Vancouver—partly because we lived there, I'm sure.

After dinner one balmy evening, I was directed by Nora to go to Aunt Kay's to fix her kitchen stove. It seemed that one of the tungsten burners did not burn. I dutifully bought a replacement, packed a few tools into an old zipper-ring binder, and boarded a bus to her home, which was but a few blocks away. She lived on the third floor of an old and elegant brick dwelling overlooking Burrard Inlet. An evening of fading skies passed as I replaced the tungsten element on the stove. It worked, and darkness had fallen.

During the repair procedure, Aunt Kay had said, "The sight of city lights from the dormer window are something to see." She spoke of how she often turned out the lights and gazed from the window for hours. She mentioned that "It is a calming sedative that helps me sleep." She then said, "I'll show you when you finish."

I sensed a note of hopefulness as she spoke. She was a lonely person. She was looking to delay my departure. She was projecting mating-activity needs.

As I finished, the night was now dark. I said, "OK, please share this calming and comforting spread of city lights with me."

She simply said, "Sure."

She directed me to the window, then turned out the lights, all of them. It was dark. I held out my hand as she approached and oriented her by placing my hand on her lower back and guiding her to the windows. She unlocked them and stepped back as the windows swung inward. In doing so, there was close contact between us, which she made no adjustments to avoid or decrease.

The view was indeed soothing. Spread across that large valley were ribbons of streetlights, and between them, a blanket of random pinpoint illuminations of unplanned beauty that defies description.

It is my nature to express thoughts, and I started by saying, "What a beautiful view. Just think, each of those little lights is needed by someone. Perhaps a student is doing homework, someone is reading a book, preparing a sandwich, working on a budget, a crossword puzzle, or just contemplating cobwebs."

She was amused and, turning her face toward me, said, "I never even thought of those things. They are just pretty lights." She laughed a soft and restful laugh.

We continued to gaze and grew a bit closer against the cool incoming zephyr of humid Vancouver weather. After a time, I said, "Thanks for sharing this view with me. Any one of those lights is probably being shared by people just like us, and I'm glad you are sharing them with me." She made no reply, but I sensed she was savoring the moment.

A light in a nearby window was extinguished. I playfully said, "Did you see that? A couple over there are going to share something nice without lights." I demurely added, "Some of life's best experiences do happen without lights!"

She laughed, turned her face to me, and with coyness in her voice said, "Yes, but you can't tell anybody about it!" She uttered a cheerful little laugh and turned back to the window.

I felt a growing connection. I went on to say, "Relations between two people should not be shared with others anyway." Then, in a softer, suggestive voice, I added, "We should just savor them for a lifetime." I hesitated, then continued with, "They are treasures."

She turned in this darkened room and, for a fleeting moment, looked at me closely, face-to-face. Then her attention went back to the city lights.

I was unsure what to say next. Had I implied feelings I should not have made known? Had I stirred an instinctive warmth that made her uncomfortable? By nature, I have always felt that being flirtatious was complimentary, but now, I sensed it was time to get away from these windows and get some lights on. I simply said, "It's chilly. Let's close the windows."

She stepped back against me and, with measured deliberation, gently swung them shut. My hand had been caressing her lower back during this time, and I knew she was very aware of it. I stepped back a bit and said, "Where is that light switch?"

She disappeared into the misty dark and suddenly, there was light.

She was about to say something to me when her phone rang. It was Nora. I heard her say, "He is just leaving!"

This visit was never mentioned in any future conversation. I mused that we had shared a little fantasy that we would savor for a lifetime.

CHAPTER 27

LIFE ON LULU ISLAND

Give, and it shall be given unto you.—Luke 6:38

Time passed. I continued to work in the Vancouver main exchange installing transmission and signaling equipment. Here I ran into an old Siemens acquaintance, Ben Litwinowich. He now worked for Lenkurt Electric, installing 33A carrier equipment, and lived in Surrey, just south of Lulu Island. He had left Siemens and St. Adolph a couple years prior. We made plans to reunite our families soon.

When I spoke to Nora of my reacquaintance with Ben, she was less than enthusiastic about the news. I sensed she did not wish to pursue a social relationship. I wondered about that. They had been our neighbors.

Nora was a loving mother to our four children. Here, on 21st Avenue, our firstborn, Gail, started school. Our family was maturing, and the time had come to get a home of our own. We heard of a builder who rented duplexes and applied a portion of the rent to a new home purchased from him. We bit and moved into one of his duplexes in Richmond, on Lulu Island.

In 1959, we bought our first house from him, located at 1019 Ruskin Road. It was a fast-growing residential community on this island in the estuary of the Frazer River. The 1,200-square-foot frame house had hardwood floors throughout, a white stone fireplace, and sparkling white plastered walls. There was a drainage ditch across the front of the lot with no culvert to get a car across. The water level in that ditch fluctuated with the ocean tide but was never completely dry. The Lulu Island soil was rich and fertile.

We were elated. Was this the just reward for our forbearance? We owned a home! We really owned a home!

I was transferred back to the Trinity Central office and came down with a spontaneous laceration on the surface of a hernia I had endured since birth. Now it was open, bleeding, and probably infected. I had it surgically corrected in the Queen Elizabeth Hospital, and it eventually healed. I returned to work, relieved that after all this time, I was rid of a physical curse I had always hidden. No more trusses and braces!

Shortly after I had returned to work, a fellow worker, Hugh Heatherington, who had just purchased a new Volkswagen van, asked me, "John, why don't you have a car?"

I simply told him the truth: "We can't afford one!"

He then asked if I had a valid driver's license. I did not.

"John," he said, "get a driver's license, and you can have my old 1939 Pontiac coup."

I was a bit overwhelmed. Was he offering a free car? What was the catch? Hugh simply told me, "A man with four kids needs a car."

I got my license renewed and offered Hugh $50 for the Pontiac. He said, "Hell no!" And I now owned a 1939 Pontiac coupe.

———————◆·◈·◆———————

Time passed. A neighbor, Gunther Hoyem, introduced us to the local United Church of Canada, and the two of us became involved in rebuilding a purchased pipe organ. It became a second job. Only someone who has ever built a pipe organ can appreciate one the way I do. After completion, it was first featured in the 1959 Christmas concert. An affecting lump in my throat returns to me even today as I remember it.

Occasionally, I hunted waterfowl on the seaward end of the island, which was littered with twisted driftwood and escaped sawlogs. On the last such hunt, I carefully selected my steps to beyond the water's edge, sat on a high drift-stump, and brought down a couple of ducks. As time passed, the sun was setting, and I suddenly noticed that water was splashing over the toes of my rubber boots.

Oh God! The tide was coming in!

I left everything behind except my gun and waded fearfully through those rising waters, step by step, feeling for slippery, submerged waterlogged driftwood to step on—fragments I could not see, just feel.

I thrashed my way to shore, sat down on littered beechwood, and buried my face in my hands. In the fading light of day, I sobbed a grateful thanks to God.

Now that we had a car, we needed a bridge over that front drainage ditch on our lot. I acquired some secondhand railroad ties and built it myself. Now in case you were not aware, railroad ties are coated with creosote, and creosote burns. That bridge cost me a trip to the doctor for burns on my hands, arms, legs, and … whatever, plus a couple days off work. It wasn't pretty!

I already mentioned the fertility of the soil on the island. A story once circulated that a man with a wooden leg had once stood still too long, and it took root. So much for folklore, but Nora planted a wide variety of garden goods, and yields were phenomenal. She picked, packed, froze, and canned everything imaginable. Life was good.

On Saturday mornings, Hugh and I would occasionally get an early morning tee on the municipal golf course in Vancouver. If anyone accomplished a hole in one, the course offered a commemorative plaque, and names were placed on a wall-mounted list of achievers. One fine Saturday morning, on a par three link, I did so.

My recognition was denied. It was midsummer, and my hole in one was accomplished on a wintertime green. Even if I had been aiming for that wintertime green, it would not have counted in the summer.

Was I actually aiming for that winter green? Only I will ever know.

Life went on, and we were happy. I worked with a great bunch of guys, and we socialized with many families from the church and the telephone company. The lawn was green and carpet-soft, and in the spring, wild daffodils sprouted. We had never felt more settled and secure than now. Hopefully, things would stay just as they were.

One day, a company official approached me at work, took me aside, and said, "John, there is an opening for a maintenance supervisor in Victoria." He went on to inform me that "it would place you on the management staff of the British Columbia Telephone Company," and added that there would be an attractive salary increase, and the company would underwrite moving expenses.

Victoria, on Vancouver Island, would mean another move, this time to one of the most beautiful cities in the world, home of the renowned Butchart Gardens in a land of fabled fishing, hunting, and balmy weather. Could this be happening?

I gave the only answer I could: "I will need to consult with the manager of domestic affairs. Moving may not be on her list of priorities."

Nora was not at all interested in leaving this little house on Lulu Island. She would go if we must, but she loved her home—the first place she had ever really felt *was* home. How many more sacrifices must she make in the name of my career?

Against my better judgment, I turned the opportunity down. That simple little decision of career opportunity would soon bring about a major adjustment in our lives.

Spring turned into summer, and rumors of staff reduction were prevalent. That concerned me. We were unionized, and layoffs would be by seniority. All too soon, the rumors were confirmed: there would be a layoff. Within a couple of weeks, I was given my notice. On my last day of work, I received two weeks' severance pay plus unused vacation credit.

I took my treasured little toolbox home that night. I was unemployed!

Fate has a funny way of catching one off-guard. All my life, some power of fortune had delivered me from adversity. Had my luck finally run out? Had the rejection of that promotion terminated the tie to my guardian angel? Had my dependency on divine intervention finally run its course? Had I made one bad decision too many?

I spent two weeks making applications to any place that would accept them: gas-station attendant, store clerk, home construction, selling vacuum cleaners, working in a sawmill, a fish canning factory, and so on. I anxiously awaited a reply, and none had yet come. I had even approached the Lenkurt carrier people, who had openings in the US. I did not consider them.

We had kept our investment account intact, but otherwise, money was running short. Nora had found nightshift work in the fish cannery, and I went door to door selling siding, with little luck. Then one evening, a call came from the telephone company warehouse manager in New Westminster. Would I be interested in working as a temporary employee in their warehouse?

New Westminster was a city on the Fraser River accessible from the east end of Lulu Island. It was but a short drive from our house, and on Monday, I reported for work. I worked amongst many union men who knew I was a recent low-on-the-list layoff. I was therefore proclaimed a sheltered individual—a scab! Life was not pleasant.

I could tell stories of being put into dangerous situations, sent on fool's errands, finding my cap and gloves missing from the cubbyhole employee boxes, and having my brown-bag lunch messed with. I ate my lunch alone among the shelves and bins, or in the office of the warehouse foreman. I was not welcome in the employee lunchroom. Union people felt I was being given an unfair benefit and were making sure that I knew it. They were very good at it.

This painful existence lasted about a month. Then, one afternoon, the PA system blared my name and "come to the front office." As I left in response to the call, my fellow workers were yelling "Good-bye, John. It's been good knowing you, John!" They were laughing, so sure that the union had prevailed.

I was greeted in the office by a gentleman named Harold Price— the man whom I had met in the personnel office on my initial visit. He was smiling and asked how I had been faring. I was waiting for the shoe to drop, but his cheerful frame of mind persisted.

"John," he said, "we have something for you to consider."

He went on to speak of the General Telephone Company's manufacturing plant, Automatic Electric, in Brockville, Ontario. They had an installation department and needed some help. "Do you know where Brockville is?" he asked.

"Oh yes," I replied. "I was born and raised a few miles from there."

Suddenly, my gloomy attitude was lifting. Could a revival be coming?

As our conversation continued, Mr. Price mentioned names of people with whom he had spoken in the Automatic Electric Ltd. Plant. He spoke of their installation department woes and of a need for leadership. "By some coincidence," he said, "I told them I might be able to send them some help."

After some further exchange of chitchat, I assured him of my interest. He simply picked up the telephone and placed a call, asking to speak with Mr. Rex Holmes. After a brief exchange with Rex, he handed me the phone.

I do not remember the details of our conversation; I just remember I was being offered a job in Brockville, Ontario. It was three thousand miles away, and it would be an on-the-road job overseeing installations and directing final testing procedures prior to turning a finished product over to customers. Was I interested?

"Yes!"

Had some quirk of fate just delivered me from another error of judgment? If I had taken that job in Victoria, I would have been immune from the layoff. Was this to be for the greater good? Time would tell.

Within two weeks, I was on a four-day bus trip, leaving my wife, four children, a new house, and an old car behind. My current fortune amounted to a suitcase of clothes and fifty dollars in my pocket. Was I on another harvest excursion or launching a bright new career? During the entire trip, I was never sure whether to be rejoicing or scared silly.

It was summer 1960.

Without the element of uncertainty, the
road of life would be about as exciting
as a casual walk to the mailbox!

CHAPTER 28

GOING BACK—TO ONTARIO!

Ask, and it shall be given you; seek,
and ye shall find; knock, and it shall be
opened unto you.—Matthew 7:7

Upon arrival at the Brockville bus depot on a Tuesday afternoon, I checked my bags and called Rex Holmes to announce my arrival. He spoke words of welcome and, seeming to understand my meager situation, immediately sent a car to pick me up. "The driver," he said, "will help get you settled."

The driver, named Lorne Driver, greeted me cheerfully and had brought a newspaper with him. After loading my luggage, he said, "Let's find you a room. There are plenty to look at."

We had an early dinner (he paid) and soon found a slant-ceiling room on the second floor of a private home. It was walking distance from the plant—perfect! It boasted a single bed, a hotplate, an old and very noisy refrigerator, and a shared bathroom. There was no bedding and no pillows, but the landlady did provide me with minimal tableware, an old aluminum teakettle, and a breadbasket. From there on I was on my own. I was also low on money.

The next morning, after spending the night on a bare mattress that emitted bodily odors of past tenants, I reported for work having had no breakfast and wearing my only other almost-clean shirt and unpressed trousers. While on one hand I had a blessed feeling of confidence, on the other, I wondered if I yet fully understood the situation.

Wednesday morning, I walked to work for the first time in Brockville and was taken directly to Rex's office. We spent a couple of hours talking, then he took me on a tour of wood-paneled offices and introduced me to supervisors, managers, general managers, and others with titles. I was certain my clothes, which had spent four days in a suitcase, left an impression.

I reported to a gentleman by the name of Jeff Chittenden. Jeff had been promoted to installation supervisor from the manufacturing plant. He had no previous installation experience and limited exposure to supervising employees. I was given a worktable beside his desk and told that I would spend most of my time at jobsites. This was all I needed.

Pay was weekly but held back one week. I was broke! I did not have a credit card. When I told Jeff of my plight, he obtained a two-week travel advance for me, in cash, for which I signed a receipt. I was informed that on Monday, I would travel to Bout-de-l'Ile, Quebec, on my first assignment. The job was to replace a 100-line PAX.

I had never seen, or even heard, of a 100-line PAX.

The remainder of the week was spent at my worktable studying the schematic of a 100-line PAX, and I was perturbed to find there was no such schematic in the installation files. In fact, there was an astounding absence of any technical-support blueprints. I mused about the first telegraph message ever, sent by Samuel B. Morse: "What hath God wrought."

I looked over Jeff's sketchy schedule of job projects, reviewed some questionable project labor estimates, got a list of installation employees (their names, contact information, seniority, and experience level), and enquired into where the crews were located and what progress each job was at.

I sensed a reluctance in Jeff's responses. He seemed to regard my enquiries as an interrogation rather than a need-to-know. Obviously, he thought I was getting a bit pushy. After all, he was my boss.

Frankly, I *was* getting pushy!

On Friday morning, I was summoned to the personnel office for a get-acquainted chat with my contact-to-be and was told that my seniority with the British Columbia company would be bridged. He seemed to know more about me than I had anticipated, as he spoke of my service in British Columbia and of references from former supervisors. He had done his homework.

While talking to him, I mentioned that I had anticipated a little more latitude in my role in the department. I had, at least, expected a desk, file cabinets, an office phone of my own, and clerical help. I also made it quite clear that I intended to get involved. With a knowing smile, he assured me he would get word to the "right people." And he did!

Friday evening, I called my parents to apologize for not being able to visit with them sooner. I had no car and no money, and I needed to do some shopping for bedding, dishes, and groceries. They said they would leave for Brockville the next day, and I should expect them.

When my parents arrived, I was bathed, shaved, and groomed. They looked at me like it was for the first time ever. We had not seen each other in eleven years.

After a visit to my exceedingly humble room, we had a hearty restaurant lunch and then shopped for bedding, dishes, tableware, cookware, and groceries. They insisted on paying for it all. I began to feel like the prodigal son and mused that they were "killing the fatted calf."

They even brought a couple of family pictures for my wall. I had a blessed feeling; I was back in Ontario and living near the picture-postcard region of the mighty St. Lawrence River. I was beginning to feel like there was hope for the future.

Before leaving in the late afternoon, Dad told me that if I needed a car, he could spare one. His taxi business had a surplus. I would take him up on that offer later. They also encouraged me to bring the family home to Ontario to live with them until we were settled. That I might do, I thought, but only after I'd established a secure presence in Automatic Electric. In some way, I still felt uncertainty.

At this point, I was an in-charge employee about to be launched on my first project. On Monday morning, I would ride with my crew of one, Chester Kraft, to Bout-de-l'Ile Quebec and had a feeling my performance would be under microscopic scrutiny. After all, they probably were still a bit uncertain on exactly what they had bargained for. I prayed for fair weather and smooth sailing!

———◆◆◆———

On our ride to Bout-de-l'Ile, I had the chance to interrogated Chester about gossip subjects and the inner sanctums of the installation department. He gave me the lowdown on many situations. Employee morale was one of them. It did not sound promising.

Chester was a cheerful individual who spoke fluent French and had previously installed a type-100 PAX. He knew the way to Bout-d-l'Ile and the local cheap hotels. He was a treasure!

Monday afternoon, we stopped by the Hydro Quebec workstation and were denied entry. Unless "Maurice" was there, no one came into the transmission control room, and that is where the PAX was located. Chester spoke with the attendant for a period, in French, and I was told that "Maurice" would be there in the morning. We were to come back then.

We checked into a local motel, ate *lingue Chinois* at a local café, then had a shower and a good night's sleep. I was already beginning to readapt to life on the road. The excitement of travel and anticipation of adventures was reemerging. I was beginning to recognize the symptoms of a restless pioneer. I wanted to venture farther out yonder.

We spent the rest of the week doing the necessary cable-running, wire-terminating, power work, and positioning of the new PAX unit. On Saturday morning, we cut the old unit dead, and by Sunday afternoon, the new unit was operational. Maurice came to do acceptance tests, communicating exclusively in French with Chester. By early evening, acceptance was complete, and we were released. My first job as an Automatic Electric installer-in-charge was over.

As we left, Maurice shook hands with us, addressing Chester in French. Then, as he shook my hand, in good and perfect English he said, "Thanks, John. You guys did a great job!"

Over the years, Maurice and I would become fast friends.

The Geen children, In rear L-R John Ritchie, Ronald Wayne, Front row L - R. Gary Stephen, Grant Russel, Glen Delbert and Gail Ellen. Their clothes were all made at home by their mother.

My parents John Ritchie and Flossie-Mary taken about 1941. On the Lawncrest Farm.

This was used on the header of my monthly column in the American Squarer Dance Magazine from 2013 until Nora's passing in 2017. The magazine has an international distribution.

Photo of Nora in a favorite square dance dress, taken October 21, 2015.

Nora and I renew our wedding vows, June 26ᵗʰ. 2015

Our final square dance club location at 618 Locust Street, San Angelo. A renovated Boy Scouts of America building on about a half acre nestled in the bend of the quiet North Concho River in central San Angelo.

The Promenade Squares entered the above float in the San Angelo rodeo parade on a cold Valentine's Day in February 2015. It won no awards but attracted much attention.

John & Nora Geen observe their 60th anniversary April 1st.
They were married in Winnipeg Manitoba in 1952 and since
have lived in Edmonton Alberta, Saskatoon Saskatchewan,
Vancouver British Columbia, Brockville Ontario,
Middletown N.Y. Johnstown N. Y. and San Angelo TX.
The had six children, daughter Gail Mulrooney and sons John
Ritchie Geen of Windesheim Germany, Ronald Geen and spouse
Julie of Port Alberni, British Columbia, Gary Geen of Red Deer
Alberta, Grant Geen of Lethbridge Alberta, Glen Geen of Sachse
TX. They have four grandchildren and seven great grandchildren.
John worked thirty-seven years in central office installation and
engineering with Siemens Bros. Canada Ltd. British Columbia
Telephone Company, Automatic Electric Ltd. and retired from the
General Telephone Systems in San Angelo Texas in 1988. He is
currently a member of the Concho Valley Telephone Pioneer's club.
Nora worked at a variety of retail sales and bookkeeping positions,
including KLST-TV and Western Shamrock Finance of San Angelo.

Nora passed away on the day after their sixty-fifth anniversary, 2017.

CHAPTER 29

PASSING THE LITMUS TESTS

*There is no silver medal for success. You either
win or lose. There is no compromise.*

After the Bout-de-l'Ile installation, I spent time on jobs that most of the installers could not, would not, or dared not touch. They required some electromagnetic circuitry skills, which I had. For instance, in Pont Rouge, I updated an old power shelf to industry-standard dial tone, busy tone, and all-trunk-busy tones, and revised the alarm systems to better monitor the heartbeat of the switching system. In Rivière-du-Loup, I replaced a power shelf with a power bay having industry-standard generating and monitoring circuitry.

I was then assigned a crew on a line addition in Contrecoeur, and again, a line addition in Causapscal, Quebec. On that crew was my friend Chester Kraft and some new faces, one of whom was Peter Elliott (nickname *Piere la Cochon*.)

It was not until fall that I was sent to a predominately English-speaking destination: yes, Winnipeg, Manitoba.

In the Fort Rouge switching center, I was comfortable. I had been there before as a Siemens installer. Our job was replacing Siemens' plunger-line switches with Strowger line-finder shelves. Here I would renew acquaintances with Manitoba Telephone Service men and a couple of Siemens technicians who knew many of my old buddies. You get the picture—I was back on familiar ground. I felt at home. I had everything except my wife and family.

Peter would be my right-hand man, perhaps because he had a car and I didn't. Together we decided to seek an economical boarding place. One was located on Tod Drive. Our landlady would be the widow Mabel Scieney. Somehow the house looked familiar, but I did not remember why.

It was but a few days later when, in a conversation with Mabel, she mentioned a familiar name: Hazel Gunderson. Wow, small world! What was her connection to Hazel? Hazel had once lived upstairs but had recently moved into the Thunderbird apartments on Portage Avenue near the airport. I just had to ask, "Mabel, do you have any contact information?"

She did.

Before long, I was talking on the phone with Hazel, first reminiscing of our acquaintance in Erickson; her brother's café, now closed; her parents' farm, now rented to a neighbor; and so forth. Our conversations warmed up, and within a week or so, we were meeting at the Airport Café for dinner.

The Manitoba liquor laws had been forever changed by the Bracken Commission back in 1955. There were no more men-only beer parlors. Now the nightlife of stodgy old Winnipeg was wide open, and people were making up for the proverbial lost time. In short, Winnipeg was now a party place, and my liaisons with Hazel evolved from that of an acquaintance, to a friendship, to a relationship.

Those liaisons became frequent. Her needs and desires were evident. She gave me her undivided attention, made frequent deep eye contact then fluttered her eyelashes as she looked away. Her eyes followed my moves. She laughed at my humor, smiled constantly, touched my forearm with her hand, and offered me bites of food from her dinner plate with her fork. She would ask me to sip and taste from her wineglass and teased me about my social transgressions. She projected the classical aura of desire that activates the mating instincts of a targeted subject.

I was the targeted subject. We both had needs, and opportunity prevailed.

Yes, we did the bars and the nightclubs. The funds I saved by being in a boardinghouse instead of a hotel or motel were spent on self-indulgence. On multiple occasions, I committed marital transgressions with Hazel for which I shall always endure recollections of shame and remorse.

> *A prudent man foresees evil and hides; but the*
> *simple pass on and are punished.—Proverbs 27:12*

I never again had an extramarital affair.

———◆◆◆———

One evening, in a fancy bar, I spotted someone I knew—someone I had worked with at Siemens. It was a couple we had socialized with briefly while living in Richmond (on Lulu Island) and lost contact with when we left British Columbia. Here were Ben Litwinowich and his charming wife, Gloria, back in Winnipeg. Lenkurt Electric had included Ben in a layoff, and he was now in Winnipeg working in an auto-supply store.

Ben was a dedicated drinker and imposed his habits on all his associates. Throughout this short stay in Winnipeg, we would indulge often and persistently. During a regular weekend phone conversation with Nora, I mentioned his name, and she said, "Oh no, not him. You don't need him in your life."

Ben and Gloria had been our neighbors back in St. Adolph.

Ben had driven her for shopping, appointments, and other essential needs when I was not there. Only later in life would I suspect why she wanted to snub him and his family. She tolerated them only for my sake.

The assignment in Winnipeg came to an end, and I was brought back to Brockville. On arrival, I found my worktable piled with stuff belonging to others. The schedule of installations I had created had not been updated. The file cabinet obtained for circuit schematics was now stuffed with unrelated folders. A feeling that I was of greater value in the field than in an office came over me, yet I felt I had been brought here for another purpose. It was time to begin fulfilling that purpose.

The winter of 1960 was coming down, and my little room under the rafters was not a comfort. Fact: I had spent only a few days in this room over a period of four months. Keep it or ditch it? Was I to be a company field hand or an organizer? Paying rent for an unused room was counter to my sense of value, and it was time to assess who and what I was.

On my first day back at work, I made my job report to Jeff and requested an audience with the manager, Rex Holmes. The request was granted, and that afternoon Jeff and I went to his office. It was time for us both to understand the purpose of my presence.

Rex was comfortable with our visit. For some reason, I had expected him to be defensive and authoritative, and he was not; he spoke of appreciation for my work in the field and of encouraging customer feedback. He also spoke of current bids on large projects, the likes of which had not yet been undertaken by the local installation department. The economics of using our own installation group could be the difference between winning such bids or losing them.

I felt a challenge coming on—and a pending conflict between Jeff and myself. He guarded his position of authority, insisting that all calls I make from the field were to him. He discouraged me from talking with the engineering staff, insisting that he be the carrier of messages and information. This was often inconvenient, and occasionally, the engineering staff would call my number to speak directly with me. Jeff insisted on knowing of such calls.

One of Rex's essential objectives was to have reliable and consistent installation labor estimates and schedules. I was assigned to develop such practices, and I would be allocated whatever resources were needed.

I now had a desk, although I kept my worktable. I was assigned a clerical assistant with her own typing table, and the junk was removed from my file cabinet. A notice went to all field installation personal that I was the field supervisor, and all technical matters were to be directed to me. I was in charge.

Thus was the beginning of my influence on the Brockville installation department that was to last nine years.

━━━◆◦◈◦◆━━━

During the October Canadian Thanksgiving weekend, I did find time to visit my parents in Stirling, Ontario. All the family was gathered for the traditional turkey dinner for the first time in eleven years. It was a warm family gathering with sister Eva and brothers Ray and Dale and their spouses.

The only family member missing was Nora. We called her long-distance after the feast for a take-turn talk with her. They really didn't know her and had not much to say.

It was during this weekend that I mentioned moving my family to Brockville. Brother Raymond chimed in: "Marg and I have never been to British Columbia. We can go get them in the station wagon. Just let us know when!" Dad offered his seven-seat station wagon for the trip.

I would remember this conversation at a future date.

CHAPTER 30

CHRISTMAS AT HOME

The moment of decision approaches.

F all was descending on the world. The Cold War was still very cold, Francis Powers had been shot down over Russia, Vietnam was about to erupt, Trudeau was prime minister of Canada, bread was twenty cents a loaf, and people were putting their faith in "the pill."

For me, it had been a year of uncertain transition, but now it was time to go home. I had sufficient accumulated vacation time to take the last two weeks of 1960 to do so. My flight was scheduled from Ottawa. Peter took me to the airport, and before takeoff, I had advised Nora by phone of my arrival time at the Sea Island terminal.

"You needed to take a cab from the airport," she said. "I can't leave the kids home alone."

The flight was without incident, and I looked forward to enjoying a two-week Christmas celebration at home with the kids. This was a worthy reward for the months of scurrying about in Ontario, Quebec, and Manitoba, demonstrating my willingness and capabilities. Had I passed my tests? I was smugly confident that I had.

When I arrived home, there was a decorated Christmas tree, and the house was adorned inside and out. Gail and Ritchie were now in school, and Nora apprised me of their progress. Ron and Gary, still toddlers, were happy to see me, although they initially approached with an air of restraint. I had essentially become a stranger.

The next few days were spent shopping, restringing the fallen clothesline, trimming the back hedge, doing dad things around the house, and overeating homemade meals. Day by day, the children warmed to me and learned they could climb over my reclining body, throw stuffed toys at me, and ride my crossed-legged foot. Some evenings, I had a sparkling fire in the fireplace, and we sang Christmas carols the children knew with beautiful off-key joy.

Life was good.

This was our first real home, the place we had purchased with hope of permanence. What was to become of our dream? I felt I was about to consolidate my position in Automatic Electric and sensed that we would be leaving it behind. Automatic Electric needed me, and I needed the job.

One evening, when the children were in bed, I sat beside Nora on the couch and brought up a subject I sensed she was avoiding.

"Nora," I said, "we will be moving to Ontario. We need to think about selling the house."

She simply looked down at her hands and said nothing.

I persisted. "I'll talk to a real estate agent before I go," I told her.

She replied, "Let's make sure before we go too far. We must have some place to move to."

I never contacted that real estate agent.

⸻

We attended a service at the United Church of Canada where Gunther and I had installed the pipe organ, and visited and partied with friends. Many were curious as to how I had fared. I told stories of my travels into Quebec, rural Ontario, and Winnipeg. To them, my life seemed one of excitement and glamorous travel.

They knew not of the pressures of performing overnight circuit modifications in functioning centers that had to be up and running by morning. Little did they know of long tiresome drives between jobs in unfamiliar communities. They could not imagine nights in ill-lit hotel rooms drawing up conversion plans and analyzing circuitry for compatibility.

Nora had heard these tales in our weekly telephone conversations, but she never burdened me with the trials and tribulations she faced raising four children alone. We were both enduring that which we must. We let our friends think that life was wine and roses.

During this blissful occasion of renewed emotion and love of family, I found reason to question Nora's strength of devotion. There was a gasoline credit card receipt between the cushions of her car; Nora had no such credit card. I found a beer bottle cap under furniture; Nora did not drink. I asked no questions, just wondered: Had I neglected her biological needs too long? Were my expectations of marital devotion too unrealistic?

Women, as well as men, desire long-term commitments, but can a husband's neglect not make a woman liable to commit a convenient coupling outside of the marriage? The affection a wife does not receive in the home can be found elsewhere, and the call of nature will prevail. This need had been embedded into the nature of woman since Eve took a bite from the apple.

In my absence, had Nora found alternate satisfaction? It crossed my mind.

Woman will lust for her paramours.—Ezekiel 23:20

———◆•◆•◆———

On Monday, January 2, I boarded a Trans Canada Airline flight back to Ottawa. It was a long-enough flight for some surfeit of thought.

> *When the unclean spirit has gone from a*
> *person, and he finds no rest he will return to the*
> *house from whence he came.—Luke 11:24*

In one respect, I felt like I was going home, to the region of my birth, to a place where there were kinfolk and friends, a place where hills, lakes, rivers, villages, and cities had familiar names. It gave me a feeling of comfort and relief.

On the other hand, I had a heavy heart leaving Nora in British Columbia, once again abandoning her with four children in her first real home, a place where she harbored hopes and dreams of happiness, a home where she was sure we would find peace and pride and forever leave behind the life of endured privations while in St. Adolph. All now seemed to be vanishing in a mist of imposed obligations.

Had she lost the strength to survive her family role without emotional support from another? I can only presume!

> *A house divided against itself cannot*
> *stand.—Matthew 12:24*

During the flight, I concluded that the house must be sold and the family repositioned to Southern Ontario, the heartbeat of the Canadian economy. With heavy heart, I harbored the realization of Nora's inability to further resist the influence of outside attention. I recalled with anguish that incident when her sister Bertha brought men to her in St. Adolph, only to find me home, and now evidence of her further clandestine interests in Richmond.

She had plenty of cause to seek the satisfaction of life's needs, and I had made insufficient contributions to those needs beyond providing economic support. Why had I not been able to deliver her needed love? Was it deficiency in genetic endowments, or a lack of ability to express heartfelt emotions? Perhaps the environmental influences of my youth may hold the answer, but I did not realize it at this time. It is not enough to love someone; they must know they are loved.

I never saw my father kiss my mother. They never embraced or called each other *dear*. I never experienced a mother's kiss or loving embrace. I cannot recall my father ever complimenting me or expressing affection. Was I mirroring my parents' emotional deficiencies?

I was aware that when a spouse no longer met the emotional needs of the other, the deprived spouse would welcome attention from an alternative source. When left at the mercy of community influences, should the results be surprising?

The ball was now in my court. I had to fix the problem or lose the battle. I had no way of knowing that I would never return to the Lulu Island city of Richmond ever again.

If we say we have no sin, we deceive ourselves
and the truth is not in us.—John 1:8

CHAPTER 31

ME AND LOVE

*Love is patient, love is kind. It does not envy, it
does not boast, it is not proud. It does not dishonor
others, it is not self-seeking, it is not easily angered,
it keeps no record of wrongs. Love does not delight
in evil but rejoices with the truth. It always protects,
always trusts, always hopes, always perseveres.
Love never fails.—1 Corinthians, 13:4–8*

I have expressed my beliefs in God—beliefs that are a culmination of lifetime observations and contemplations, a look-back at influences collected over time. Now let's consider a subject I seem to understand more than many: love.

What exactly is it? What exactly does *love* mean? Can a fleeting sense of deep affection be love? Can love be temporary and still be love? Can the very word *love* stand alone, or must it always be clarified by a compounding adjective?

Can there be love without emotion? Loyalty? Trust? Confidence? Security? Desire? Dedication? And perhaps many more? Let us consider a few compounding examples.

Emotion

If a spouse never calls the other *dear* or *sweetheart,* does that mean the marriage lacks emotion? Can love endure on feelings of emotion without expressing it? (That may well be the difference between *faith* and *loyalty.*) Emotions of sadness can be conveyed by a bowed head and downcast eyes, while happy emotions are exhibited by smiles and laughter, but emotions stirred by personal attractions are much more subtle.

The strategies women use to signal their sexual interest in men are subtle and nonverbal, such as eye contact, an eyelash twinkle, open body posture, body language, and coy glances and smiles. Men are more likely to use overt strategies, like moving into close proximity, presenting a profile view of themselves, and even initiating conversation, but they often wait to receive a woman's come-hither signals before making their move.

Loyalty

The terms *loyalty* and *faithfulness* are often interchanged. Is it not possible to commit adultery and still love a spouse? Is it not possible to still love a spouse who has committed adultery? Is intercourse an expression of love and devotion, or an outlet for personal desires?

Some feel it is relief from stress, but few recognize it as a primitive call of nature, an instinct placed deep in some corner of our cerebral cortex by the hand of God to perpetuate our species. Is it not present in every living thing? Perhaps few really care.

Trust

For love to prevail, there must be trust. There cannot be doubt about the ability of a spouse to resist temptations. Or can there?

An absent or inactive spouse creates a state of mind for the other to seek alternative relief. The resulting social mating rituals can be subtle, and some who are the targets of an approach may not even recognize it as such. There can be, and often is, a point of no return. The call of nature is highly and often tragically misunderstood.

Confidence

Confidence is not something one can demand; confidence is something one must feel. All too often, we suffer the illusion of overconfidence. Simply, we do not understand the underlying nature of nature. The Bible concedes that the flesh is weak, and indeed, it is the will of God that demands us to go forth and multiply. God's will is powerful.

Security

For a couple to be together and stay together requires that both feel safe from harm while in the presence of the other. Harm can be emotional, financial, or physical. Physical possessiveness is often misread by women as being protected and cared for. Red flags of caution are therefore missed and can result in a life of spousal abuse.

Desire

Desire is a feeling or longing for the coital services of another. Telegraphing of personal desires is done in many ways. Suggestive expressions can be used by a suitor to seduce a targeted participant into willing surrender.

Physical displays to entice are numerous. We see it in someone's manner of dress, body exposure, body language, and facial expressions, and in the gestures and faraway eye focusing of a longing individual.

Dedication

Dedication is adherence to something to which one is bound by a pledge or a duty. Love requires commitment and can only prevail with a constant awareness that emotions can shift and stray. A dedicated individual will neutralize enticements by exercising good and worldly judgement. Is anything less still love?

By the time our family was finally gathered together in a house with relatively modern conveniences in Vancouver, I had already imposed much pain and anguish upon my wife and children. An ingrained obligation to provide for them and my willingness to go to any lengths to do so blinded me to Nora's need for current comforts. At that point, my mission was to secure respect for myself and provide future comforts for the family. I had not understood that for them, the future was now.

While I was still mentally escaping memories of the poverty and inconveniences of that old farm, my family had experienced the very thing I was working to escape. Yes, I was living an illusionary future, while they had been living a very real present.

The future was important to me; the present was important to Nora. It must have taken enormous courage for her to leave that inadequate place in St. Adolph, Manitoba, and place trust in my support and comfort in Salmon Arm, B.C. Did she do so for love, loyalty, security, desire, or was there a measure of desperation? I will never know.

Did she have reason to love and cherish me as our vows had stated? Does love have boundaries?

When I was living my career, the fear of failure perpetually loomed in my mind. I dared not fail; that would not happen. But from Nora's viewpoint, had I not already failed? Had my vows to love and cherish not already been brought into question? Did abandoning a wife and family time after time in the name of job necessity not constitute neglect?

God will judge!

CHAPTER 32

RECOMPOSING OUR LIVES

Hope springs eternal.

On the first day of work, 1961, I now had a desk, a worktable, and a stenographer to handle my needs, plus a clerk who would file documents and ink the mimeographs. The formalizing of installation estimating forms had been achieved. Our marketing organization now quoted all sales with the option of installation.

Along with office obligations and procedural developments, there were many field obligations scattered hither and yon throughout southern Ontario and Quebec. Jeff encouraged me to go forth and do my thing in the field and seemed happy when I was away from the office. As a result our installation competence was steadily improving.

Occasionally, I had the luxury of relaxing in my Hubble Street room, staring at the sloped ceiling and remembering the days on the farm. Memories of plowing, cultivating, harrowing, and harvesting the fields that now were but a few miles away came to mind. I had lived and worked in many communities of the vast prairies and rugged mountains of the west, and on the Pacific coast. Now I had returned to the land of my youth, of my heritage.

I would drift off to sleep believing I had an influence. I was making difference.

Field trips, I made by bus, train, air, or company station wagon, when appropriate. The station wagon was by far the most practical, since I could haul tools, test equipment, and supplies when necessary. Many of these trips were to facilitate frantic in-service deadlines. We did have some installers with good function-testing capabilities, but we needed more of them.

The installation department manager Rex Holmes had undertaken the following: The engineering group would draw up plans for a model training exchange in the factory section of the building complex. An engineering circuit designer was appointed to conduct circuit study for an installation test staff yet to be selected. Assigned test personnel would be given instructions on Strowger switch, rotary switch, and relay adjusting, taught by a highly skilled factory assembly technician.

New employees were already being taught cable-securing essentials, cable color codes, terminal block wiring, and soldering techniques, plus many other components of installation in a makeshift training area. This had previously been done on jobsites on an as-needed basis.

The installation tools and test-equipment inventory had been, at best, unsuitable. There were pretty good records of what we had, but not always where it was. It was often shipped with inadequate packaging and subject to damage. To address this, Roy Howard, a former drafting employee nearing retirement, had been assigned to our department to inventory all tools and test equipment and to oversee the building of a tool and test equipment crib in a company warehouse and have standard tool-chests built by the shop.

A standard inventory of tools was being placed at each jobsite, and Roy was keeping records on who had what and where. In addition, small toolboxes with essential hand tools had been issued to each installer. Test-equipment shipping boxes were being built in the shop, and custom keyed locks had been purchased from the Corbin Locks Company for all installation needs. Keying was exclusive to our installation department.

By April of 1961, we were realizing benefits. Time estimates were being met, and the quality of our installation product was becoming exemplary. Automatic Electric was becoming the second-most-purchased switching equipment in eastern Canada, exceeded only by Northern Electric, a Bell Telephone associate.

Installation crew capability was steadily improving. I was confident it would soon be equal to or surpass those in the British Columbia Telephone System from whence I came. At this point in history, many independent (non-Bell) telephone companies were converting from manual switchboards to dial service. We were competing.

Since my return to Brockville, I had spoken weekly to Nora by telephone, assuring her that my position here at Automatic Electric was secure. When I asked her to contact a real estate agent and place the house on the market, there was a notable hesitance. Then she said, "Do we really want to do that?"

I was momentarily taken aback but asked, "Do you want to stay there?"

There was no response.

I added, "My job here is secure—it is permanent. I will never return to the British Columbia Telephone System."

She quietly said, "I know."

The conversation ended with an unenthusiastic agreement that she would put the house on the market and relocate to Brockville with the family when the children had finished school. My obligation was to have a house to move into when the time came.

I was an optimist by nature and felt a new dawn of light breaking into our life. But I still felt a pressing need to get her out of Richmond.

———◆·◆·◆———

The remainder of winter, then spring, had passed. Most of my time has been on jobsite inspections in southern Ontario and Quebec. Jeff had acclimatized to the new installation procedures, and we had developed a more tolerable relationship.

The department now numbered over a hundred and thirty installers, and installation estimates and job-planning charts were helping to meet marketing pressures. I often worked at jobsites during the week and in the office on weekends, compiling those estimates and progress charts.

I had an occasion to visit with Rex at one point and made a proposition: locate another person in the office to do job estimates and schedules along with the basic training of new hires. I would select the candidate.

He asked, "Why not have Jeff do it?"

I replied in a rather sarcastic manner, "He can't teach what he doesn't know! He has no experience to call on. None!"

I reminded Rex that accurate labor estimates were essential to the marketing people, and job-progress charts were one of the greatest tools we had in monitoring progress. Weekly progress reports based on those charts indicated that jobs were either on schedule or not. Those charts not only motivated in-charge people to stay on schedule but to call for help when a need arose.

As the conversation ended, I remember saying to Rex, "Remember when you had vague labor estimates and no job progress charts? How confident did you feel about the status of those remote jobs then?"

This conversation ended with a promise to take the matter under consideration.

———◆·◆·◆———

It was now early May, and the house in Richmond had not sold. School would end in June, and I had taken a lease on a home in Tincap, about four miles from the plant. I had given my notice to my little-used "rafter room" on Hubbell Street and would move to the Tincap house on June 1. Everything seemed to be going great, except … what if the Richmond house did not sell?

The Realtor had assured Nora he could rent the house for enough to make the payments and his commission, with a few dollars to spare. Most renters would require a minimum lease. Nora told him, "Find one!"

Meanwhile, she had arranged for the Hudson Bay Company to give a credit on the furniture we owned, with the credit applied to an account with Morgan's furniture stores in Ontario. There would be minimal furniture to move, just kitchenware and personal goods to be shipped by train.

Our plans were taking shape. Now, how to get them here? Train would be the most practical.

On May 14, Mother's Day, I had dinner with all the Geen family at my brother Ray's place in Belleville. In conversation, my plans came up, and Ray reminded me he had offered to take one of Dad's seven-seater station wagons to Richmond to bring Nora and family to Ontario. We agreed, and plans were made.

Finally, our family would be reunited. I had not seen Nora or the kids since Christmas. It could not happen too soon.

In late May, Ray and Marg left to do some vacationing in western Canada, and on the return trip, they would bring Nora "home." Our new home was to be established in Tincap in June.

One evening, in my crowded little room on Hubbel Street, with the window open and the sound of birds fluttering about in the whispering trees, I lay on my bed and stared at the slanted ceiling. My mind went back to that conversation asking Nora to place our house on the market. I recalled her hesitancy to commit.

Yes, I suspected that she was being asked to leave behind a satisfaction for her womanly needs—needs I had not been fulfilling. I vowed that she would never feel that neglect again. She had found sensual comforts without me, but her support was with me. Our lives would be good.

I always try to live in the present and let the past be the past, but the past had imposed obligations upon me. Those obligations make the past part of the present. A family was dependent upon me now. I felt alone, but I was not alone. I was just by myself.

Hope springs eternal!

CHAPTER 33

STARTING OVER

All that the Father giveth me shall come
to me; and him that cometh to me I will
in no wise cast out.—John 6:37

R ay and Marg arrived in Stirling with Nora and family on a
balmy mid-June day. I had taken time off from work to be
there, and most of the family was on hand to greet them

My mother hugged Nora, then my father gave her a big hug with
words of welcome. My sister Eva, my brothers and their spouses,
all gave her hugs and smiling welcomes. They fussed over the kids,
and in the evening we all enjoyed one of Mother's legendary feasts.
Nora was being welcomed to the home of my youth. She was being
accepted. She was to be a Geen.

Later, she tearfully told me her own parents had never hugged
her and told her they loved her. I believed Nora sensed she would
never again be alone.

Although our genes produce a blueprint for our development,
they do not determine what we will do. The environment of our
homes creates our fate or fortune, but instincts placed by God
determine our biological needs.

Next day, the relocation was complete as I drove the family to
Tincap in the company station wagon and ceremoniously presented

to Nora her new home. The furnishings consisted of an eight-chair chrome dining set purchased prior to their arrival, and the household possessions from the Hubbel Street room, which consisted of little more than a few essential dishes, a coffee mug, a coffee percolator, a drop-side toaster, a breadbasket, some cutlery, and bedding. Mother had anticipated our needs and sent additional kitchenware home with us.

Our first night together was spent on a floor-mounted mattress while the kids slept on borrowed sleeping bags. With but humble possessions, we were starting over.

When the Hudson's Bay store credit transfer was complete. Nora bought a master bedroom suite and living room furniture, which included a fold-down davenport. She furnished the kids' bedrooms and bought a desk for me, saying I should use it at home instead of spending so much time at the office, and so forth. The allowance on our old furniture was minimal, so some savings bonds were cashed in to avoid monthly payments.

There was a feeling of renewed purpose in our relationship. Once more, the children had the benefit of a father in the household. A new life lay ahead, and the failed hopes of creating a home in Richmond faded into the mist of the past. Disappointments would influence our future determinations when self-confidence permitted. This time would be different.

Meantime, I had a job to attend to.

———— ◆ ◆ ◆ ————

The installation manager, Rex Holmes, was aggressively building the department to be productive and efficient. During the remainder of the year, the training room was built and equipped, the tool crib in the warehouse was finished, and all new employees were now trained in basic installation techniques and standards prior to job assignment. The instructor from circuit engineering was a talented circuit analysist who instilled capabilities and confidence into our technicians.

We were accumulating adequate test equipment and developing the talent to use it. Our installation department capabilities were second to none and finally being recognized as such. Thanks to the growing confidence of our marketing representatives, customers were now buying almost exclusively EF&I (engineer, furnish, install).

Some noteworthy consumers we served included Hydro Quebec (which was buying custom consoles for its control rooms plus intersystem switching), Quebec Telephones, the Newfoundland Telephone Company, Northern Ontario Telephones, Manitoba Telephone System, Saskatchewan Government Telephones, and numerous privately owned and community telephone systems in Ontario and Quebec. All were converting manual switchboards to dial service. Our orders for Strowger (step-by-step) central office equipment was increasing, as was confidence in our product.

My place in the company was still making jobsite visits, attending cut-overs, putting out flare-ups of job disruptions, placating anxious customers, working with difficult extended-area service companies, and so forth. Some weekends I would be home, sometimes not. My travels were far, fast, and constant.

Meanwhile, back at Tincap, the children were placed in a school that was just a stone's throw from our backyard. Nora now had her Ontario driver's license and a Ford station wagon donated by Dad's taxi business. She had joined a neighborhood euchre club and, during the summer and fall, enjoyed some special-occasion visits with the Geen family, including weekends at Harry and Eva's isolated cottage on Eagle Lake. She and the kids were delighted with the lengthy boat ride from Tichborne Landing on the quiet lake, getting to and from the cottage. Nora was blending into the family.

Summer passed, as did fall, and now it was winter of 1961. At Christmas, I had a week of holidays and spent them at home, except for attending the annual family Christmas dinner at Mother's. We had a well-decorated natural tree of our own and a few outdoor lights that blended us into the Tincap neighborhood.

New Year's Eve had an exciting moment or two when some drunk tried to break into our station wagon. The local police came and carted him away. The kids were all sleeping as we listened to the Guy Lombardo's New Year's celebration on the radio. At midnight, we sang "Auld Lang Syne" along with Lombardo and his Royal Canadian Orchestra and went to bed.

New Year's Day we spent at home. Our transplant to Ontario was complete.

CHAPTER 34

MORE OF THE BROCKVILLE STORY, 1962–1964

Go back to the land of your fathers and relatives
and I will be with you.—Genesis 31:1

I have never kept a journal or much of anything that tracked my history. I just knew where I was in the here and now, and there was a growing relief in being where I was.

There had been much comfort in returning to this land of my childhood. I now felt an unshakable self-confidence from having a family safety net should I falter. Family gatherings, be they few, were precious. This, then, was my family.

I prayed that Nora would come to feel the same secure comfort. Without realizing it, I had left much uncertainty behind in British Columbia. Yes, we'd had many friends, but friends are not family. Friends are not apt to go that extra mile when the trail of life encounters trauma. Though we still owned a house in Richmond, in my heart I knew we could never return.

Our life at Tincap was good. Nora had assumed leadership of a girls' 4H group. We had paid off our moving debts. My travel obligations were still extensive, and I was often gone for weeks on projects, but I did get home when possible.

Many of my duties were in the southern Ontario vicinity, which allowed me to get home on weekends. Even some activity in Quebec was within driving distance. Through good weather or bad, winter or summer, I trekked the highways and byways with increasing familiarity. It got so I seldom needed a road map.

Nora's attempt at gardening was foiled by shallow topsoil over shale rock. Being from southern Manitoba, she really did not know what shale rock was. She once said, "How come they didn't put any dirt over this?" It took daily watering, or it died. There was not enough soil depth to grow potatoes, or even radishes. After the first attempt, she abandoned the garden. For some reason, the weeds seemed to thrive.

Some family developments were encouraging. Each year on opening day of bass season, my parents spent the weekend with us. Dad and I would take my little red rowboat to fish in Stump Lake and Temperance Lake. It became an annual ritual that lasted all the years that we lived in Brockville. Dad loved it!

My brother-in-law, Harry, drove a truck for the Royal Canadian Air Force. One of his functions was recovering military planes after emergency landings. His regular duties took him through Brockville often on his trips between Toronto and Montreal.

Many family activities centered on Eva and Harry's home and cottage. At the cottage, Harry would give the kids a ride in a fast little overpowered boat on Eagle Lake. Nora always rode with him to assure the safety of the kids.

At their farm north of Frankford, Harry would take the kids for rides up into the hills on an off-road vehicle, where they enjoyed a spectacular view of the mile-wide Trent River. Nora sat with him and kept the kids in line.

In the winter, they rode with him on his snowmobile through

the fields at top speeds with much shrieking, squealing, and laughter. Of course, Nora sat on the back and secured the kids. Nora and the family were dovetailing securely into the Geen coterie. Life was good.

I do not remember life in exact chronological order, so at this time let me write of some individual experiences as they occur to me. I'll start with some adventures in the province of Quebec.

Do you recall my initiation into the Quebec environment in a previous chapter? In that instance, our customer was Hydro Quebec, a government-owned power company that relied almost exclusively on hydro sources for energy. That location was the Bout-d-l'Ile station located on an island in the St. Lawrence River near Montreal.

At a Drummondville project, on the mighty Rivière-Saint-François, I expressed my intrigue with the size and volume of the great water-powered turbines. Over a beer or two with my Hydro Quebec contact Maurice, he offered to have me escorted into the inner workings of a working turbine. (Probably several beers were involved in this decision.)

On the appointed day, I was taken down to the turbine enclosure, and as I stood near it, the sound it generated defied description. It was penetrating; it suffocated any other sound. It was a feeling that engulfed the entire body. I'd already had some reservations about the close encounter I was about to experience, but I had asked for it, so I would do it.

There were two persons assigned to accompany me into the turbine enclosure. Ear pads were place on me, and a hatch was opened. One of my guides entered first and gave me a hand to guide me through the entry. The second attendant quickly followed, and we stood on a walkway about four feet wide beside a gigantic whirling mechanical thing that had no distinctive surficial characteristics. It was a blur!

Air movement was swift. Flesh crawled on my bones. My sight became blurred, and a feeling of lightness came over me. I tried to speak to a guide, and he just smiled, patted his ears, shook his head, and shrugged his shoulders as much as to say, *There is no sound in here.* It lasted but a few seconds before a tug on my arm guided me back through the hatch.

My crew and a few Hydro Quebec employees watched as I emerged and applauded. Apparently, I had just experienced a forbidden activity. No one but authorized personal with a purpose were ever permitted to enter a working turbine.

While I never wish to experience that feeling again, should not everyone volunteer to experience a fear-provoking encounter at least once in a lifetime?

Bear with me as I mention a further memorable experience in the province of Quebec. It was the installation of a PAX (private automatic exchange) in the bowels of a mountain.

The location was a copper mine, and I am not sure if there was a real named town there or just mining-company accommodations. The name Murdochville comes to mind.

Upon arrival, we were accommodated in a mining-company rooming house and, the next day, taken into an enormous adit by personnel vehicle to a cavity carved from stone. There was a level concrete floor and a framed-in room to accommodate the equipment, which was piled along one wall, still in the crates. I was comforted to see our installation toolbox and test equipment already there with it.

Several outside plant cables protruding from a panel would connect different locations inside and outside the mine and smelter with dial technology. It was our job to install the needed equipment. There was also a power panel to provide us with lights and outlets, plus connections for the converter that would power the equipment.

Before our host left, we were given a map showing us how to come and go by foot. There was to be no personnel vehicle for us.

The walk in and out was about two hundred yards through this enormous tunnel with giant Euclid ore trucks speeding by, close enough to be scary. They had a schedule one could set one's watch by.

The walk from the rooming accommodations to the adit was about a half mile, but complimentary bus service, run by French-speaking-only drivers and occupied by French-speaking-only employees, was available. I was learning a bit of their language and amused that many cuss words they used were English. I won't elaborate!

At one point during the installation, a copper-company employee took me for a tour of the smelter. I cannot relate much detail of what I saw, but try to imagine the heat radiating from, and the sight of, molten metal flowing in a trench and being poured into molds to make large copper ingots. The guide mentioned that gold, silver, zinc, and other minerals were found in copper ore.

"How do they separate the copper from other metals?" I asked.

It was explained, but I did not comprehend. What I do recall is that a tremendous amount of white birch wood was used in the process.

Once more, I felt privileged to observe a phenomenon that few would ever see in their lifetime. It is difficult to imagine occurrences of life if we have no way to know they exist.

Another job experience of significance started with an air of mystery. Rex called me into his office one day, closed the door, and asked me if I had worked on a key system.

"Yes," I said. "I am quite familiar with the key systems."

He said "Good!" and began to ask me about my life history.

Had I ever been arrested? Had I ever been involved in controversial political activities? Did I have proof of citizenship?

I started to get fidgety about these questions and asked, "What's this all about?"

"You'll soon know," he said. "Do you have a birth certificate?"

"No, I lost mine in the Lake McKernan flood in Edmonton," I answered.

He said, "Get one. You will need it!"

He then asked me to name the five people I would like to take on a select project. I named some names, then he told me to go to personnel and pick up a clearance application for myself.

I felt a twinge of excitement.

I obtained the birth certificate, completed the application, and went about my assigned duties. A few weeks later, I was once again in Rex's office, and he announced that I would oversee a job requiring top security.

"Where?" I asked.

"Carp Ontario, a government experimental army signals establishment." He added, "You and your crew will go into on-site confinement for periods of time, and there will be no unsupervised communication with the outside world while there." He added, "You will all be required to take an oath of secrecy and never speak of anything about the site."

He named the crew I would be taking, which included a consulting engineer, Art Chamberlain. The work was to begin in a couple of weeks.

Now my curiosity was aroused, and I mentioned that I had seen no specifications, made no estimate of installation hours, and drawn up no job plan. Rex replied that I would get the specifications when we arrived on-site, not before. "Good luck!"

That year, 1962 I think, soon after the opening of bass season, I reported for duty at Carp Ontario along with my workers and the consulting engineer.

Upon arrival, there wasn't much to see, just a large high-fenced parking area, many military vehicles, a large guardhouse, and a guarded adit to something. We were taken into a room in the guardhouse, recited an oath of secrecy, and were told for the first time that this was the Government of Canada bomb shelter. (Later it would be referred to by many as the Diefenbunker, a play on the name Diefenbaker, the prime minister of Canada.)

In the Diefenbunker we ate, slept, and worked. The clocks on the wall were twenty-four-hour clocks with the day of the week displayed on each. In here, there was no day or night, just time. There were restricted areas with armed guards, where we did not go without a guard standing by us with a weapon. The equipment in the room would be covered before we entered.

Arrangements for this took much time, but it was a government project. No one questioned efficiency. We spent four twelve-day stints in the bunker, with a two-day break between them.

Today that four-story underground Diefenbunker is but a tourist attraction. I will not burden you with further details.

———————◆◆◆———————

On a Sunday afternoon in June of 1963, after I had come home from a weekend of fishing in Harry and Eva's cottage, Nora put the children to bed and told me to come sit on the living room couch. I wondered, *What now?*

She simply said, "It's time to tell you, I'm pregnant."

Child number five—yes, but, while discussing it, Nora simply said, "What will be will be. We can handle it."

Number-four son, Grant Delbert Geen, was born in the Brockville General Hospital on February 11, 1964. This development had little effect on my career, nor on our life in general. Nora was very adept at child-rearing, and disposable diapers were now available and affordable on our budget. I am sure they brought about the dawn of clothesline obsolescence.

Grant was welcomed to our home.

The remainder of the year passed, and in June 1964, I was assigned to a major expansion of service in Newfoundland. The activity, centered in Stephenville and Stephenville Crossing, was extensive. I had little choice but to accept the assignment.

Nora and I talked it over, and surprisingly, she said, "Why don't I just go with you?" I was flabbergasted at the suggestion, but after some *how are going to do this* conversation, it was decided. It would be the first time in ten years that she would live a life without caring for children. We hired a local nanny, known to us, and set out for Newfoundland in the old Ford station wagon donated by Geen's Taxi Service.

We drove the Canadian route through Quebec, taking the coastal route along the Gaspe Peninsula, where sheer cliffs at the side of the highway dropped to the rolling waters of *le fleuve Saint-Laurent*, then through New Brunswick and Nova Scotia. We had brought a tent and camping utilities and enjoyed the parks and recreational areas along the way.

We visited the Alexander Graham Bell Museum at Bedeck, and finally boarded the MV *Carson*, leaving from the city of Sidney on Cape Bretton Island. We took a sleeper on the overnight trip to Port aux Basques in Newfoundland, but spent most of the night on deck looking at nothing but reflections of boat lights on the water and listening to gulls.

In the morning, we unloaded at Port aux Basques and made our way through Trainwreck Pass, arriving at Stephenville in the afternoon. The Newfoundland Telephone people were known to me; I had been here many times before and had equipment and tools delivered from their warehouse. Work would begin on Monday.

Some of the crews were already on hand. We made contact with them, and then we set up housekeeping at a cottage near Stephenville Crossing. This cottage was normally rented to hunters and fishermen from the mainland. It was rustic but clean and comfortable. There was an additional charge for bedding, towels, and the like. We had not brought sufficient of our own.

Occasionally, we visited with the old couple who owned the cottages, who spoke of Newfoundland customs and lore, of times when they were still a colony of England, of the stripping of the land by the Bowater paper company, of the migration of the young to Canada for jobs before confederation.

When I was not working, Nora and I walked the local trails in the surrounding bush, scattering the deer and flushing the partridges. I fly-fished the pristine streams and ponds, and Nora fried the catch for our meals. We made an occasional visit to the local pub, where I drank Moosehead beer with the employees and sampled some of the famous Newfoundland "Screech."

Back at the cottage, we fought off the aggressive mosquitos in the evenings and went to bed. This was the most carefree time we were ever to spend together. It was good!

In July, we came home to find the family safe and sound. They did have a frightening experience to relate. Late one evening, someone had attempted to break into the house. A call to the police brought swift response, and the perpetrators were apprehended.

Weeks later, as we settled back into our routines, Nora had a message for me one evening. She was once again with child.

Her children arise up and call her blessed; her
husband also, and he praiseth her.—Proverb 31:28

CHAPTER 35

A NEED FOR A PLACE
OF OUR OWN

The road to our next new home.

L ater in the year, I arrived home from a work site visit, dined on the usual home-cooked meal, and listened to the radio news. As bedtime neared, Nora reminded me her time was "getting short."

Some things don't wait. I vowed to stay put and stay in the office until our sixth and last blessed event took place.

Baby Glen Stephen Geen was born in the Brockville General Hospital on May 27, 1965.

———————————◆◆◆———————————

Meanwhile, my presence at Automatic Electric Ltd. was gaining recognition. Occasionally, Rex had me visit his office to talk, just talk, about what was going on out there beyond his line of vision. Jeff was keeping him posted, but he wanted my on-site point of view. He was probably mining our conversations for rumor and buzz.

Rex was a former British Columbia Telephone Company central

office installer from way back and valued graphic information he could relate to. It made my chats of value to him.

I expressed a need to hire extra hands, based on conversations with the Montreal sales representative. Selection of hires started with the personnel office, then the selected candidates were interviewed by Jeff and for final approval by Rex. The firing of individuals was my bailiwick. If I said there were gone, they were gone.

Most discharges were for conduct principles—drinking and insubordination. Resignations were frequent. Most marriages could not withstand the degree of separation that our job demanded. Each time we lost an installer, many hours of experience and training were lost too. It seemed like I was always pushing a stone uphill, but we were gaining ground.

Only a few will reach the summit, so I learned
to appreciate the view from where I was!

Spring, 1966. Trees were breaking into leaf when our landlord hand-delivered a letter to advise us he had sold the house. We had about six weeks to move.

Family accommodations were not plentiful in Brockville. We were, in fact, fortunate to have what we had. Thus began a search for alternative living accommodations.

After an extensive search, Nora located an upstairs apartment in a private home in Lyn, a few miles from work. It was unsuitable, but available. It meant having to carry the baby up and down stairs as we were coming or going. With little to choose from, we signed a six-month lease.

It was but a block from the United Church of Canada we had been attending, and we found the village friendly. The children started school in the fall, and life went on. We ultimately overran the lease, but with no formal extension agreement, we just stayed.

As the end of the school year approached, a three-bedroom house on the east side of Brockville, by the St. Lawrence River, came available. It was perfect—we were blessed! We would once again live in a real house.

These little interruptions in life can be more than just inconvenient; they can be downright disruptive. Moving from Tincap made little difference to me. My job was my world, and my life just went on.

On the other hand, the small circle of friends Nora had cultivated in Tincap were now miles away. In a manner of speaking, she was again a friendless person. Her introvert tendencies needed familiar faces to minimize loneliness.

I had my workplace associates; she didn't have that. On occasions when we had a night out together, it was just us, going to a movie, the racetrack, a school sports event, or just for dinner. We had but few functioning friendships.

Because of the nature of my ever-changing job schedule, we could not participate in group activities like a bowling league, a square dance club, or any other activities with a recurring schedule. My non-schedulable job took precedence over all.

Sebastion Junger's book *Tribe* claims that there can be no happiness outside of group survival. Loners, or outsiders, create no bonds essential to happiness.

The only Tincap friendship that Nora retained was Dona Jensen. She treasured their friendship, be it from afar, until her death.

The house we would move into was on an unnamed laneway leading from Highway 2 to the river. We were the second house on the laneway, which was fenced on one side, dividing us from the grounds of the White House Motel and their otherwise open swimming pool. Across the highway was the Ontario Mental Hospital.

The house was large enough to accommodate us in comfort and gave a feeling of privacy. The overgrown vacant lot between us and the river was a playground for the kids, but the steep shale bank to deep water was of concern. Nora repeatedly warned them, "Don't go near."

Some evenings when I was home and the children were secure, Nora and I would walk to the water's edge, where we sat, talked, and watched the seaway freighters pass in the night. The twinkling lights of Morristown, New York, on the other side of the St. Laurence fascinated us. We often speculated as to whether someone was on the other side looking back at us. We never ever visited Morristown.

The mosquitoes would eventually drive us back to the house.

———————◆•◆•◆———————

My schedule for the next few months was scorching. I was hither and yon, from final testing of new operators' toll positions in Newfoundland, a progress visit, to a large dial conversion job in Val d'Or, Quebec; another dial conversion in Sudbury, northern Ontario; still another dial conversion in Serpent Mounds, Ontario; and visits to many small jobs in many nameless towns and villages in between.

One obligation took me to a Hydro Quebec console installation at Shawinigan. We achieved an in-service cut at two o'clock on a Sunday morning that went well. We monitored the project and did the cleanup work on Monday, then on Tuesday, after work, I decided to just drive on home. It was my third week on the road. I checked out of the hotel, filled the car with gas, and took off for an all-night drive.

When I arrived home during the wee hours of the morning, Nora and the kids were asleep. With as little disturbance as I could muster,

I entered, undressed, and went to bed. She did not acknowledge my arrival.

It should be no revelation as to what a husband's needs are after an extensive absence. I managed to make my presence known, maneuvered her into position, and upon penetration, immediately knew there had been a previous encounter. It was wet and slippery, and I detected an odor of activity generated by another.

I was devastated. I rolled away, clenching my fists for a moment of trembling rage. She was now paying attention. She pressed herself against my back and asked, "What's wrong?"

All I could blurt out was "Nothing!" My mind was bursting with unspoken anger. I dared say no more.

Where did the encounter take place? I wondered. *This is our home with six children under the roof. Surely not here!*

I had always attributed her extramarital connubial needs to my absence and inattention, but right now, this was here, in our home …

As I lay in the darkness, I recalled going to the car with her recently and noticing from the corner of my eye that she made an apparent brief wave to someone at the motel, then quickly looked to see if I had noticed.

Had I imagined that? There was nothing between us and that motel but a collapsed wire fence one could easily step over in many places. I thought, *God no—let it not be!* I drifted briefly into a fitful sleep.

———◆•◈•◆———

Next morning, after the school-age children had left, I confronted her at the kitchen table with "What the hell is going on? Why? You know exactly what I'm talking about!"

There was a prolonged pause, and then she quite calmly asked, "Are you ever going to be a full-time husband?" There was another brief pause, and she continued, "Am I supposed to spend my life just staying home and raising kids?"

There were further words and discussion, but another statement came out of the blue and cut me to the quick. Looking down toward the hands in her lap with no expression on her face, she said, "You know, I never do feel that good feeling with you."

That good feeling? I immediately made the connection. It left me speechless. Suddenly, too many things knotted up in my head. I left the house.

As I sat in the car for God knows how long, the words kept turning over in my mind: *That good feeling.* I knew exactly what she meant. *That* good feeling I knew to be essential for a woman's satisfaction. Soon I calmed down enough to drive to work.

I had never even guessed!

Never did Nora ever admit to having coital relations with anyone. I did not push for confessions; it would have been pointless.

Back at work, I buried myself in the backlog of duties and pondered my purpose. *Work hard, be loyal to my employer and prosper.* That I did, but there must be more. Each time I had a salary increase, half of it went into payroll-deducted Canada Savings Bonds. They paid good interest rates of from 5 to 8 percent.

Those savings brought little comfort to Nora. Life for her was a thankless obligation to family needs. She made their clothes, cut their hair, dressed their wounds, soothed their bumps and contusions, and comforted their sorrows while I was out there, somewhere, living in expense-account comfort. (Little did she know!)

Nora had her own moments of anxiety. For instance, Grant once fell into the motel swimming pool. Gary pulled him out. I didn't find out about that for weeks, but it must have terrified her.

One of the boys broke the motel neon sign with a rock. Nora

paid for the repairs from household money, and I didn't found out about that for years.

Their pet dog was run over on the highway, and I had the job of burying it when I came home. The children were devastated. I hardly knew that dog.

Perhaps I needed to take stock of where I stood as a husband.

> *By the grace of God, I am what I*
> *am—1 Corinthians 15:16.*

But is that enough?

I had no idea where to go from here, but our lives had to merge into a workable marriage or lose it. I did not want that to happen.

I recalled a recent conversation with one of my employees, Wayne Larocque, who had mentioned buying a lot from a farmer on Murray Road. He and his wife, Karen, were in the process of building.

I checked Murray Road, a short distance beyond Tincap. Turning left from Highway 6 onto Murray Road, I saw a residence on each side, beyond which ran a trickling stream, the banks lined by enormous weeping willows shading the water they so dearly craved. Beyond that, the south side of Murray Road was lined with mighty elms that twisted, groaned, and squeaked during strong winds, but never gave up a limb or a twig. As the road sloped upward, there to the north side was the initial construction activity on Wayne's house.

A thought occurred: *A place where we could grow roots. A place of our own. A place back at Tincap. A place we could once again call "our" home.*

Wayne put me in touch with the family that was selling the lots. We cashed enough savings bonds to pay the $800 cost of a seventy-foot frontage by two-hundred-foot-deep lot on rich farmland next door.

The Richmond home was placed on the market, a necessity to qualify for a CMHC mortgage. Wayne's home builders from Smith Falls were contracted, and in June of 1967, we had sold the Richmond house and owned a new and beautiful home on Murray Road. We were back in Tincap.

Had I once again moved my family from another peril of my own creation without solving the real problem? Was my infatuation with my job more important than being a "full-time" husband?

I pondered that question often. "Someday," I told myself, "I will be that full-time husband she needs!"

To paraphrase Walt Kelly's comic strip character, Pogo, "I have met my foe, and it is me."

CHAPTER 36

MY RISE TO SIGNIFICANCE

Achievement is to credit oneself.
Success is to credit many.

had an occasion, or should I call it an obligation, to pay a visit to an ongoing project in Chibougamau and was given a prepaid air ticket as far as Baie-Comeau. From there, I was to take a bush flight to Chibougamau and apply for reimbursement. The flight had already left, and the clerk suggested I ride the freight. I would be there before dark.

Now, "riding the freight" means riding in the locomotive of an ore train that runs between Baie-Comeau and Chibougamau. Somehow, I qualified as a "company rider." There was no charge. I took my suitcase and briefcase to the train yard and boarded the next one out.

Ore trains run fast. There is one set of tracks between Baie-Comeau and Chibougamau, and trains run both ways. Southbound units loaded with hundreds of tons of iron ore have priority, and northbound trains must pull off onto sidings at the appropriate time. I will give them credit for this: their schedules are breathtakingly precise.

As the crew was pulling off onto the first siding, I could already see the approaching southbound. I could also look out the rear window and see our trailing cars still on the through track. My thoughts? *Oh my God, a train wreck!*

Need I say it? Seconds after the last empty ore car pulled onto the siding, the fully loaded ore cars went roaring by. The noise of a fully loaded ore train on iron rails is hard to describe. I'll let you use your imagination.

I realize people go to amusement parks and pay good money for frightening thrills that would hardly match this experience. However, on the return voyage from Chibougamau, there was an even more frightening experience ahead, one in which I felt my life was threatened.

<hr>

In a morning phone conversation with Rex, I was advised in an authoritative tone to take the next plane back to Brockville. The reason? He just said it was important that I be there.

Good God, I thought. *What have I done now?*

I left the jobsite in good hands, returned to the hotel, packed, and went to the airstrip to catch the one and only bush-plane flight of the day. It was near noon, and I would be the only passenger.

I recognized the pilot as he looked through the large picture window, mostly at the gathering clouds, the angry wind bending reluctant trees and scooping up swirling lines of dust from the graveled runway. I approached to ask when we would take off. He recognized me from previous flights and, in broken English, said, "There is a storm between here and Val d'or. I don't know if we should …"

I interrupted and said, "I am traveling with some urgency, I need to go!"

He once more looked out the window, then turned to say, "I do have a big bag of mail. It should go." Then, looking me straight in the eye, he said, "If you're willing to do it, I will."

Leaving the gusty wind and dust behind, we were soon airborne in his six-passenger Cessna. He gave me the privilege of sitting in the copilot seat with the warning, "Don't touch anything—nothing!"

I agreed.

I am not sure just how far we had gone when a strengthening wind started tossing the plane like a butterfly in the wind. Looking ahead, I saw approaching hail. Big mushy hail soon pelted the windshield, and spray from the propeller distorted all visibility. While Gaston (yes, that was the name on his shirt) was struggling to keep the plane in balance, I saw him lean his head against the side window with a look of concern. He said, "Where the hell is he going?"

Gaston was soon on his radio. He made some selections and said something in French. A short conversation took place and, by now, the ferocity of the storm was subsiding. Gaston turned to me and said, "Marcell was lost in the storm—no compass. He didn't know where the hell he was." (Yes, bush pilots all seem to know each other by name!)

Anyway, Marcell followed us to Val d'or.

Late in the afternoon, I caught an Air Canada flight from Val d'or to Ottawa, where a driver awaited me. I surprised the family by my arrival and found them well. That was one worry off my chest. This was obviously not about my family. Why was I being called back to Brockville?

Some concerns were crossing my mind. Was my career as secure as I had thought?

Upon arrival at the office in the morning, I felt like a kid who had just been called to the principal's office. I wondered, *Why am I here?*

On presenting myself to Rex, he just said, "Be in the conference room at nine!"

At nine o'clock, I walked in to find Jeff, Rex, and Walter

Ashcroft, general manager of engineering, already there. I made a flash attitude assessment of those present and felt no negative vibes. All seemed calm, comfortable, and amiable.

After I was told to "be seated," Walter spoke. It was a brief prepared scenario lauding me on my efforts and conduct. He then said, "Jeff is moving to another position, and Rex has recommended that you succeed him—congratulations."

Rex made a few comments, which included, "We have come far but have much more to do. Much more!"

After some further talk, Jeff accompanied me back to our work area and announced the change to Stella and our file clerk. (Somehow, I think they already knew.) I thanked Jeff for doing so, and he walked away.

The installation department was in my care.

My title was now installation supervisor. The station wagon I had been driving was no longer in the car pool—it was exclusively mine. (It pretty much had been anyway.) I had been assigned a reserved parking space. (I hoped to get to use it frequently.) The selection of, and assignment of, staff was now my sole responsibility. (I had been doing it for the past couple of years anyway.)

In short, I was doing the job that I had pretty much been doing but now had some authority to do it. I quickly settled in.

Installation estimates were being made by the engineering staff using the forms I had introduced. They often complained about the forms being too involved, and I often questioned the accuracy of their estimates. I wanted these estimates done by our people, under my supervision.

Many small jobs were in progress without the critical path progress charts. Why? Because I had not had enough time to generate them and no experienced staff to do it for me.

I needed someone to visit installations in progress to assure quality, maintain jobsite morale, and show a presence and concern to our on-site customers.

In short, I needed help.

I spoke with my personnel contact person and told him I planned to offer a job to someone in whom I had great confidence. He lived with his family in Winnipeg. Could we offer him relocation reimbursement if he were to accept the job?

The short answer: no.

That evening, I called Ben Litwinowich and offered him the job. He accepted the salary I offered and the move at his own expense. They did not own a house and had no other encumbrances. Ben was ready!

Next day, I told Rex of the offer and of my intent to locate Ben in a cubicle in this office where he would do estimates, compile critical-path job charts, review weekly progress reports from the field, and bring any concerns to me. He would also visit the field on occasion when I would have needed to do it myself.

I came away from this discussion with much more than expected. Rex approved my ideas, approved the cubicle, and suggested I move to a larger, high-walled glass-top cubicle like the engineering supervisors.

Rex set the wheels turning.

That evening, I told Nora about the job offer to Ben. She just said "Why? Why him?" In a whining voice, she said, "Why would you do that!" I was not too sure why the subject always struck a nerve with Nora.

Ben would start in a week's time, and he, Gloria, and family would soon move to Lyn, a village near Brockville where we had briefly lived. It was a done deal. Ben would be my first senior foreman.

As I settled in at the helm, there were but few quirks and faults to work out. I began to appreciate the roll Stella played in office procedures. She knew where every one of the installers was located at any given time. Expense reimbursements were submitted to accounting without delay. Paychecks and per diem checks were always directed to proper addresses, and on time.

Through the travel department, she arranged to have airfares and train tickets available at points of departure when staff was being relocated. She relentlessly dunned the in-charge installers for late time and progress reports, and she kept me apprised of potential concerns that I needed to consider.

Stella was a gem.

When Ben arrived, it brought relief to my frantic schedule. Ben was soon compiling all installation estimates, which delighted me and the engineering department. No longer did they have to listen to me bellyache about inaccurate estimates. He soon became adept at drawing installation progress charts and handling technical questions from the field. He also made field visits for quality assurance and jobsite morale purposes.

Over the years, many installers of notable capabilities contributed to the abilities of the installation department.

Wayne Larocque came from the test line in the shop. A brilliant circuit man, he had an amazing memory for circuit numbers and details. He was productive, trustworthy, and a leader by example. After a couple of years in the field, he became my second senior foreman.

John Goodwin, a graduate of Queens University in Kingston, Ontario, started as an installer, soon was a job in-charge, then a job foreman, and eventually became my third senior foreman. He would eventually transfer to exchange engineering.

Cliff White worked for the Newfoundland Telephone Company for many years. During a job visit to Cornerbrook, we spoke of him joining our installation group. I hired him, and he, his wife, and his daughter rode to Brockville with me on my return trip. He worked in the field for some time and eventually replaced John Goodwin as senior foreman.

Years later, John and Cliff would start their own sales and installation company of electronic PAX exchanges.

As for me, I felt that I was finally doing the job I had been brought to Brockville to do.

CHAPTER 37

BEATING AN ADDICTION

Yea, though I walk through a cloud of
smoke, I will fear no evil. Nicotine will
comfort me. My ashtray runneth over.

In the fall of 1967, I paid a compulsory visit to the company clinic for my annual checkup. A requirement for our health insurance, I was told. The attending nurse took my pulse, temperature, and blood pressure and passed me on to Dr. Bird for further assessment.

The doctor slowly and purposefully ran his cold stethoscope over my warm chest, up my back, then back to my chest before finally laying it aside. "John," he said, "it has been a pleasure to have evaluated you over the years, but your time could run out if we don't do something."

Pointing to the yellow Sportsman cigarette package protruding from my shirt pocket, he asked, "How many of those things do you smoke in a day?"

I was not about to own up to the whole truth. I said "Close to a pack a day." The traditional flat pack of cigarettes in Canada is twenty-five cigarettes. I often opened a second pack in any given day. He shook his head and said, "We are going to have to do something. I will state my concern in your annual report."

Returning to my desk, I took the flat pack of Sportsman

cigarettes from my pocket, placed it on my desk, and just stared at it. The doctor was right. I had made many attempts to quit even as I worked in Vancouver. Many times I tried, many times I failed. I wondered what the company could do about it anyway.

I chain-smoked, starting when I awoke in the morning, another after breakfast, and again on the way to work. Upon arrival in my office, my first act was to light up another cigarette. At no time during the day was I apt to be found without a lit cigarette. If I wasn't smoking one, it would be smoldering in my nine-inch desktop ashtray.

My mind mused on the twenty third Psalm: *Yea, though I walk through a cloud of smoke, I will fear no evil. Nicotine will comfort me. My ashtray runneth over.* Wait a minute, this isn't funny.

I vowed to cut back with some limited success and was encouraged when Stella mentioned that she didn't have to empty my ashtray quite so often. She had noticed!

Nothing ever came up about the insurance checkup. I speculated that probably no one ever read them anyway. Soon I just forgot about the whole episode.

Time passed, and in early 1968, Brockville was hit with a glazing ice storm during a Sunday night. Streets, sidewalks, roadways, and anything capable of getting wet became a slippery patch of dangerous black ice.

On that Monday morning, on my way to work, I stepped out of the door onto the entry stoop. There was a frantic blur, a feeling of being launched into thin air, followed by a collapse at the bottom step. I felt stunned.

Then a sensation of pain sliced through my right arm and shoulder. My briefcase and lunch went sliding across an icy surface. The sound brought Nora to the door, and as she opened it, I was beginning to realize just what had happened. I yelled, "Stay in the house—it's ice!"

I inched my way to the door by shoving my backside up one step at a time and finally slid in through the open door. As I stood up, my right arm dangled painfully and helplessly. It was obvious my shoulder was broken.

The roads had already been salted and sanded. Nora called Steve, the Tincap storekeeper across the street, and asked him to somehow get me to emergency. With some cautious maneuvering that approached valor, he managed to do just that. The break was right at the ball joint, so no cast would be effective. I was bound up and sent home.

Now, you may wonder what exactly these two incidents had to do with each other. Here it is: I was home, helpless, and without cigarettes. Nora suggested that maybe I really didn't need them. Thus, an abusive personality bubbled up inside me. It affected me in many ways for many years. No, I'm not exaggerating.

Nicotine addiction is much more severe than many may imagine. I had been truly hooked since I was about sixteen. Now my temper flared. I was a vocal menace to anyone who came near me, including the kids. I begged for Nora to get me just one package of cigarettes. She declined.

Life was miserable, and I made life miserable for anyone who came near me. Nora brought my meals to the bedroom to shield the kids from my wrath and did her level best to placate me. Somehow, our marriage survived.

This went on for one whole week at home. Then I took the residual anger to the office with me.

On returning to work, I visited the clinic. Dr. Bird's nurse gave me some pills she said would help—and perhaps they did, but I didn't notice. In any case, when I was settled in at my desk, I opened the top center drawer and there, staring up at me, was a pack of Sportsman cigarettes.

I called Stella and said, "Get those things out of my sight." In a slow menacing tone, I continued, "I don't dare touch them."

Stella had a different idea. "John," she said, "you can't go through life frightened by a pack of cigarettes. You've beaten them so far. Just put them in your pocket and, when you get the urge to smoke, tell yourself that you are stronger than a cigarette. Use your own determination. You can do it!"

While I felt that I would soon fall off the wagon, I put them in my shirt pocket. For the next few days, whenever Stella saw me reach my hand up to my shirt pocket, she would say, "No!"

I never opened that pack of cigarettes. I now believe that knowing they were right there in my pocket stopped me from panicking and, consequently, buying some. That's my story and I'm sticking to it.

Without the perpetual cigarette smoke congesting my lungs, I found it difficult to enjoy a beer. My determination to not light-up diminished my thirst for beer, and I was experiencing life through a much clearer lens.

But it was otherwise taking a toll. My usual mellow and forgiving personality was turning aggressive. I faced life not as an adventure but as a personal affront. I tended to make swift and harsh judgments even if and when they affected the fate and future of others. It would have an impact on my relationship with just about everyone I knew and worked with.

Nora endured. For that, I shall always be grateful for God giving her the strength to do so!

CHAPTER 38

OUR HOME ON MURRAY ROAD

Another Plateau in My Career

Our new four-bedroom home on Murray Road was a dream come true. It was built on an elevated lot, and a high terrace behind the backyard featured a fertile garden with a productive raspberry and strawberry patch. The house overlooked a terraced front yard, and the final descent dropped to the level of the road. Beyond the road was a well-grazed pasture ending at the edge of a distant woodlot.

The lower half of the front structure of the house was red brick; the upper, a sand-colored aluminum siding with window shutters and door trimmings painted brick red. It was a pretty house. Nora chose relaxing pastels colors for the interior, which she applied herself. The floors in the halls, living room, and dining area were hardwood; the bedrooms were carpeted; and the kitchen floor was vinyl. Ours was the third home to be built on Murray Road, and it set the trend for future homes.

Nora was comfortable being back in the Tincap community with friends and acquaintances nearby and living in a house which many envied. Her ties to my family remained close. Dad and Mother came every spring on the opening day of bass season, and while

Dad and I fished Stump Lake, Temperance Lake, and occasionally Graham Lake, Mother and Nora prepared our meals.

Our whole family regularly attended Thanksgiving and Christmas dinners at my parents' home in Stirling, or my brother Ray's or brother Dale's place in Belleville, and often at Harry and Eva's farm near Frankford. I was pleased that Nora was blending well into the Geen clan. She had no close relationships with her own.

My position in the company now gave me some control of my own scheduling. There were senior foremen I could send hither and yon on field support chores. My responsibilities and duties shifted to hiring, training, evaluating, solving personal problems and disputes, and firing. Yes, there were a few!

My new post-nicotine personality made me a force to be reckoned with, but I always praised and complimented employees when the occasion called for it. I remembered the lack of recognition for the many thankless duties I had experienced in the past. I did what I did then because there was no choice. Skill levels can be changed through training, but we can only change attitudes through recognition of achievements.

Our new training facilities were developing efficient and capable installers. Some of my own contributions were designing a simple dry-cell battery-driven electromechanical device to find the location of short circuits hidden somewhere in the many possible appearances of selector banks and distribution terminal assemblies. It required a low-impedance headset created by hand-winding discarded telephone-operator headsets recovered from dial conversions.

This "drop" system saved many hundreds of hours a year. I developed a transistorized version and applied for a patent but was advised there could be so many workable variations that a patent would be difficult to enforce.

I also developed a short-circuit "burner" that cleared very fine copper and/or tin wire shavings often left in selector banks after the shop assembly process. This too saved a multitude of man hours every year and cleared switch-bank short circuits quickly and effectively. Some engineering staff expressed concern that a residue might cause subsequent problems. This never occurred.

I then introduced a method of locating in-bank short circuits I had learned while working with the telephone company in British Columbia. It took time to perform on each selector bank prior to turning into service but avoided the discovery of embarrassing problems too late.

Over a period of two years, most installers would get up to 120 hours of formal training, which contributed to increased quality and efficiency. Previously, any training that was done was on-the-job, and much was never done at all.

As time marched on, we were a player in establishing the first ever US/Canada international extended-area telephone service between Clair, New Brunswick, and Fort Kent, Maine. I was involved in that operation and took great pride in the quality of our installers vs. the ones across the border. On a couple of occasions, we helped guide their technicians to successful solutions.

Meanwhile, at home, Nora had exchanged holiday and birthday greetings with her sisters but there had been no visits since we moved to Ontario. In the summer of 1968, she received a letter from her sister Bertha, who was now married and had moved to Toronto. They were living in an apartment just a few blocks north of the 401—the Trans- Canada Highway.

Highway 401 was kind of like a long driveway to me. I was up and down it frequently. Just about every trip to Quebec and the Maritime Provinces started northeast on that highway, and just about every trip to the population centers of Southern Ontario started southwest on the 401.

Bert enclosed her return address and telephone number. The ingredients for a family connection were being reestablished. Nora responded to the letter saying we would visit soon. We did!

It was now late summer 1968, and a major dial conversion in Gimli Manitoba was under way. The supervisor, John Goodwin, and a crew of nine men were on-site. I visited during the testing stage, starting with a flight from Ottawa to Winnipeg. It was a Vickers Viscount —one of my favorite passenger planes.

The flight was full and included a family with a preteen son and a lap baby. All was well until somewhere over the vicinity of Kenora, Ontario, the plane depressurized. The pilot announced a steep descent—"do not panic"—but the negative pressure on eardrums was almost instant. While many adults screamed, groaned, cussed, and held their ears, the children shrieked in acute pain.

The flight leveled off at a low altitude and soon landed in Winnipeg. The pilot advised the passengers by intercom that medical consultants would be on hand upon landing, and hearing-damage claims would be acknowledged by the airline.

John Goodwin was on hand to pick me up, and on the drive to Gimli, I could not carry on a conversation! My hearing slowly returned to near normal in the week ahead.

In Gimli, fall weather was approaching, and flocks of Canada geese had begun gathering in the wheat stubbles for the flight south. The sound of shotguns could be heard in the distant slews and fields, but my hearing was still deficient. I mostly heard only the whistles and ringing generated inside my own head.

John had the job well organized and very much in order. Feeling the project was in good hands, I made it a short visit and returned home early the following week.

Back in Brockville and relaxing after the evening meal, at about eight o'clock, the phone rang. I answered—it was Harry! I noted that his first word was "John?"—yes, "John?" with a question mark, like he had not expected me to answer. In any case, he quickly recomposed and said he was staying the night at a nearby hotel, would I like to join him in the pub? I would!

During a relaxing beer or two, he mentioned spending nights in Brockville on his Toronto/Montreal runs. He also asked when I had gotten home from Manitoba. That question exploded in my mind. I had not told him I had been to Manitoba.

A bitter recollections flooded into my mind—a memory of the night I had arrived home unexpectedly from Shawinigan, Quebec. Surely it could not be!

I excused myself and drove home.

On the way, I recalled those joyful boat rides, him with Nora and the kids at the cottage, and the off-road vehicle excursions they took into the hills near Frankford. The high-speed snowmobile runs on his farm were thrilling experiences for both Nora and the joyfully screaming kids. I had noted an attraction between them then, but this? Surely not!

I now wondered how many stops he had made when passing through Brockville when I was out of town.

I will never know ... I don't ever want to know.

CHAPTER 39

THE REST OF THE BROCKVILLE STORY

Awake, arise, the hour is late
Angels are knocking at thy door
They are in haste, they cannot wait
Once departed, they come no more
—Henry Wadsworth Longfellow

S ummers and winters came and went. We had a couple of deep-snow winters, and some almost barren of snow. Summers were breezy and humid. The mayflies swarmed in a cloud of green around our yard light each spring. A thrush would sing on Gail's bedroom window in the mornings and cause her to yell, "Go away, bird."

Number-two son Ronald Wayne was in constant fights with a neighbor's kid, and number-three son, Gary, spent much time swimming in a neighbor's flooded quarry during school shutdowns or, otherwise, reading. Number-one son Ritchie worked on our neighbor's market garden all summer, sleeping in the attic of his barn.

The annual visits from Dad and Mother at the opening of bass season continued each year. They coincided with the Canada Day holiday in July.

With the children in school, Nora went to work for Zellers Department Store, her first employment since the fish-packing plant in Richmond, British Columbia. She was pleased to be out of the house and circulating among peers as well as able to contribute to the family income. Life was good.

My senior foreman, Wayne Larocque, and spouse Karen lived next door, and one of my field foremen, Thomas Schweige, and his wife built a house on an adjoining lot to the east of us. Our lives on Murray Road were the perfect example of normality.

Meanwhile, back at work, the Dunnville Telephone Company contracted to convert its manual switchboard system to a local dial and direct-toll dial system in one grand combined cut-over. It would be our first and only venture to do so.

The project was going well until the final testing of senders. They were to transmit information by frequencies to connecting Bell Telephone toll carriers, and they were faulty. John Goodwin, the on-site foreman, called to say, "The senders are way off frequency." I told him to take the problem to the engineering group, which subsequently involved the shop-testing people. Their final tests had indicated all frequencies within the permitted 1 percent.

I was already on the road while the problem was being probed.

On arrival in Dunnville, I spoke first with John and the Bell testers on-site. They simply said that all frequencies appeared to be off by a percentage. "OK," I said. "This is not a random thing. It is common to the frequency generators in the units. Let's find out why!"

Consulting the blueprint and comparing the specified values of components to those on the circuit boards, I could see that there were discrepancies. I called the final testing people in the shop to ask if there were reasons for this, and I was told that to make the units pass inspection, they had to substitute the values of some components.

Upon hanging up, I told the Bell Telephone technicians that I had a Hewlett Packard sign-wave generator, and they had an oscilloscope. With those two pieces of test gear, we could fix this.

They agreed to lend me their oscilloscope.

About now, John received a phone call from engineering that the units—all of them—would have to be unwired, repacked, and returned to the shop for changes. This would result in the postponing of the cut-over.

I quickly phoned back and said, "Don't do it. Let's see what I can do here." I was told there was nothing I could do. It required some very sophisticated test equipment. I said, "Give me twenty-four hours. I can fix it."

I then made a frantic call to Rex who reluctantly gave me until the next day before he would notify the customer of the need to delay the cut-over.

Oh, ye of little faith, why are you so afraid?—Mathew 8:26

I made it to a local radio repair shop before their closing time and bought a handful of resistors and capacitors in the values listed on the blueprints, plus a few trimmers. I had dinner, returned to work, and sat cross-legged on the floor at the level of the lowest sender. I plugged in a soldering iron, powered up the sinewave generator, and, setting the oscilloscope to the desired output frequencies, began replacing components on the circuit boards with values as shown on the schematics.

Before midnight, and with the use of some of those trimmer components, I was producing perfect circles on that oscilloscope. The generated frequencies were dead-on specification. They just had to work.

Once more I phoned Rex, who was not yet in bed, and told him, "I fixed one unit. It will work. Do not let anyone even think about delaying this cut-over."

I would like to say that Rex was delighted to hear this, but he questioned my conviction. He had been advised by shop personnel that it could not be fixed on-site. I finally said, with emphasis, "Rex, for Christ's sake—it works!" I added "I'll fix the rest of the senders tomorrow!"

He simply said, "We'll talk tomorrow."

I went to a hotel and went to bed.

Three weeks later, the cut-over happened on schedule.

This was as close as we ever came to an industry embarrassment, and it was my last, and probably most significant, rescue mission for the Automatic Electric Company of Canada.

The Strowger switch had been the anchor in the telephone industry since 1891. The Bell Telephone Company and Siemens paid patent fees for use of the design, and the Stromberg Carlson Company had its own design based on the dial-generated vertical/ horizontal control features of Almon Strowger.

In 1947, Bell Laboratories created solid-state circuitry that led to the development of the transistor. How would that affect our industry? In a nutshell, electric current could be started and stopped without a manual or solenoid-driven mechanical device, and current could be regulated without a glass vacuum tube that needed power-hungry short-life filaments. Hence, the transistor radio and a multitude of other power-saving technological devices were born. Binary technology was about to affect our lives at different levels. Soon, we would not even have to wind a clock.

The Northern Electric crossbar system already dominated the larger market areas of Canada. It was a low-maintenance common-control system that was quiet, fast, and readily adaptable to touch-tone dials made possible by the development of solid-state circuitry. Our company would ultimately tumble from a leadership role in dial switching to oblivion.

In Canada, the Automatic Electric company attempted to stave off the inevitable by adapting the Leich Company Crosspoint switch (owned by General Telephone since 1950) to electronic common control. It was developed by our engineering department in Brockville, which took sole responsibility for its manufacture and installation. Those who ran the projects were graduate electrical engineers. We had but one such person on staff, and they took him—my friend and supervising foreman, John Goodwin.

There were many units sold, and they performed well, but total solid-state switching would soon take the market away from all manner of mechanical switching systems.

In recent years, others of my staff had bought or built homes in Brockville, including Cliff White and John Goodwin. Both now had homes in the preferred district north of the 401. While we had sensed the gathering storm, we'd also had confidence that the parent company in Northlake, Illinois, would come up with a system to keep us in the game. After all, the General Telephone Company in the United States was a big player. We had confidence that nothing could go wrong.

Late summer, 1970, my personnel department contact (whose name I still do not remember) asked me to "drop by." I sensed it was not for one of our occasional visits to just keep in touch.

As I entered his office, he asked Mabel (yes, I remember his secretary's name) to bring us a coffee, and we chatted about the direction our company was going—our hopes and fears. He informed me that he had been in contact with the personnel manager of the General Telephone Company of Upstate New York. "John," he said, "have you ever considered moving to the states?"

I had a sudden concern for what might be ahead. Why was this suddenly coming from out of the blue? He obviously knew something I did not. No! This was not idle conversation. Something was about to be unveiled.

He continued, "They could use you in the southern tier of New York. They need management."

He said all was above-board, and that Rex and Walter knew of this. Would I like to have him set up an interview in Middletown, New York?

He added, "John, I believe you should seriously consider this." I perceived that he had my best interests in mind.

That very evening, Gail babysat as Nora and I went for a Chinese dinner to discuss the subject over some won ton soup and out of earshot of the children. I had located Middletown on a road map and found it was in the tri-state area, not too near "the city" but far from the Canadian border, and our family.

Until now, I had been hiding my concerns about the company's waning sales from Nora. While dining on sweet and sour pork, she lamented, "Are we ever going to settle down and stay somewhere— anywhere?" She continued, "What do the states have to offer we don't have here?"

Without saying it aloud, I thought, *A job!*

I reminded her of the statement, "I believe you should seriously consider this." And added, "He may well know more than he has said."

On the following Monday, I asked that the appointment be made. I could almost hear the flutter of gossamer wings as my guardian angel once more flew away from a successful rescue.

The road to tomorrow will always be fraught with
the danger of failure. Even the most confident
will accept the possibility of failure. It often takes
as much courage to fail as it does to succeed!

CHAPTER 40

A RELUCTANT DECISION

Opportunity does not waste time with those
who are unprepared.—Idowu Keynesian

My journey to the Middletown interview was taking me deeper into the United States than I had ever been before. As I crossed the Ivy Lea bridge at Gananoque, I slowed to view the scenic Thousand Islands seaway. It extended over twenty miles from here to beyond Brockville, and I wondered, *Am I destined to leave this beautiful, pristine land behind?*

Now, as I headed south on Highway 81, the sun was gaining altitude, and the roads were clear. I was feeling a twinge of excitement mixed with misgivings. Was this really happening to me and my family—again?

Driving the undulating terrain of upstate New York, I wondered: was my career is still on the incline? Had it plateaued? Had my glide to retirement already begun? Was the General Telephone Company of Upstate New York looking for my technical capability or my somewhat aggressive management skills? Was this to be an expedition into progress or a dignified escape from a failing company? Whatever, I perceived that this undertaking was now a necessity and felt compelled to pursue it.

As the miles went by—through Watertown, Pulaski, and

Syracuse, and then at Binghamton, turning onto Highway 17 through Liberty and beyond—my mind evaluated the past decade. During the years at Automatic Electric, there had been career peaks and valleys, conquests and calamities. My personal life had experienced triumphs and sorrows. Was I pursuing distinction or being driven?

Finally, at the junction of Highway 11, I spotted my destination: the Howard Johnson motel. During the final miles of this journey, I recalled the day in New Westminster, B.C., when I accepted the challenge to improve a dysfunctional installation department. How desperately I had needed a job then! How confident I had felt even though I didn't understand the situation.

At that point, there had been little to no choice. This time, there was—or was there? When your life starts with nothing, you never want to go back there.

How well I remembered the challenges faced. I encountered problems; I found solutions. I gained the respect of peers and the fear of employees. Now I was an unneeded entity. The company had granted me a great deal of latitude in my management endeavors, and Rex had given me his support and confidence. The results were a functioning, viable department with capabilities second to none in the industry.

The dilemma? Progress! The era of solid-state switching was upon us. My expertise in electromechanical switching was of little value to this new generation of technology. What would my job be here? I surmised I would be overseeing the salvaging of electromechanical equipment from switching centers now being replaced by electronics and reinstalling it in rural offices to stave off the cost of updating. Would this bide me until retirement?

I checked in and spent the night in absent-minded deliberations. Did I belong in this foreign land? Was necessity determining my destiny, or was I in control?

That night in the darkness of my motel room, my mind drifted to the distant past. For years, I had virtually abandoned Nora with four preschool children in that forlorn little house in St. Adolph, Manitoba. How had she endured such an existence in that unfriendly neighborhood for so long?

Finally, in desperation, she had put the furniture into storage and, with four children in tow, boarded a train to Salmon Arm, British Columbia, to seek security and comfort with a neglectful husband. Had that been an act of faith or desperation? Had she exhausted all reserve endurance? Was she seeking the comforts of a loving mate or the security of an employed husband?

Our later move to Vancouver had been a near misfortune. Yes, by the grace of God, I did get hired to a job for which I was not academically qualified. The thought of the alternative still sends chills up my back to this day. (Nora was never told about that.)

When I took the job in Brockville, she faced the necessity of leaving our first-ever new home in Richmond. Surely she was once again experiencing both practical and emotional abandonment. She had found personal satisfaction and comforts in Richmond, but for family security, she needed me. She then came to me in Ontario, a true demonstration of faith that I have never been sure I earned.

Now she was to leave our nice new home in Brockville to live in a foreign land. As I lay there in the darkness, I wondered—how much more could I expect? How much more could she give? What other options did we have?

I gave thanks to God for giving me Nora, and finally slept.

A gracious woman retaineth honor: and
strong men only riches.—Proverbs 11:16

The next morning, I appeared for my appointment at the selected location and was first greeted by Ralph, the supervisor of the installation group consisting of less the thirty employees. Ralph was a pleasant, alert, and well-spoken individual with a history of central office equipment maintenance and outside plant.

He gave me a rundown of his duties, which included central office equipment warehouse supervisor with a shop where recovered telephones and PBX and key-phone units were restored (cleaned, polished, tested, and cords replaced). He also managed a tool crib from which many departments could draw tools, and he ran the carpool. My duties, he informed me, would be confined to equipment installation.

We had a brief chat about my background, discussed our mutual concerns about many things, and went to coffee.

My next interrogation was with the plant manager, Mr. Richard ("call me Dick") Brott. He was bigger than life in every respect, jovial, talkative and yet I felt that just beneath that seemingly relaxed surface there was a pool of firm resolve. We discussed my experiences of the past, and he stated that my reputation had preceded me. I came highly recommended.

As we swapped some experience chitchat, he mentioned that the company was run from the headquarters in Johnstown. "We in this southern tier are a stepchild!" he chuckled. Then he leaned forward in his squeaky chair, looked directly at me, and asked, "Have you any experience supervising a union crew?"

"No, but B.C. Telephones, where I worked eleven years ago, was a union company."

"*Working* is not the same as *supervising*," he said. He pushed a half-inch-thick five-by-seven-inch union agreement book toward me and said, "This is what we work by." Tapping the book with his finger, he continued, "You won't get away with some of things you did in Brockville."

Apparently, Dick had held conversations with my Brockville

personnel contact. I sensed that beneath that cheery personality, there was someone you would rather not mess with.

We went to lunch, after which a personnel manager from the headquarters in Johnstown would be there to talk with me.

The personnel manager, Robert (Bob) Hausman, met with me in a conference room. He made no inquiries into my experiences but went right to my history, asking, "Have you ever obtained a high school equivalency certificate?"

I had never heard of a high school equivalency certificate, but I told him about my circuit-analysis course in the Manitoba Technical Institute in Winnipeg. I also pointed out that I had a radio and electronics certificate from the British Columbia Board of Education, and there were several company technical courses to my credit.

I said, "I have never thought of my lack of high school as a handicap." He did not further comment on that subject.

The next item of discussion was immigration. They first must show evidence to a Labor Board that there was no citizen available with suitable or equal qualifications. He stated, "The wheels are already turning on that."

This was the first indication that my move was already in the works. He did note that I had top security clearance from the Canadian government, so immigration should be no problem.

I was given some papers to take to the American Embassy in Toronto and told to file for a temporary work permit as soon as possible.

I left for home that night with a briefcase filled with a union work agreement, immigration applications, bundles of the General Telephone Company of Upstate New York information, and a local newspaper.

Our future seemed to have already been determined.

Would Nora finally have that full-time husband she craved? Would she once again find peace and purpose in her life? Was she always to be first a mother, secondly a wife, and lastly, an individual?

> *If you make the mistake of looking back*
> *too much, you aren't focused enough on the*
> *road in front of you.*—Brad Paisley

CHAPTER 41

LEAVING THE WORLD WE KNEW

But I tell you in truth, it is to your advantage
that I go; for if I do not go away, the
Helper will not come to you; but if I go, I
will send Him to you.—John 16:28

I t was 1969. During my tenure at Automatic Electric, the friendly culture of Canada had been shifting. While the Canada centennial was celebrated with a successful Expo '67, a visit from the president of France, Charles de Gaul, stirred much political conflict with his Montreal *"vive le Quebec libre"* speech. Mailboxes were still being blown up by supporters of a free Quebec.

In the media circus election of 1968, liberal Pierre Trudeau was elected prime minister of Canada. (That was to be the last election in which I ever voted.) We now carried Social Insurance cards, and our country was plunging toward socialized medicine. We also adopted our first-ever official flag, the red maple leaf. It has become one of the most recognizable emblems in the world.

Roman Catholics were celebrating Mass in English. Laws concerning abortion were liberalized, and homosexual acts were decriminalized. Sexual orientation was now included in the Canadian Charter of Rights and Freedoms. Ontario became the first province to allows same-sex couples to adopt children, followed by Alberta, British Columbia, and Nova Scotia.

We lost Saturday postal delivery, and the Ontario Provincial Police were using breathalyzers to test for drunk drivers.

It didn't seem like the same old conservative Canada.

------◆◈◆------

When, at the age of seventeen, I had left Ontario to seek my fortunes in the cold, desolate, remote plains of Manitoba, I had not envisioned returning with a family and with skills of commercial value. Was I now destined to leave this land where we were comfortable and secure? Was I once again being rescued from an uncertain future by people who, for some mysterious reason, cared?

Developments were swift. We drove to the American Embassy in Toronto and filed for my temporary work permit and green-card status for all. The temporary work permit was granted, and the wheels for immigration clearance were turning.

Nora was working at the Zellers store in Brockville. When I was to leave for the states, she would needed a car. Soon, we purchased a suitable used Pontiac Parisienne, a model unique to Canada.

A decision was made to leave the children in school until the summer break, and meanwhile, I would shop for living accommodations in Middletown. An optimistic plan was made to place our home on the market sixty days prior to moving date. We also determined I would make the 290-mile trip home on alternate weekends until the family could relocate.

On September 12, I left my Brockville office for the last time. My tenure in Brockville was at an end.

My parting from the Automatic Electric Company was not without regret. On the recommendation of Rex Holmes, I had been rescued from a situation of despair in British Columbia, and in return, I had given all I had to justify his confidence. Now leaving, I felt neither pride nor prejudice. I had paid my debt.

> *In everything give thanks: for this is the*
> *will of God.—1 Thessalonians 5:18*

————◆————

Upon reporting for work in Middletown, I arrived at the timeworn plant and warehouse building and was guided to my assigned gray metal desk, in a bullpen of several other grey metal desks. As I eased into a well-worn leather upholstered swivel chair, I wondered if I was gaining a secure future or doing penance for transgressions of the past. Ralph's office was just behind me, and I shared floor space with his—make that our—secretary, stenographer, and file clerk.

A self-serve coffee area was at the far end to my left, near Dick Brock's office, and the installation and plant crew dispatch room was in the warehouse behind us. In front and across an aisle facing me was a plant supervisor, John Webber, and his support staff. The floor space was otherwise cluttered with file cabinets and drafting tables. A far cry from my spacious glassed-in office in Brockville.

This was reality. This was a cost-conscious company. I would have to become accustomed.

My initial hours were spent with the secretary and file clerk delivering a well-rehearsed explanation of where things were and providing some insight into the personalities of the foremen who would report directly to me. This took me through to coffee time, of which I partook with Ralph, John Webber, and Dick Brott.

The rest of the morning was spent on keep-busy stuff. After lunch, Ralph took me on a tour of the nearby town and community exchanges where installation activity was ongoing. His driving suggested that at some time, he many have been a stock-car driver.

I began to get a picture of my future as we visited step-by-step switching exchanges like those in British Columbia, but on a much smaller scale. In my mind, I felt the oncoming confinement of a closing circle.

On Tuesday, I was introduced to the foremen I had not yet met. They regarded me with apprehension, like I would burn them if touched. I was not sure if this was fear or respect and shamefully found myself enjoying their anxiety. They scrutinized me in the manner of a bull approaching an electric fence.

Bob then took me on a visit to the main city exchange, where I met the central office maintenance supervisor, a man whose body had expanded almost beyond the capacity of his chair. Next, it was the manual toll office, where the chief operator was much too busy to chat, then the vehicle upkeep and building maintenance shop. Here, the in-charge, Mary Ellen, seemed to have wide-ranging influence. I would deal with her many times in the future, and in any confrontation, she seemed always to win.

In the afternoon, I was chauffeured to far outlying exchange locations that included Dingmans Ferry, Pennsylvania; Montague, New Jersey; and Port Jarvis, New York. Finally, my geographic orientation ended.

On Wednesday, I accompanied Ralph on the morning duties of the dispatch room, and the next day, I would be handed the reins and start to drive the team.

I sensed that much was expected of me.

During the fall of 1969 through the spring of 1970, I made long weekend trips to Brockville whenever possible. Through sunshine, wind, rain, sloppy snow, and hard freezes, my Chevy Acadian served me well. Canadian immigration waved me through with a smile and a "good-day" wish.

On the return trip, American immigration agents were thorough. They questioned my purpose and scrutinized my work card. Once, an agent discovered the three-cornered zipper opening that once accessed the roof light on my secondhand police car. He almost tore the headliner down looking for the contraband, obviously thinking he had hit a jackpot. He expressed only disappointment.

For temporary living accommodations, I found a boarding place in the house of a stately widow of an attorney. I was her only tenant. Her riveted attention was almost a discomfort, as she continually asked me what my favorite this or that was, and provided it. She once even asked about my favorite wine. I thought I would stump her this time and said, "Barnes Catawba." Now Barnes Catawba wine is exclusively a Canadian Niagara region wine—but she found it! Never again did I doubt her resourcefulness.

During my early days in Middletown, there was a noticeable difference in social protocols and customs, one of the most annoying being the habit of chewing gum, both in public and in the workplace. People smacked and popped their gum with all the tact and aplomb of a hog at a trough. I never became accustomed to it.

Another was related to customer relations, one of which took place when I inquired as to the cost of welding a cracked muffler support. I thought the price was high and simply said, "I'll think about it."

The welder said something to the effect of, "Just try and get it cheaper somewhere else, and if you can't, don't come back!" I was to experience this attitude many times in the years ahead.

I quickly learned that in the United States, sandwiches came without butter unless specified upon order. Shoes were not shed at the door by visitors to your home. Victors in any game or group endeavor flaunted their jubilation in the face of the vanquished, and there seemed a noticeable lack of compassion for the underprivileged.

Was this a fact, or was I just looking for social differences? Sometimes I wasn't too sure.

As spring approached, Nora drove to Middletown on several weekends to house-hunt. One weekend, she experienced a blinding blizzard just north of Binghamton and was rear-ended on the highway. Nothing bad came of it but inconvenience, yet it did emphasize the local attitude. The party who hit her boisterously gave the investigating officer a story of Nora's irrational driving that simply was not even logical.

Yes, many New Yorkers quickly turned nasty to deflect blame in the face of conflict. I had already experienced some of it myself.

In any case, eventually we found an attractive split-entry house on Whipple Road just outside of Middletown. I moved in and batchlored it until the family arrived in June.

Diminishing voltage of domestic power source would occasionally trigger what was locally known as a *brownout*. Our house, having an oil furnace, depended on full power for electric ignition. During one of these brownouts, the thermostat called for heat, and oil was released to the fire chamber. Without sufficient power to ignite it, there was a substantial accumulation. Then the power level was restored, and the excess oil ignited.

When I got home from work, the fire department was on hand watching the flames from the chimney and preparing to do … who knows what?

I learned to turn the furnace off when leaving the house and to leave an electric heater on. What exactly did that do for the power inadequacy? New York logic!

Meanwhile, upper management expectations and my apparent inability to energize my support staff to improve that which was apparently expected of me was taking a toll. Nobody liked change, and I stood for change! Union people resisted any effort to alter any standards, most of which were not documented procedures to begin with. They would not have this foreign person coming to their little corner of the world and telling them how to do things.

While the job foremen understood, they simply informed me, "It's all been tried before."

One day, I left work before lunch, went to our still-empty house, sat on the floor, and cried. That was as close to a complete mental breakdown as I ever came.

I questioned my own ability to change. Perhaps a carrot would be more effective than a stick. I decided to try it.

Months passed. The weekend trips to Brockville during the fall had featured a view of highways bracketed with colorful deciduous hardwood foliage, followed by a few weeks of sloppy wet snow. Then came the winter chill and danger of drifting snow, followed in spring by soft, budding greenery and fair weather.

I was now ready to leave Canada behind.

> *Yesterday I was clever, so I wanted to*
> *change the world. Today I am wise, so I am*
> *changing myself.—Jamaluddin Rumi*

CHAPTER 42

OUR LIFE IN MIDDLETOWN

Adapting has become a way of life.
A new thing is a good thing. He is making
a way for us in the wilderness. "The old has
gone, the new is here!"—2 Corinthians 5:17

t was the 1970s, a decade with many historic highlights—some good, some not so good, but anything but dull. The voting age was lowered to eighteen (a blunder that will never be corrected). An exciting new Walt Disney World theme park opened in Florida, and a new stock market index called Nasdaq was created that changed the course of investing. Yes, we were now a part of this dynamic world.

When school ended, the family made the move to Whipple Road in Middletown. Everyone quickly adapted to our spacious house that looked across a well-grazed pasture beyond which, on a clear day, we could see the New Jersey High-Point monument.

I should now have felt more content than I did. There were no more extensive travel obligations, and I enjoyed good earnings. I felt secure in my job and was living in comfort, yet there were no close family ties, no longtime friends nearby, no community bonds of common interest. My life seemed a social island of my own making.

I vowed to become someone other than just a telephone company employee. I had new hopes!

Nora now landed a retail position with Curtain World, a major supplier of custom draperies. Soon, she attended a three-day designing seminar in New York City and was further included in several overnight buying trips. Her rapid progress from salesclerk to design specialist and then assistant manager gave her a sense of confidence and accomplishment.

She reveled in this job and received many accolades for her talents. I had never seen her happier. Need I mention that our living room picture window sported regal satin drapes of her own design?

There were community house parties in our remote little neighborhood on the hill. The residents ranged from a New York City policeman to a Wall Street financial banker. I was saddened to meet a nearby neighbor lady who took her husband to the train station each morning to commute to "the city" and earn their daily bread. At about seven in the evening, she would pick him up at the station, noticeably inebriated; bring him home; feed him; and put him to bed. They would repeat the whole procedure over again each day of the week.

How sad! Would he someday look back and regret this behavior? Or would he justify his actions as the necessity of making a living? I still wonder. (That hit a little close to home.)

In this way, seasons came and went.

It was not long before Ralph was taken from the chain of command, and I reported directly to the installation manager in Johnstown. Ralph considered the role of a warehouse supervisor to be beneath him and quit.

Over the next three years, my endeavors to increase productivity and quality met with some success, but were minimal. Yes, I now had full control of the southern tier installation group, but I made very few inroads into the apathetic attitudes of those I looked to for support. They were the first to feel union resistance to change.

That which has been, is what will be, that which is done is what will be done, and there is nothing new under the sun.—Ecclesiastes 1:9

Some of my less-than-spectacular experiences involved a lack of understanding of the union mind-set. Let me relate a couple to you.

One morning, about 8:10 p.m., the car pool clerk came and requested an unauthorized car for one of my installers. Reason? He was late and had missed the crew-car that left at 8:05 a.m. I told her yes, but he had to come talk to me first.

He was a minority; I'll call him Bubba.

My conversation was brief. First, I asked, "Why didn't you just drive your own car the seven miles to the jobsite?"

He replied, "I don't have a car, and I don't have to anyway. The company has to provide one."

I gave him the car and decided to read the union agreement to see just what the extent of the company's obligations were. They were quite clear: employees had the option to report to the assembly location and ride the crew-car(s) or provide their own transportation and be given equal travel time. On locations over fifteen miles, they would be paid a mileage allowance.

Next day, same situation. He didn't get to the assembly room on time to catch the departure of the crew.

I spoke with him again and let him have a car, but I was firm in my message: "This will be the last time. No more personal pool cars. Be on time or find your own way to the work site."

Need I say it? On Wednesday morning, same scenario—but this time, I simply told the car pool clerk no!

That afternoon, I was sitting face to face with Bubba and a union steward who handed me a written complaint and let me know "we are going to take this to the wire. You are obligated to provide transportation to the assigned remote job location."

I will spare you details, but Walt Rickrack, my manager from Johnstown, came and handled the negotiations. Walt won. No more private pool-car transportation due to tardiness.

Bubba was vindictive. Months later, while assigned to the main Middletown central office, there appeared on a support beam, well above the cable runways, in yellow floor marker, a very degrading message directed at me, on a first-name basis.

When it was called to my attention, I told Phinn, his foreman, to have him paint it over. He said, "I already have."

Great, but now there was no evidence that it was ever there. I felt somewhat vindictive myself and asked, "Who and how many have seen it?"

"Just about everybody," Phinn said, trying to hide a grin. "They make jokes about it!"

Now, I am not a person who angers easily, but this was an affront. I phoned Walt, my superior in Johnstown, and discussed it. Walt simply said, "Leave it with me."

Walt and someone from the personnel department came and conducted interviews with many on-site employees, both maintenance and installation, and came away with a case.

Bubba was fired.

I would like to say this was the end of the story. It wasn't. In fact, it ended before a magistrate several weeks later, and I, the official complainant, was called upon to testify—about something I had never even seen!

In any case, Bubba was gone, and I sensed that I was regarded with a great deal more respect amongst the ranks thereafter. End of story.

On a different subject, a contract installation foreman from the Northlake Automatic Electric Company visited my office one afternoon and woefully told me he had a notification of a layoff. Dennis Terwilliger had worked on expansions to our main exchange for over a year, and we had become friends.

Now, coincidences in life do happen. For a purpose, or for naught—they do happen. I had spoken with my friend in the Brockville personnel office recently, and he mentioned that they were looking for experience on a Saskatchewan project.

With Dennis sitting beside my desk, I called Brockville and told my personnel friend, "You're looking for experienced installers? There is someone sitting right here who can help." After some brief chitchat, Dennis got on the phone, and soon he had an appointment for an interview in Brockville. Good things happen to good people.

Dennis went to work in Canada. I was not to see him again for over a decade.

In 1972, I heard that a reorganization of executive staff was about to occur in the General Telephone Company of Upstate New York. Would I be involved?

Yes!

I soon learned we would move again—this time, to the Johnstown, New York, headquarters of the company. We had spent less than four years in Middletown. For me, it was a promotion. For Nora, it brought depressing hurt. This would tear her away from what she regarded as her first career occupation.

My heart was heavy at her reaction to the news, but the move was not an option.

Church and state alike have demonstrated—
that woman was made after man, of

> *man, and for man, a subordinate being,*
> *subject to man.—Corinthians 11:12.*

The Bible apparently is not subject to social amendments.

⸻◆•◆⸻

Meanwhile, back at the house, Gail was attending Orange County Community College and about to graduate as a licensed lab technician. Number-one son Ritchie had finished high school and was working full-time in the produce department of a supermarket.

We discussed the move with family, and it was decided that Gail would get an apartment and a job with the telephone company when we moved. (Yes, I did have the influence to get her a night-shift operator position.) Ritchie would move to Johnstown when Nora and the rest of the family moved. Career development had not yet become part of his lexicon.

In the fall of 1972, I moved to a rental house in Johnstown, New York, which I shared with my good friend and fellow employee Al Dill. We would house-hunt together with the hope of getting our families to Johnstown by Christmas.

It was four years almost to the day since I had started my employment in Middletown. News from Brockville told me that many step-by step production lines were closing, and the EAX switching unit orders were drying up. While this job was not the stirring adventure I had enjoyed in Brockville, it was secure.

Life was good.

CHAPTER 43

COMMITMENT TO USA RESIDENCY

*Am I fated to one day reflect on the sacrifices
others have made for my good fortunes?*

In Upstate New York, fall foliage shows color early. Chill breezes carry cool misty moisture from across Lake Erie, and people contemplate less fishing, more deer-hunting, and high school football.

The United States had ended involvement in the Vietnam War, Secretariat had become the first horse since Citation to win the Triple Crown, construction was beginning on the Alaska Oil Pipeline, Roe v. Wade became law, and I was named installation manager of the Upstate New York Telephone Company. Yes, to me, it was just as big a deal as those national news items.

Manager had been a wish almost too unreal to even hope for. I moved into a glassed-in office with an attached workroom furnished with a small drafting table, a large cork-based bulletin board, a chalkboard, and a worktable.

Meanwhile, Pat, the former Northern Area supervisor, had been demoted to job foreman. Pat had given his best, but the rumored conflict between him and Walt rendered the result predictable. To add more salt to the wound, Pat would now report to his former charge, Bruce Becker, who in turn reported to me.

Pat owned three rental houses and invited me to look at them as potential home. He was unable to hide his disappointment when none qualified. Other transferees from Middletown, John Webber and Al Dill, also took no interest in Pat's houses. I felt a twinge of sympathy for him. He seemed not to deserve what had been dealt him.

The Upstate area covered about twice the subscriber count of the southern tier and was widely spread from Pulaski, on Lake Erie, to Tribes Hill, in the east, plus a scattering of towns in the vast Adirondacks Forest reserves. My job was to increase quality and production, in that order. It was to be a challenge.

Upon visiting the main exchanges in both Johnstown and its twin city, Gloversville, I was not encouraged. Unsecured cable hung over the edges of overhead runways. Feeder cables that ran down the rear of bays were largely unsecured. Distribution terminal assembly strapping was sloppy, to the point of near short circuits between bulging solder joints. A trunk bay that did not quite fit into its specified location between two previously placed bays was left askew and placed in service.

I spoke with the maintenance supervisors at each site, and they had few positive words for my inherited installation department. In the background, I could hear the incessant spinning of rotary preselectors. I mentioned to the supervisor, Carl, "That shouldn't be."

He replied, "I know, but that's how your installers leave them, and I can't fix them." I perceived I was really here for a purpose.

I can do all this through him who gives
me strength.—Philippians 4:13

258

That glassed-in office with its attached workroom suddenly didn't look as appealing.

———◆•◆•◆———

One morning I sensed someone standing in the doorway of my office. I looked up and, to my astonishment, there stood Art Chamberlain, the consulting engineer on the Diefenbunker project in Carp Ontario. His first words were, "Looks like you have done OK for yourself, John."

I don't recall exactly how I responded, but we visited for a few minutes, in which he informed me that Brockville was continuing to cut back on production and personnel. Concerns for his future had motivated him to leave the Brockville engineering group. His workstation was now but a short distance from where I was located. We agreed to have coffee together at break.

An old friendship was renewed.

———◆•◆•◆———

On a Monday morning, a call beckoned me to Robert Hausman's office. "John," he said, "we have just received a second renewal for your temporary work permit. Why haven't you got the permanent residents card? What's holding you up?"

I sheepishly told him that the last one required me to report to the embassy in Montreal. I had requested my case be transferred back to Toronto, where it had originated. Time had passed, they had not responded, and I had neglected to follow up.

He simply said, "Get it. This is a nuisance I don't need!" Thus, we made our Montreal appointment and gathered the whole family together for the journey—in January, 1973. There are worse places to be in January, but not many.

Our hotel rooms were only a few blocks from the embassy, and we checked in on a cold Tuesday afternoon. In January, there is no other kind in Montreal.

Ritchie was viewing the Montreal metropolis from the hotel window and suddenly called out, "Come and see this."

We could see a sloped parking lot, typical of the rolling terrain of Montreal. A car had parked in a parking space when another, pulling in beside it, stopped, then slowly slid on the frozen surface against the one below. Two people emerged and were slipping and sliding around observing their predicament when another pulled into the next vacant spot, stopped, and slowly slid into the previously parked cars. Now this wasn't funny, but we laughed. Yes, someone else's misery was our entertainment for the day.

Our afternoon appointment at the embassy next day was one of painfully slow progress. We were, after all, a package of eight people. As we sat with our bundle of necessary documents, we had time to look around at other applicants awaiting their turn. I hoped that some of them would not become our neighbors. By closing time, five o'clock, we were unprocessed and told to return at eleven in the morning.

That evening, I called my friend Ben Litwinowich in Brockville to say hello and to mention that, if time permitted, we might drop in for a visit on our way home the next day. He bade us to do so and said we would be expected. As I have previously mentioned, Nora still had an unaccounted-for dislike of Ben but agreed it was a convenient pit stop.

We checked out of the hotel in the morning, loaded our luggage, and proceeded to the embassy for processing—which did not commence until after lunch.

Processing eight people through immigration is time-consuming. The clock was ticking: two o'clock … three o'clock … still in progress. I cringed at the thought of another night at that hotel.

The clerk processing us was a cheerful young bilingual lady who expressed amazement and gratitude at how well Nora had organized our material. Every document came out of each Manilla envelope in the exact required order, and all were complete and accurate. She said, "That seldom happens—not here."

By about four o'clock, all was done except reciting the oath and the presentation of green cards. She bade us wait and be patient.

A well-dressed gentleman approached us, introduced himself as the ambassador, and administered the oath. He presented our immigration cards and said, "I don't usually perform this duty, but [clerk's name] told me how impressed she was with your family and how well-organized you were." He continued, "I know you all will be an asset to our country."

He addressed each of our children with appropriate earnestness, shook hands with me and Nora, and said, with sincerity, "Welcome to the United Stated of America."

By five-thirty that evening, we were pulling onto old Highway 2, Brockville-bound. This would be the last time I would ever travel this route. It had been my road to many adventures over the past years.

Somewhere along the way, Highway 2 merged into the new multilane 401, and by early evening, we had arrived at the home of Ben and Gloria Litwinowich.

We were greeted with much enthusiasm, and Gloria had held dinner for us. After enjoying a lovely meal, we contemplated taking a hotel overnight. Middletown was still six hours away on winter highways, in a car loaded with eight people.

Ben and Gloria would not hear of it. They made sleeping accommodations on beds, couches, and on-floor sleeping bags. They even put Nora and I into their master bedroom. I felt much gratitude for their hospitality.

We drove home on Thursday and spent Friday resting. We were now permanent residents of the United States of America. It felt good!

CHAPTER 44

ANOTHER MOVE TO ANOTHER LIFE

A sorrowful farewell to maturing family members.

During a long cold snow-ridden winter, Al and I had house-hunted when practicable and took turns driving to our Middletown homes on weekends. In Johnstown, we did our own cooking and laundry and such, and on weekends, we were fed and pampered by our spouses at home. Despite the pressures at work, for both of us, life was good.

Finally, the winter weather receded, but our house-hunting had not been fruitful. We had, in fact, visited almost every worthwhile listing in town and were both contemplating the same solution: build. Yes, we had learned of lots and plots of land available. Our endeavors shifted to building. To get to the point, we found a five-acre dividable plot and decided to split it, find a builder, and get on with it.

A prebuilt home supplier was selected, suitable floor plans were decided upon, and a builder was engaged. As the frost was seeping from the soil, our homes were in the making. Al selected a two-story four-bedroom plan for his family; Nora and I went with a six-bedroom two-story to be built on the wooded uphill side of the sloping lot. My builder would leave the inside finishing to Ritchie and me.

Our location faced Johnson Street, across from which were acres of farmland and a view of the Adirondacks foothills: a calendar-worthy landscape setting. This would surely be our final home. It couldn't get any better!

Construction progressed.

With our housing needs now being met, I had all but forgotten Pat and his disappointment at not selling a house to me or any of the other transferees. He did not hide his feelings for me and avoided me when possible. One Monday morning, he unexpectedly entered my office and handed me a paper saying, "This is my resignation. I got a job with Continental Telephones."

He took a breath, hesitated as if to say something more, then began to turn to walk away.

"Pat," I said, "I truly hope you are happy with the Continental people."

As he turned back, I extended a hand for a handshake. He took it and said, "Thanks." He paused, as if suppressing further feelings, and added, "I saw this coming. Be careful. Don't let Walt screw you—and he will."

Bruce and the crew held a party for Pat and his wife that evening. I did him the favor of not attending.

Meanwhile, during a visit to the installation reporting station and warehouse in the industrial section of Johnstown, I found random caches of equipment, some never having been removed from the manufacturers' shipping crates. There were non inventoried units of recovered equipment, much of which had been cannibalized, and some depressing collections of nondescript paraphernalia that had accumulated over the years.

A bin of copper wire with the insulation burned off caught my attention. Was it being sold as scrap, to whom, and by whom? I wondered!

One discovery amazed me. I stood looking at it for a full minute and wondered, *Can it be?* Yes—a split iron tank had been transformed into a fire pit and mounted on a triangular frame fashioned from equipment-bay guardrails, with an overhead rotisserie driven by a busy tone interrupter motor. The explanation? "We use it on company-sponsored outdoor events!"

Oh boy!

———◆◆◆———

Our new home was soon enclosed and weatherproofed. Ritchie had moved into the rental house with Al, and I and we began full-time interior finishing. He did the wiring and placed insulation while plumbers installed water-heating radiators and domestic plumbing.

In the meantime, the oil furnace and water-pressure systems were placed by appropriate tradesmen. In the evenings, we worked together to place hardwood flooring, added Sheetrock and spackled the walls. We then painted, placed baseboards and door frames, hung cupboards, and so forth. By early summer, the house was livable. There was still landscaping, building a redwood sun deck, clearing brush for a garden, and other make-busy stuff to be done on a post-move-in basis.

Nora had given notice to her employer and, as Al and I drove the now-familiar Highway 87 to Middletown on a Friday night, I was aware that this day would be her last at Curtain World. At 7:30 that evening, she called to say she would be a bit late—it was her last day, and a farewell gathering was in progress.

Gail made dinner, and we watched some TV and went to bed. I am not sure just when Nora arrived home. Her cherished Curtain World career had come to an end.

The following week, she finished packing; on Thursday, the movers came; and on Friday, they delivered our furniture to still another new home. We were once again turning a page to a new chapter in the chronicles of our life.

Gail had graduated from college, found an apartment, and

was now working full-time for the telephone company. We had furnished a small upstairs room for her visiting convenience. She seldom used it.

Soon after our move to Johnstown, Ritchie made it known to us that he had enlisted in the US military. Nora was saddened, but her protests were in vain. In Johnstown, he had no friends, no one to wish him well, and no one to say good-bye as he departed. We alone would say our sad adieus as he boarded a military bus and woefully watched it fade from sight over the crest of the Johnston Street hill.

Nora cried outright, and I concealed a few tears of my own.

My mind drifted back to 1950. When I boarded that train in Stirling, I had left with a soul full of hope to seek my fortunes on a harvesting excursion. As I stepped aboard, I looked back and watched my mother turn away. I now wondered, was she then concealing a tear? Did my parents have that empty let-down feeling we now felt?

Our family was melting into another generation. Our two eldest, having taken control of their lives, no longer needed our shelter or influence. Suddenly, our six-bedroom house seemed inappropriate. It was not to be the all-encompassing warm family home we had envisioned.

Never again would there be a full dinner table enjoying a joyful roast turkey or ham celebration for Thanksgiving and Christmas. Never again would they be opening birthday gifts or proudly presenting trophies of their achievement. They had exercised judgment and made choices just as we'd encouraged them to do. We should have been rejoicing, but somehow that was not how we felt.

Choices are a selection of current options; once made, they become decisions, and options no longer exist. Nora and I once made those choices, and we understood our children had their own challenges to face, their own goals to pursue, their own lives to live. Home would be where they made it.

Our two eldest were essentially the product of Nora's parenting. I had contributed little more than funding. Nora had tended to and comforted them on multiple relocation journeys. We had packed them into our old cars along with household goods, our total wardrobes, and baby needs.

She had rescued them from an unsuitable St. Adolph house and single-handedly brought them by train to reestablish us as a family in Salmon Arm, British Columbia. She had loved, protected, and cared for them during my many years of consistent absence. A miracle had been accomplished in giving them life and preparing them for the future on which they were now embarking.

Had we achieved all we could? Had we done enough? Had we done it right? Only God would ever know.

The cocoons we spun for them went now empty as they scattered to the winds of the world. Would they choose happy and productive lives?

Time would tell.

> *Her children rise up and call her blessed;*
> *her husband also, and he praises her: "Many*
> *women have done excellently, but you*
> *surpass them all."—Proverbs 29-29)*

CHAPTER 45

OUR JOHNSTOWN DAYS

The taming of the beast I once created.

Now settled in our house nestled peacefully in the palm of a gentle wooded hill slope, we had cleared the garden of brush, stumps, and stones, and established a lawn. The house was an ivory-colored prefinished siding with red brick highlights framed by an abrupt hill to the north that melted into a gentle incline to a wooded area at the rear. The terrain leveled off to the south toward Al Dill's colorful dwelling punctuated by white birch.

A black iron weathervane perched on the cupola of our north lower roof gave it an air of New England tradition. We beheld it with pride.

I often toiled outside after work until the mosquitoes drove me in for a late dinner. The rototiller shook my body and took more energy than I cared to admit, but I suffered little more than a few broken fingernails and did some cussing.

We also enjoyed early evening dining on the redwood deck accessed from double sliding doors. Beyond the deck, a brief upward-sloping lawn blended into the shaded woods. Our oversized three-burner hibachi sizzled flavor into everything from steak and burgers to jumbo shrimp. Then, the mosquitos would emerge, and a hasty retreat was beaten to the inside and those sliding doors closed.

Life was good and getting better. We were blessed.

Our two youngest, Grant and Glen, were enrolled in the Meco grade school, while Ron and Gary attended Gloversville High School.

Grant and Glen joined a Boy Scouts of America cub pack that appointed me the troop leader, and Nora found employment in Britts Department Store, a prominent retail outlet in Gloversville. She worked a split afternoon/evening shift.

I enjoyed the privilege of being an eight-to-five employee and no longer felt that there was something I had to prove, confront, or defend. My nature had softened. There were no threats to our future or comforts, and no obstacles to overcome. We made occasional visits with family and friends in Canada, and they in turn reciprocated. A measure of serenity settled into our lives.

I must mention a family story about brother-in-law Harry. After being denied access to the United State during the Second World War because he was of draft age, he vowed to never again enter the United States. Well, after some coaxing, he and Eva came to visit us in Johnstown.

Eventually, they bought a lot in Kissimmee, moved a camping trailer onto it, and spent the next twenty or so winters in Florida.

Please do not expect me to explain it!

Over the years, Nora and I made ends meet financially and accumulated some investment resources. We did not live in opulence, but in comfort. Our savings comprised of government savings bonds and payroll-deducted payments for employee stock-option purchases of General Telephones with reinvested dividends.

John Webber often brought his *Money* magazine to our morning coffee breaks, and we discussed investments. I had absolutely no knowledge and not much understanding of investing, but John explained what a mutual fund was and spoke of them returning many times bank and bond yields. He gave me his discarded magazine each month, and I consumed the material with gusto.

The company stocks I had purchased appreciated in value and paid dividends, and government savings bonds were a convenient payroll savings vehicle, but the interest on them merely compensated for inflation. I wanted a little more.

Nora was the family banker and bookkeeper, and I paid little attention to our cash flow, at least not until one day when she happened to mention we had over a thousand dollars in the savings account. The thought of investing crept into my mind. I looked upon it as an adventure.

One evening, after a satisfying dinner, I broached the subject of investing that one thousand dollars in a mutual fund. Nora's reaction was, at best, lukewarm. "What is a mutual fund?"

With some support from *Money*, I showed her month-by-month earnings of some recommended funds. Invested dollars were working dollars. Savings account dollars were dormant dollars.

Without going into further negotiation details, in a month's time or so, we mailed an investment of one thousand dollars to the Vanguard Wellington fund. It was our first step toward investing prosperity.

It is difficult to explain the hesitancy we felt as that check for our hard-earned money went into the mailbox. I remember us walking to the mailbox together, placing the envelope ceremoniously into it, raising the flag, and then standing there for a few seconds looking at each other. The moment was fragile, but hand in hand, we walked back to the house.

She laughingly said something to the effect of, "If we lose this money, you are in trouble, you know that, don't you?"

Investing would ultimately become our main source of wealth.

Time passed. My department did, bit by bit, gain respect. For example, the busy hour spinning of rotary preselector switches I previously mentioned did get fixed. I solicited help from the engineering department and had Art Chaberlain put a course together and present it to a select few of my upstate and southern-tier installers. I then had a crew go from exchange to exchange where the situation persisted to get the inter-shelf ATB chain properly equipped and wired. Finally, no more complaints!

During the next five years, my position in the company never changed. Day by day, week by week, and month by month, time marched on. The department was not expanded. In fact, I was permitted only to replace losses, and slack was taken up by contract labor. Soon I had several capable contractors on my approved vendor supply list. All major purchases of new equipment from the Northlake plant were "engineer, furnish, and install" (EF&I).

This brought Automatic Electric salesperson Dick Hignight into my life. Dick was not your typical salesman. He was low-key and would take Nora and me to dinner whenever he was in town. We became friends, and he would ultimately influence another life-changing decision I would soon make.

Other contract salespersons kept me well supplied with good rye whiskey. One even brought a large smoked Easter ham to the house.

———— ◆ ◆ ————

During the summers, we enjoyed company-sponsored social activities in a little wooded park beyond the head-office parking lot. At these company events, we dined on succulent "steamer" roasts prepared by my installers on the rotisserie I had discovered in the installation storeroom. My field supervisor, Bruce Becker, would have the roast skewered and seasoned, and the cooking was tended by our installers.

Somehow, I no longer begrudged the time they spent on this

activity. Those roasts were yummy. Yes, I was blending in with company values.

At home, I managed a half-acre of lawn and each spring prepared the soil in the garden plot for Nora. She tended to it with delight and canned the vegetables or preserved them in the freezer. Perhaps our minds floated back to the peaceable farm life of our youth. There we consumed what the land had to offer.

We bought beef by the half-carcass to best utilize our twenty-nine-cubic-foot freezer. Our family ate well.

The woods on the hill behind the house was a shaded playground for the two youngest. Perfect! If Nora could hear them, she knew all was well.

Each Easter, I drove the boys to sell Boy Scout hot-cross buns door-to-door and delivered them on Easter Saturday. The older boys, Ron and Gary, created a prize-winning history log for a Boy Scout exhibit by mounting a three-inch-thick, thirty-nine-inch-in-diameter slab from a white pine log onto a framed four-by-eight plywood sheet. It was sanded and varnished, and each ring identified a listed milestone of history. Ring counts indicated it sprouted in about 1783, the year Great Britain acknowledged American independence.

Nora and I finally felt like a normal working couple contributing to a community that accepted us. Days of doubt were fading into the past.

CHAPTER 46

OUR MATURING FAMILY

*Parents defer many needs and desires of their
own to favor the needs of their children.
Therefore, they develop a nobility of character
and put into practice the selfless truths taught
by the Savior Himself.—James E. Faust*

L ife was good, but the world around us was changing. During
our tenure in New York, Patty Hearst was kidnapped by the
Symbionese Liberation Army, the ugly Watergate situation
reached its climax with the resignation of Richard Nixon, Saigon fell
to the Vietnamese, Jimmy Hoffa went missing, Elvis Presley died,
and John Paul III became pope.

The seventies also brought us the first video game: Pong.
Apple and Microsoft launched technology that would change the
world. An OPEC embargo raised the price of our heating oil from
eleven cents a gallon to twenty-nine cents, and lines formed at
filling stations. The seventies brought an erosion of public trust
in the federal government that persists to this day, but they were,
nevertheless, good years for the Geen family.

One morning I noticed Walt, my boss, and the department manager, Jack Conklin, talking in serious closeness, and looking across the work area toward my office. Something of a serious nature was obviously being discussed. I was soon to find out.

Jack called me to his office and, in a serious tone of voice, asked, "Have you heard?"

Puzzled, I said, "No!"

He continued, "Gail, your daughter, has been terminated."

"For what?" I stammered.

"Her cash drawer had been left unattended and unlocked, and was cleaned-out." Jack continued, "When Gail returned to her post, she discovered it, reported it, took responsibility for leaving it unlocked, and pleaded it was an oversight on her behalf." She was, nevertheless, immediately terminated.

Nora spoke to Gail at length on the phone, and I would later learn that she loaned Gail money to make restitution in exchange for waiving of legal charges.

We had bought number-two son, Ron, a subcompact Chevy Vega, the one with the lightweight aluminum motor, which he used to service a rather extensive paper route. He made us proud by putting half of his earning into a savings account. Yes, he was obviously a chip off the old block.

The bad news was, that car burned almost as much oil as it did gasoline. I had the engine reboarded and steel sleeves inserted into the cylinder shafts, and that solved the problem. It cost just about as much as I had paid for the car.

Now for the rest of the story. Shortly after he graduated from high school, Ron left the house one morning and did not come home. We worried, but next day a police officer came to inform us that his girlfriend's father had reported her missing. At least we now had a clue as to his motivation.

Apparently, the cops were told that Ron had access to a large amount of money. Were we financing him? I assured him that he was spending his own savings.

After a couple of days, the wayward couple contacted her father to assure him both were safe and sound. A week later, they came home. His money was gone.

Before long, we were attending their pretty backyard wedding at her parents' home in Gloversville. Their daughter, Christie, was born on January 12, 1975.

After marriage, Ron worked for the local glove factory for a while but approached me one day and asked, "What are my chances of employment with General Telephone?"

I spoke with him about how most of the people who lived in this area were born here, got married here, live their life here, died here, and were buried here. I really wanted something better for him and his family. I called upon my friend in the personnel office at Automatic Electric in Brockville, and he agreed to get Ron employed in the installation department that I once ran. There he would get quality training for a career in communications.

Along the way, I had purchased an old pop-up tent trailer, stripped it of all its pop-up apparatus, and painted it green. When closed, it was a roomy and weatherproof cargo box. It would also hold about all of Ron and Teresa's worldly goods.

On a warm spring day, Nora and I bid adieu to them and sadly watched Ron and his family fade over the brow of that Johnstown Road hill by our house. Their little green Vega was towing my little green trailer, which I never saw again. Ron was on the road to a career. Teresa was on an adventure that would change her life forever. She was making her escape from Gloversville! They made Canada their home.

And I promised you: You will inherit the land,
since I will give it to you to possess, a land flowing
with milk and honey.—Leviticus 20:24

A year later, number-three son, Gary, graduated from high school and chose to go to Fulton County Junior College. We bought him a Plymouth compact station wagon for his transportation needs, and upon graduation, he too enquired about joining the General Telephone Company. This time, I called my old friend Ken Kaiser, manager of the Northlake Automatic Electric installation department. Ken assured me could put Gary to work. "Send him on over!"

We purchased some luggage for him. Nora selected some living essentials and packed them in the back of his station wagon. With a few dollars in his pocket and an Exxon gas credit card, Gary was off to face the world.

He did well with the Northlake people. After spending time with them, he transferred to Brockville to do contract maintenance in Saudi Arabia. Upon his return to Canada, he found employment with a communications group in Red Deer, Alberta. He never returned to the United States.

Now our household was down to two sons, Grant and Glen, and a Manx cat called Fifi. Meanwhile, back at work, there were dark rumors that the ongoing conflicts between the New York Public Service Commission and the company had motivated General Telephone to yield the New York properties to the Continental Telephone Company. On a blustery fall day in 1978, all head-office employees were assembled in the cafeteria, and the rumor was confirmed.

Many management people were offered an escape: a choice to move to other General Telephone operating companies with moving expenses paid. We were given a month to decide.

Shortly after this offer, Dick Hignight, the Northlake salesperson, took Nora and I to dinner, and over the meal, he said, "John, if San

Angelo, Texas, is a choice, take it. If any engineering department ever needed help, they do." He further advised, "Be sure to ask for General Telephone Company of the Southwest engineering" He added, almost as an afterthought, "In a couple of years I will retire, and we plan to move to San Angelo. Perhaps we can go fishing."

I took Dick's suggestion. It was to be another turning point in our lives.

My request for transfer to General Telephone of the Southwest was approved. Nora had mixed emotions, even though she had shared in that decision. She was sensitively involved in her position at work but also aware that our house no longer reflected family needs. Would we ever again get a place so well located, so beautiful?

The decision was made, and I was jubilant at the prospect of moving to an engineering position. On the other hand, she was being torn away from the comfort and warmth she was enjoying at Britt's Department Store.

Upon her departure from Britt's, a farewell party was thrown in a private home. I drove her to the party and was ushered into a connecting room with other nonparticipating spouses. From where I sat, I could see across a hall into the party room.

I watched as Nora positioned herself on a bench-seat near the end of a long table. Shortly afterward, a gentleman I recognized as a fellow employee of hers entered. There was much oohing and awwing from the guests as she made room for him beside her. Someone said, "Here he is, Nora," and laughter ensued.

It hit me that those after-hours obligations at work had become frequent. Were they motivated by dedication to the store, or to other interests? I didn't even want to think about it. I drove home.

I went to bed in emotional distress and kept asking myself *why*. There had to be a reason, an explanation. I just didn't know the answer.

Later, a car came. There were muted voices as the door quietly opened, then a rustle of paper as gifts were brought in. Then the car left. I feigned sleep as she climbed the stairs in stockinged feet, quietly prepared for bed in the hall bathroom, then, without turning on the lights, positioned herself on the far edge of the bed and slept.

I never did ask how she got home. I never confronted her with my suspicions and concerns. She took obvious delight in showing me her gifts and keepsakes and told me how honored she was made to feel. Peace had fallen upon her. Strong comfort and assurance bathed her whole being. Life was solid, and splendid, and good.

I have since wondered: Did I harbor false suspicions? Had my anxieties of self-inadequacy overcome reasoning? Were my past inabilities to satisfy her with "good feelings" making me cynical? Would I ever be the full-time and satisfying husband she needed?

She never asked why I left the party waiting room.

Comforting memories of illicit love affairs should
forever be confined to the perpetrators, and to God!

CHAPTER 47

THE TRAIL TO OUR FINAL HOME

*Each chapter of our life starts as a blank page on
which we compose our destiny word by word.*

Preparations for our relocation were quickly made. The house
was placed on the market, cars were serviced, and movers were
contracted. We made unfortunate choices on the purchase
of walkie-talkies by selecting emergency channel 9, the trucker's
channel 10, and a commercial channel 14 seemingly used by all kids'
two-way radios in the country.

In any case, on September 30, 1978, we drove over the brink of
the Johnson Street hill as our sons had done before us. I glanced back
and bade a repentant farewell to that beautiful six-bedroom country
home with a view that we would never see again.

Sadly, a chapter of our life ended at the brow of that hill. Surely, I
thought, this nomadic lifestyle will have a happy ending—somehow,
somewhere, sometime.

The journey to Texas had begun. Nora drove the Plymouth
Volvo with Glen, a treasured potted Boston fern, a Manx cat, and
much clothing and survival needs on board. I drove the Dodge
Dart with Grant and much personal luggage. Grant's assignment
was to watch for fifty-cent-a-gallon gasoline for fill-ups. Those were
getting scarce.

Along the way, we were entertained by the truckers' colorful vocabulary on channel 10 and the chatter of locals on channel 14 of our walkie-talkies. Nora got a few propositions from truckers. I got ignored. The overall journey was an adventure worthy of many stories, but I shall desist.

As we eased into West Texas, we spotted unfamiliar flora and fauna along the byways, like cactus, mesquite, and armadillos. The flatlands were somewhat reminiscent of Manitoba, where one can go farther and see less than anywhere else on earth. We became aware of a need for air-conditioning in cars.

My first San Angelo sightings were of barrio bungalows that caused me to utter, "Dear God, let it not be." As the real San Angelo began to materialize, I felt better. It looked friendly and warm.

It was Friday, November 3, when we pulled into the La Quinta Motel along the developing but still incomplete Loop 306. Living in one room with two beds, with two kids, a cat, and a potted fern, is definite motivation for timely house-hunting.

Obtaining a city map, we spent the weekend scouting real estate localities from ads in the San Angelo *Morning-Times*. My reaction to affordable community locations was, "Who can live on such tiny lots in such crowded neighborhoods?" We would learn to live with it.

On Monday, Nora enrolled the boys in the John Glenn Middle School and had to drive them daily. There was no school bus pickup at the La Quinta Motel. She checked real estate ads and spent her days with agents looking for that perfect house. (Those we couldn't afford.)

Also on Monday, I reported to the Johnson Street business and engineering building and was escorted to the sixth-floor engineering wing by a lovely young lady who said she had been expecting me. There I was greeted by Melvin Gray, the exchange engineering manager.

One of his first questions was, "Why engineering? You have no work history of engineering!"

I could not very well tell him Dick had told me his engineering department needed help. I simply said, "I need a change. I am well versed in engineering practices and protocols."

After some routine conversation, Ray Couch, an engineering supervisor, was called in, and we chatted. I was led to a desk, a table, and a chair in the open-floor engineering bullpen.

At ten o'clock, Hugo Bose invited me to coffee break, where we joined Ramie Miller and Dale Wells in the cafeteria. They would be my cultural influence for the many years ahead, with Ramie being from Louisiana and Dale a dyed-in-the-wool Texan.

The next day, Tuesday, I was taken to the office of Joe Lee, the installation department manager on north sixth floor. Joe offered me a more elevated position in the installation department, but it would be in an East Texas city. As tactfully as possible, I declined.

Yes, I had just breached one of my most consistent rules: to never turn down a promotion or relocation opportunity. It puts a tarnish on one's corporate loyalty forever. I failed to feel guilty, however, as my motivation to prove something was waning. I had already done that. Now serenity was more important than recognition.

I returned to my desk. A fellow engineer, Al Dodson, had been assigned to guide me on my first assignment, a simple two-hundred-line addition to some distant exchange. I sensed that my first specification would be scrutinized by both my supervisor and manager, and I was determined to make it worthy. After reviewing past engineering files, that appeared not to be a real challenge. Dick Hignight was correct: they needed help.

It was the fair and favorable type of weather that generated house-hunting optimism. As we viewed many units in many neighborhoods it became obvious that we would have to compromise. What we wanted; we couldn't afford!

Homes are statements of who we are. We use our homes to display the stature we have achieved. Our homes are a place we share with those who are near and dear to us, our family, our friends and neighbors. It is a personal sanctuary where we are sheltered from evil. We had left a series of such homes behind. Could we develop an emotional attachment to still another?

One afternoon, our real estate agent called to say we had a "hot opportunity." It was new construction, totally without landscaping. Dr. Bates and family had lived in it for less than three months. Some urgent need was taking them to Houston, and they wanted a quick closing. I left work early for the showing.

It was not exactly what Nora had in mind, but it did have an enormous living room with a full-wall brick fireplace, and it was located in a developing area of the city. We bought it. "We will," I said, "learn to love it." (I already did!)

To accommodate the quick closing, I cashed our Vanguard Mutual Fund and every savings bond we owned. We closed on December 1, 1978.

Nora lived there the rest of her life. I still do.

Later, back at work, Hugo invited Nora and me to go for square dance lessons. "Last chance," he said. "Lessons close tonight." He and his wife, Irene, picked us up at the La Quinta, and we made our very first venture into San Angelo social life. (My involvement with square dancing would last forty-four years.)

About those square dance lessons. I had square-danced during my teen years and felt that just a tune-up would be needed. Not so! Square dancing had evolved from asymmetric routines to symmetric patterns. It was now much more involved. The good news was that we, the Yankees from New York, were warmly welcomed by the Southern members. We felt blessed!

Furniture was soon delivered, and we settled into our comfortable three-bedroom two-bath home. It was located on a modest lot on a short street lined with typical brick-and-mortar boxes that all looked a little different.

I felt to be on the verge of a less challenging career, and it was OK to coast. On the other hand, Nora was anxious to get into a profession with significance. For too long, she had been a dedicated housewife and mother and subjected to many minimum-wage jobs. The Curtain World design and sales position she cherished had been pulled out from under her by another family relocation. She was again ready for a meaningful career, too long denied. The hour was at hand. It was to be now or never!

Finally, she felt deliverance from the bonds of domestic convention and about to be released into the wild. She was ready. She was confident. She was determined. It was overdue.

> *See, I am doing a new thing! Now it*
> *springs up; do you not perceive it? I am*
> *making a way in the wilderness and streams*
> *in the wasteland.—Isaiah 43:19*

CHAPTER 48

MY WANING CAREER

To fit in or stand out, that is the question.

M y search for reassurance and security was being replaced by a need for peace of mind and comfort. Yes, you may say I wanted to coast for a while. A sense of relief runs deep when a race is over and there is no longer a drive to win. I had overcome. I had earned my place in the sun. I belonged.

Shortly after my arrival in San Angelo, Melvin Gray called me into his office and closed the door. Rocking back in a squeaky swivel chair, he said, "Your record shows you don't have a high school education. Is that correct? Is there some mistake?"

The short answer was "No!"

Melvin kind of rolled his eyes and, gazing upward to the ceiling, said, in a hushed voice, to no one in particular, "How did you get here?"

I gave him a brief history, and he shook his head at a slow idle pace and said, "You need to get a high school equivalency certificate." Sitting up, with a sharp squawk from his chair, and tapping his finger in a meaningful gesture on his desktop, he looked directly at me and, in a critical tone, said, "I'll need it!"

Nora and I investigated that high school equivalency thing, made an appointment, and applied for the exams. We found our way to an old abandoned red brick school building, where we were greeted by a member of our square dance class. (Oh shucks, now our secret would soon be exposed!) She would also proctor our exam appearances.

While sitting the first exam, I was placed near a scantily dressed young lady. Her near nakedness was distraction enough, but she was chomping and popping gum with all the tact and aplomb of a hog eating slop. Approaching the proctor, I asked as quietly as I could, "Can I come back later? I can't concentrate with that gum-chewing."

She simply smiled and said, "Get your things together."

I did, and she led me to an abandoned classroom across the hall, leaving the door open. A few seconds later, she led Nora to a nearby desk. We continued with the test.

We passed this and the remaining exams, and the blemish on our prerequisite records we had so long concealed in shame was gone. Now we could represent ourselves as high school graduates. OK, thirty years late is better than never. Isn't it?

The proctor lady never revealed our educational status to anyone we knew. It would be another twenty years before I outed myself as a high school dropout.

Frankly, no one seemed to care.

I began to be comforted by the reappearance of past acquaintances. Art Chamberlain was transferred from Johnstown engineering and assigned to a nearby desk. We had been friends since Brockville.

A few months later, Dennis Terwilliger was hired and assigned to the nearby traffic engineering group. Dennis had "established" himself at the Automatic Electric Company in Canada but, in 1979, the Automatic Electric Company Ltd. of Brockville, Ontario, Canada, ceased to exist. He too became a refugee of circumstances.

This brought about the appearance of still another familiar

name. One day, I was called by the personnel people and asked, "Do you know Ben Litwinowich?" I did! Within a few weeks, Ben was in our engineering department. The Litwinowich family soon bought a home only two blocks from us.

While this would not be a moment of celebration for Nora, she and Ben's wife Gloria were friends. We socialized with them often.

In the months ahead, the engineering manager, Melvin, was replaced by John Bright. John, a man with a big body and a bigger voice, dressed for comfort, not style. He, like me, had progressed through the ranks from technician to management. We felt a connection and, except for the dress thing (I always wore a tie), we were two of a kind.

Soon after John became manager, there was an IBEW strike, and non-union employees were assigned hither and yon to maintain service. John assigned me to a Stromberg step office.

"This is your opportunity," he said, "for Stromberg step experience." He continued, "It will come in handy for you in the future."

I was soon airlifted, with three others, to Sulfur Springs, Texas.

In the weeks ahead, I did as much routine testing of the Stromberg switches as I could and found and fixed numerous malfunctions. I also did polarity checks on distribution frames and found untold numbers of tip/ring jumper reversals. If the strike had lasted a little longer, we could have had that office in perfect working condition, and John was right about this assignment. My exposure to the Stromberg system did benefit me in a future engineering position.

Now that I was back in San Angelo, John's objective was to increase the quality and productivity of central office engineering, which found us on the same page. Sometimes he even reviewed the engineering specifications he approved, and one day he asked me, in a cheerful way, "Why all these notes and diagrams?"

I told him, "I just like to confuse the installers with facts." We laughed.

The joking over, he asked me to teach a course on rotary-switch circuit applications and engineering. Yes, they had the same constant-hunt problems during busy hour peaks we had experienced in New York. I mentioned that Art Chamberlain had put such a course together for me in New York, and perhaps he could present his course.

"No," said John. "I want you to do it."

I did the course. He monitored it occasionally and apparently approved. Shortly, I was promoted to engineering supervisor.

Time passed. I was not a popular supervisor, but neither did I want inadequate specifications generated on my watch. Many previous specifications were little more than an equipment list, and an incomplete one at that. It gave installers far too much latitude to deviate. Engineering records should, to some extent, reflect that which actually existed in the central offices.

Another of my functions was the recovery and reassignment of electromechanical equipment for all districts. I had extra clerks to keep track of it, and I alone had the authority over all electromechanical engineering groups as to whether to salvage or discard retired equipment. This also gave me authority to determine if equipment needs were to be purchased or reused from recovered stock.

I often took the liberty to direct alternate trunking options to better the reuse of recovered equipment. While this was often resented and sometimes challenged by fellow supervisors, I very seldom lost a protest.

I once accompanied the vice president of engineering to Houston to evaluate a CAD (computer-assisted drafting) system. Frankly, I was impressed by what it could do, but I had no idea how it did it. This was totally contrary to my nature, which was to focus on how a circuit did something, not just what it did. In my world, if something didn't work, you fixed it. In the computer world, if something malfunctioned, you replaced it.

My inability, or unwillingness, to accept and trust the amorphous functions of integrated circuitry was a liability. I did recommend the adaption of the CAD system, however. It was expected of me.

During the mid-1980s, the computer age firmly descended upon us. I had received data-retrieval training, which helped, but my staff was working with keyboards, not pencils and paper. Reviewing their specifications on my monitor was frustrating. I could not change their text or make marginal notes on their specs. It was annoying!

Soon, my employees were producing keyboard-generated specifications and entering equipment locations directly onto rack locations by access to the CAD system. They were adapting.

An interim electronic technology briefly came along that I did embrace: a printed circuit-board version of the step-by-step switch. It reacted directly to dial pulses or push-button dial input, and it was space-saving and cost effective. But it was an interim bridge from direct-dial input to the common-control switch. Its useful life was brief.

In the meantime, our life outside of my workplace went on.

CHAPTER 49

FAMILY LIFE IN SAN ANGELO: THE EARLY YEARS

*He hath brought us into this place, and hath
given us this land, a land that floweth with
milk and honey.—Deuteronomy 26:9*

Nora and family had moved with me on this relocation. Previously, I had preceded them to each new career location. I felt our marital relationship growing warmer and closer and felt that Nora was leaving the feelings of abandonment and neglect behind.

More and more, we looked forward to Tuesday evening square dance lessons, and our circle of friends grew. Some were retired, others were professionals or business owners, and still others were working folks. We had never felt more welcomed into any previous community.

Square dancing involves a dependency on formation and structure that requires hand and eye contact. There was much handshaking and hugs. It took a bit of getting accustomed to, but Texans enjoy warm and easygoing social intermingling that would be frowned upon in our previous environments. We felt more together than at any point in the past.

An occurrence of sadness does come to mind. One Tuesday evening, when we went to lessons, Grant and Glen were home alone—just them and the Manx cat, Mimi. They would normally be in bed by the time we arrived home, but one evening, they were not. They were searching the street calling for Mimi.

Mimi was an adventurous soul, accustomed to the limitless woods and fields of Johnstown, New York. She never accepted the confines of our backyard. That evening, Mimi went out and never returned.

I never told them I later found Mimi and buried her in the backyard. I did so with a lump in my throat and a tear in my eye. Mimi had spent many evenings lying on my lap as I petted her and watched TV. Her purring was as soothing to me as a symphonic lullaby. Nora also grieved for the loss of her kitty.

Our home had seldom been without a pet, and after a few months, Nora was told of some surprise pups at a friend's house. She brought home a tiny black poodle-whatever mix. It was raised with love and cherished by all in the family. We called her Brigit. She had a home!

The first spring was upon us, and the need for air-conditioning in the cars became evident. We had it installed. We worked together on landscaping and accomplished little more than planting a pecan tree and leveling, raking, and seeding the tiny lawns. As we watered and watched with anticipation for the first sprouting of Bermuda grass, we were overtaken by a feeling of comfort and serenity. We were adjusting to the pace of San Angelo living.

Meanwhile, at school, Grant had put his heart into building a thirty-inch-high Tesla tower for a craft project. Using a neon-sign transformer and a four-inch polyvinyl chloride pipe wound with enameled copper wire, it would make a florescent lamp glow at over six feet. It was a masterful piece of workmanship, for which he was awarded second prize. He tried to hide his disappointment. Words of comfort do not often heal, they merely confirm sympathy.

Later, his term teacher confided that the first prize went to the son of an influential community member. She expressed understanding and empathy.

I have been known to disagree with Bible viewpoints such as this from Romans 13:1–3: "Everyone must submit to governing authorities. For all authority comes from God, and those in positions of authority have been placed there by God."

I rest my case!

Time passed quickly. In May, the square dance class graduated, and we danced locally and visited many clubs in the west central area. Soon, we had enough confidence to attend the San Angelo Square and Round Dance Festival in the fall, but the powerful callers of national renown were a little much for us. Frankly, we did not do well.

Years passed, and we were soon attending state festivals, dancing with the best of dancers. We eventually expanded our skills from mainstream level to plus and on to advanced levels I and II. Square dancing became a major activity in our life. It cemented the bond we had been seeking. Square dancing knitted us into the fabric of a community. Over the years, we went from fringe participants to become an influence on that community. I shall expound on that later.

After obtaining her high school equivalency diploma, Nora attended several Angelo State University continuing-education courses. She soon accumulated diplomas of proficiency in typing, bookkeeping, computer accounting, and data entry, and coveted a skilled position of respect and dignity long denied her for twenty-seven years of marriage. After years of complying with my will and raising our children, she pursued her own level of recognition and appreciation. No more retail clerk positions!

———◆·◆·◆———

One day, Grant brought his books home from Central High School and proclaimed he would not return. He was a timid soul who had been bullied unmercifully and wanted us to take no action. He said, "That would only make it worse."

He bused tables at the China Gardens restaurant until we convinced him to do the high school equivalency thing. He did so and aced every test. With renewed confidence, he enrolled in Texas State Technical Institute (TSTI), a community college in Sweetwater, Texas.

We rented an efficiency apartment for him and furnished it. He was an exemplary student and went on to pass the Texas general-class FCC radio licensing exam in Dallas. His instructors, whom we later met, said he was a brilliant student.

His first employment was an oil-drilling enterprise in Midland, repairing in-well monitoring devices. What he referred to as the rough and cussing redneck crowd was not to his liking, so he quit.

Once more, I called on my old friend Ken Kaiser in Northlake, and yes, Ken put him directly in the #5 EAX electronic switching school. He had a golden career opportunity.

Grant's experience with Automatic Electric of Northlake was short-lived. His inability, or was it reluctance, to take responsibility was his downfall. He was terminated.

After spending some adjustment time at home, he packed his things in his car and returned to Canada. His life accomplishments had been dispiriting.

Meanwhile, Glen graduated from Central High School and enrolled in Angelo State University. After one disappointing semester, he dropped out and worked in a pizza place for a while (they promised him he would make a lot of dough), but it was not his thing. We then enrolled him at TSTI. That was his thing. Two years later, he graduated with an associate degree in computer programming and went on to have a blossoming career with Texas Instruments.

◆◇◆

Years passed. Nora and I found ourselves home alone.

Her early employment included keeping books for a plumbing wholesaler and later a plumbing business. One job she treasured was the accounting position at KCTV-TV where our neighbor, Melisa Hornik, was a news anchor.

During that period, the station call letters were sold to a station in Kansas City and suggestions for new call letters were solicited. I gave Nora some to submit: KRAP, KORN, KNAP, and a couple I shall not mention here. (She never submitted them. She did not appreciate my creative talents!)

Later, a new station manager was hired, and he decided to streamline and economize the business. It cost Nora and a few others their jobs. (He lasted less than two years.)

Meanwhile, I had taken an investment course at Angelo State University and established a brokerage account. When Nora went to work for the USPA&IRA, an investment firm managed by a long-time square dance acquaintance John Muckelroy, it proved to be of a mutual benefit. I switched my brokerage account to that firm and had access to some first-hand investing insight. Over the following years, my return on investments fared well.

When Congress passed the Revenue Act of 1978, it included a provision that was added to the Internal Revenue Code—Section 401(k)—that allowed employees to avoid being taxed on deferred compensation. During my remaining years with GTE, I maxed out my allowed contributions and purchased all the employee stock options I could. This, coupled with the brokerage account, showed positive results. We were on our way to financial comfort.

Meanwhile, there was another life, a "we" life. Nora had her work, I had my work, and together we had a very satisfying social life that primarily involved square dancing.

I will share a little of that with you later.

CHAPTER 50

THE COTTAGE OF HOPE AND GLORY: 11193 TWIN LAKES LANE

And I will give to you and to your offspring
after you the land of your sojourning's, and
I will be their God.—*Genesis 17:8*

A developing community near Knickerbocker caught our attention. Five-acre plots were offered by the Runion Development Company. With dreams of ultimately building an elegant country home of our own design, with acreage, we bit. On May 1, 1984, we bought a lot on Twin Lakes Lane.

There is comfort in owning acreage. Somehow, ownership of land gives one a feeling of security. Land gives us tenure. Land produces nourishment, and land can be defended. But we decided not to rush into building our dream home on a caliche road that was unnavigable in wet weather. There was to be no paved surface until a large percentage of lots were sold. No time frame quoted!

What to do with a five-acre lot? We decided in a moment of weakness to first build a cottage. We visualized visits from our scattered family flocking to the fold with grandchildren. (Perhaps this was in penance for the years of deprivation we had imposed upon them.) We were sure they would gather from Europe and Canada, and we would have a place for them to recline and appreciate the wilds of West Texas. So went our delusions of grandeur.

Reality now: We had an unfenced plot of land in the middle of the old XQZ Ranch, indistinguishable from any other piece of land that could be seen in any direction. All were covered with second-growth mesquite, prickly pear, and horse-crippling cactus, and accessible only by a dusty caliche trail that seems to start nowhere and go nowhere.

The situs was, however, ideal. It was a shallow valley between two gently sloping lots with a west-facing frontage. Yes, it would be great—sometime, someday.

First, it had to be fenced. I bought a secondhand El Camino to haul wire fencing, barbed wire, and steel posts over these dusty caliche roads. Simple tools like a post-hole digger, steel-post driver, and the usual hand tools were obtained, and I and the little dog Brigit spent many weekends clearing the fence line and erecting the fence.

I had also bought cowboy boots as protection from rattlesnake bites, and a brown wide-brimmed hat for protection from the fierce sun. Little by little, our lot became a patch of fenced property in the middle of an expanse of ranchland. I was proud of it!

An occurrence that still gives me shivers to this day: When handling a piece of metal-top tubing for the front chain-link fence, I heard the sickening clank of pipe on the overhead power line. Fortunately, it was the bottom wire, hence was at earth potential. I was but a few inches from not coming home!

The fence was built, and I had cleared a lane allowing me to drive a vehicle all the way around the lot, inside the fence. Next, we decided on a location to build and had a caliche driveway laid to our still nonexistent cottage.

Now, what to do with the remaining mesquite and prickly-pear-overgrown acreage? A vineyard would be nice, and would provide an income in our retirement years still ahead. We consulted with a

Ballenger vineyard owner who advised me that the land too alkaline. Forget it!

Next was a consultation with an agriculture agent regarding a pecan orchard. No source of water, I was told, so I had a well-drilling crew do their thing ... and they hit salty water. There would be no pecan orchard.

Time passed, many lots were sold, and the road was improved with a promise of being paved soon. Time to build that cottage! We drew up plans and secured approval from the Dove Creek housing authority to build.

Nora and I built the cottage ourselves. We dug the footing, poured the concrete foundation, cut every piece of lumber, drove every nail, and placed every shingle. We had a contractor place a small pool and pour a slab that we covered with ceramic tile. And voila! we had our cottage.

I will not burden you with further details, but it was almost two years in the making.

During the years we owned the cottage, we had two visits from our son, Ritchie, and his family from Germany. One of those visits was a family gathering affair with all our children present except number-three son, Grant. There was one visit from my sister and her spouse, Harry, still living in Frankford, Ontario, and some of our square dance friends came and stayed in it a few times. That was the extent of family and friends' visits, but there were personal benefits.

Nora and I would spend weekends lounging in the pool and at poolside. When mosquitos drove us inside, we would take off our wet bathing suits, cozy up on the couch, watch TV, and ... well, you know!

On one of these cozy evenings, we were cuddled together watching TV when, in a soft voice, like someone conveying a thought rather than passing a message, Nora said, "Let's not build." I waited for the other shoe to drop, and it did. She continued, "We don't need a bigger house. We don't need to move again. We don't need to spend all that money. Let's just leave what we can for the kids."

All the plans I'd drawn up for our dream house remain unopened to this day.

The recollections I have of family at the cottage have been fond memories, but I do recall an occasion when our daughter Gail and her husband, Jim, spent some vacation time there. One stormy evening I called to see if everything was OK. There was no answer.

After a few well-spaced tries, I decided to drive the El Camino over those still unpaved, slippery caliche roads in the dark of night expecting … I'm not sure what. On arrival, I learned that Jim didn't want his sleep disturbed and had unplugged the phone.

Many a night when a brisk breeze kept the mosquitos at bay, we lay by the pool and watched the masses of stars in an unblemished sky. We viewed passing satellites and listened to the *whoomph* of the bull hawks diving for prey. There was no sound of angry tires on pavement, no sound of tormented auto horns, no streetlights polluting the night skies, and no barking of neighborhood dogs, just the rustling of feeding deer, the mournful call of owls, and the harmonic chirping of crickets. It was a place of peace.

Coming home one Sunday afternoon from such a weekend, we observed evidence of severe wind damage: felled trees, dislodged roofs, and random piles of windblown trash. What had happened? Apparently, a downburst had happened, and we missed it. Mercifully, our own home had been spared.

Eventually, the Dove Creek neighborhoods became populated. Roads were paved, beautiful homes were built, and all-night yard lights became numerous. The peace and quiet of the country had evolved into a populous neighborhood. Good people to be sure, but it was not the same.

Over the years, our cottage visits dwindled. A swarm of honeybees built a home in an outer wall. One winter, a freeze broke a waterpipe, and thawing water seeped under the half-empty fiberglass pool, lifting it from its moorings. The mesquite and prickly pear I had battled crept closer and grew bigger near the cottage, and part of the pool privacy fence had blown over. It was no longer our refuge from civilization. It had become a nuisance.

On June 26, 2012, we sold our treasured little cottage on the former XQZ Ranch.

CHAPTER 51

THE END OF BONDAGE

You have to leave room for God's grace.
Perfection is God's job.—Karen Kingsbury

Picture us seated behind a red-cloth-covered table. On one end stands a framed photograph of Nora and me. On the other, a standing framed photo of me seated behind a desk. In the center of the table is a large and elegant leather-bound register book for visitors to sign.

The date: December 9, 1998. The location: the San Angelo Convention Center. The occasion: a retirement reception. Many had elected to accept an early retirement offer. I was but one of those many.

May this moment in time be the severance of my obligations to others. Let it be a commitment unto myself. It is the most significant turning point in my life.

My self-imposed bondage had ended.

I normally do not recognize any one point in my life as a turning point more significant than another. Human nature tends to overemphasize the importance of the here and now, and true turning points are recognized only with the benefit of hindsight.

During my lifetime, tractors replaced horses, the light bulb replaced coal oil lamps, and e-mails replaced Western Union telegrams, but only when common-control telephone exchanges replaced the Strowger switch was there a true turning point in my life. It ended my means of making a living.

During the recent years at GTE Southwest, I had lost my value to the company. While I was supervising an engineering staff doing routine additions to dial-pulse activated electromechanical telephone exchanges, the GTD-5s and EAX 100 common control switching systems were proliferating. The silent world of solid-state telephone service was going on around me, managed from keyboards by people who had no idea how it functioned, just how to make it do so.

Exchanges I had once mastered took about two thousand square feet of floor space per thousand lines. New technology could accommodate the same service in a ten-foot square room.

I had been left behind.

On this final evening of my career, many with whom I had worked for the past decade visited my red-cloth-covered table. Others were casual work-related acquaintances who wished only to greet and remind me that we had met or communicated somewhere at some time in the past. Still others were community members who came to honor retiring friends. There were square dancers by whom I was widely recognized. Others I did not know at all.

President "Buddy" Langley visited each table for a photo op. At this point, I was presented with my final token of service: a beautiful signet ring.

The throngs of milling people were at last summoned to silence while dignitaries made noble speeches about historical progress, valiant productivity, and the greatness of the corporation that was built by employees like us. We were congratulated as a group, some mentioned by name, and all offered the traditional great wishes on future endeavors.

Evening entertainment then commenced, with Coy Moses and his violin and his band entertaining the milling crowds. At this point, many left their assigned tables to sign the guest registers of other retirees.

Late in the evening, it was over.

I never again entered the Johnson Street headquarters where I had worked the final ten years of my career. I never looked back, and many who had signed my guest register I never saw again.

I still savor reminders of my thirty years with the GTE Corporation. A decorative wooden clock hangs on my dining-room wall, ticking the passing of my remaining time. I wear my ornamental GTE belt buckle with its two diamonds for dresswear. Every Sunday, I wear a watch to church with a diamond in the GTE logo on the wristband along with my retirement ring with eight diamonds bracketing the initial G. These are symbolic of the blessings I feel for the career I have enjoyed. God's guardian angels had done their job, and I had done mine.

When it became known that I had accepted this escape option, a curious few had come to my office to ask about my post-retirement plans. Did I have another job lined up? Was I going to do contract engineering? What was my secret?

Perhaps they never took notice that I lived in a modest paid-for house and never in my life ever bought a brand-new off-the-showroom-floor car. They never noticed I had no boats, Jet Skis, or motor homes, and my extravagant vacations were well spaced. Did they notice that the summer cottage we had was constructed piece-by-piece by myself, and the in-ground fiberglass pool was of modest size? I didn't need a job!

Looking back, I will always wonder if John Webber has memories of his coffee-break investing advice and the hand-me-down *Money* magazines he gave me. I am sure he would be pleased to know he had put me on the road to financial comfort.

Some fellow retirees went on to earn fortunes, and others simply died on the vine. The difference between them was the difference between spending and investing. The line is somewhat obscured by illogic. Whatever results they achieved, it was probably due to an example set by family and/or friends. Perhaps they never met a John

Webber, or perhaps they chose to disregard any words that may have inconvenienced their chosen lifestyle.

My retirement package had included a generous cash severance offer that, well invested, was another yellow brick in my road to financial comfort. Our destiny is predicated by our ability to understand economics and our willingness to work. Back on my father's farm, I learned to go without that which we could not afford. While working the fields and stables, I learned that "by the sweat of thy brow shalt thou eat bread." I regret that more people have never had that opportunity.

Too many I know toiled to build their path to nowhere in particular. They bought larger dwellings than needed, traded in low-mileage cars for newer ones, purchase adult toys for leisure pleasures, and spent extravagantly on vacations for personal gratification.

In the recent past, some of them had even approached me requesting salary increases, complaining that the salary they received was never enough. No amount of salary increases I could authorize would satisfy their thirst for spending. They knew only the value of nothing.

> *Woe to you who are rich, for you have received*
> *your consolations in full. Woe to you who are filled*
> *up now, for you will go hungry. Woe you who are*
> *laughing now, for you will mourn and weep. Woe*
> *whenever all speak well of you, for this is what their*
> *forefathers did to the false prophets.—Luke 6:24-26*

Sometimes, the Bible just gets it wrong.

CHAPTER 52

THE TRANSFORMATION

As I go along life's way,
Reaping better than I sowed.
I'm drinking from my saucer,
'cause my cup has overflowed.
—*John Paul More*

After retirement from GTE, I launched my future careers by taking necessary courses to qualify for a real estate agent's license. I was first associated with a Better Homes and Gardens real estate franchise, bought into the franchise, and eventually sold my interest. In the meantime, I obtained a real estate instructures license and taught at the Southwest College of Real Estate for ten years.

Those were my professional careers. They were "me" careers that enabled me to earn adequate income to support our modest lifestyle, which included square dancing.

Showing real estate was a study in human nature. I never failed to be amazed at some of the transactions I conducted. Some were bound for happy endings, some were not. The job was to sell, not advise. There were at least a couple of dealings in which I wanted to say, "Don't do it—for Christ's sake, no—it is not in your best interest!"

I never did.

-------- ⟡ --------

Let me relate an interesting story that occurred during my real estate showing days. I am not a believer in apparitions, but this is a story about a perceived phantom.

A California family wished to see a vacant house for sale in Mertzon, located far to the north of the local football field, up on a hill. It was already under contract, but they insisted. The husband had been raised in that house and wanted to put a full-price back-up contract on it and was not to be denied.

I agreed to meet them on-site. There was a husband and wife, an adult daughter, and an elderly, somewhat stooped old gentleman who uttered not a word. The whole group followed my presentation, room to room, then agreed to return to my office to compile that full-price back-up contract.

The showing was over, so I proceeded to close windows, turn off lights, check door locks and so forth, then I would meet them at my office. In an upstairs bedroom, there stood the old man—and I heard their car pulling away. I rushed downstairs to hail them, but it was too late. They were gone!

I returned inside to offer the old gentleman a ride to the office and could not find him. I searched every room—he was not there! Checking outside, around the house, in the outbuildings, everywhere, he was nowhere to be found.

Against my better judgement, I drove back to the office in San Angelo, expecting them to be anxiously awaiting us—me and that old man.

They were not. They quietly filed into the office and were prepared to make their offer.

I never mentioned that old man, and they never brought up the subject. I really wanted to know about that old man. I shudder to think that, apparently, there *was* no old man.

To this day, I could describe him in detail. I was that sure!

------◆-◆-◆------

Let me relate one last story of a real estate transaction that left me with troubled emotions. Ben and Gloria Litwinowich had listed their home with me. He was taking a subsequent retirement package and they were moving back to Canada. When I informed Nora, she simply said, "Good! We won't have to be near him anymore."

From the tone of her voice I sensed that he may have imposed himself upon her during those years we lived in St. Adolph. I didn't ask, what was done was done.

------◆-◆-◆------

Meanwhile, Nora had left the USPA&IRA and worked several years with the Shamrock Financial Group. She was the family economist; she kept meticulous books and monitored our accounts. By now, we had narrowed our brokerage accounts down to two firms: Fidelity and Edward Jones.

Both of us had sprouted from the roots of poverty. Both of us feared a future of uncertainty. Ever since that first foray into the Vanguard Windsor Fund, we had invested brazenly, with confidence in growth-oriented funds. I wanted to get all there was to get.

One Sunday afternoon, Nora came wandering from our office into the living room where I was watching football. She positioned herself in the recliner and calmly said, "We did it! We are millionaires!"

She had my attention. I questioned the statement, and she reiterated that our investments plus our real estate holdings were valued at over 1 million dollars.

Why is the figure *one million* heralded as an astounding number of eminence? Why do people herald a million dollars as real wealth? Why do so many believe it's an utterly unattainable dream?

The truth is that the 1 million mark is readably attainable.

More important, to live comfortably through the octogenarian years, a nest egg of at least 1 million in investments—not savings, investments—is needed. My current rule of thumb is, one needs a million invested for every forty thousand of annual income required during retirement, not including Social Security, benefits.

So we took risks and invested aggressively. We played the game and won! I did not feel privileged.

Time passed, In June 1995, Nora retired from Shamrock Financial. Our lives were now very involved in our chosen pastime: square dancing.

Nora was still treasurer of the San Angelo Square and Round Dance Club, and I hired the guest callers. It was almost inevitable that I would be lured into calling. Many callers who stayed the night at our house gave me encouragement.

In 1991, our local caller, Arnie Wariner, approached me saying he could not do lessons this year. Our problem? He was the only available caller in town, and after consulting the club books, Nora informed me that the club could not afford an out-of-town caller.

Arnie offered a solution: he would teach me enough calling skills to do lessons.

This would probably not work, since my popularity in the San Angelo club was not great. There were many complaints that I did not hire enough of the quality callers we couldn't afford. They wanted more of the best! Nevertheless I offered our living room for practice, and we rounded up three other prospective candidates that included Earnest McFarland, Janet Barth, one other I cannot put a name to, and I made a fourth.

The calling classes were conducted in our living room during the summer. The fall brought about decision time. Who would conduct the San Angelo Club lessons?

All agreed that Earnest, who had previously called while in college, would do them.

He did well!

---————◆◆◆◆◆————---

In 1992, I was given a Hilton seventy-five-amp caller rig by a caller friend and scads of records by others. Some updates on the Hilton put me in business. I obtained the appropriate license to use copyrighted music and proclaimed myself a caller.

I started with guest appearances for the Ozona Levis & Lace club and gained a little confidence. The transformation to entrepreneurship was complete. I was now to be fully self-employed,

Yes! I could be a caller!

CHAPTER 53

THE STAR PROMENADERS STORY

We followed a rainbow in search of a star
The clouds were many the distance was far
At last we found it, our place in the sun
It is Promenade Square, for frolic and fun.

t was 1992, and after some unspectacular attempts to impress our local square dance community of my unique calling ability, I realized we must find a way or make it. The decision was to make it: start our own club!

Now, to have a club, we would need a place to dance. To find a place to dance, one needs some luck, influence, or money. We were woefully short on all counts and woefully undereducated on just what the investment could be.

Nora sensed my envy of the many callers we counted amongst our friends, and in typical Nora fashion, she encouraged me to go for it. "Get a group together and try your wings for real." She seemed sure we could do it. I wasn't too sure just when this became *we*, but that was the way it was from then on.

Our first attempt was in the fall of 1992 when we put together a group of singles and acquired donated dancing space in a church basement. The area was modest but adequate. Despite our best efforts to recruit, we started lessons woefully short of male participants. To salvage the lessons, some ladies volunteered to dance the male part but switched from part to part from one week to the next. I soon concluded that this attempt was futile. With some reluctance and much regret, we abandoned this endeavor.

Our next attempt was in the fall of 1993. This time, we accepted an invitation (which we had solicited) from the YMCA to present a square dance program on its behalf. This resulted in a group more balanced in gender, more diverse in age, and numbering two squares and some spares. We made it to our first club graduation in March 1994. Our obligations to the YMCA were over.

Our initial plan was to dissolve the group after lessons and allow them to go their separate ways, to find and dance at local clubs. During lessons, we did some "floor time" dances in a church fellowship hall for fun and practice. The dancers now wanted to continue those dances; thus, in the spring of 1994, we formed a club, albeit a nameless club.

We danced two Saturdays a month throughout the summer, but come lessons time in September, we needed weekly Tuesday evening hall time as well as our Saturdays. Alas, the deacons decided that square dancing was not part of their mission. Our dance area privileges were revoked. We needed a new place, fast.

An intensive search began to border on the frantic, but as September approached, it yielded a nice auditorium hall in a day-care center. This was my fourth location as a caller and second as a club, which by now had taken the name Star Promenaders.

Our second class graduated in March 1995. There were fourteen graduates who were a welcome expansion to our modest little club.

By fall 1995, my venture into teaching square dancing was finally being acknowledged. Yes! I was invited to do lessons at the elite San Angelo Square and Round Dance Club. The terms were, they would be the only square dance lessons in town. Graduates could go their own way upon graduation. To this I agreed.

In January 1996, we moved our Star Promenaders dances from the day-care center to the beautiful San Angelo Square and

Round Dance Club building at 3711 N. Chadbourn Street in San Angelo. We were at last a recognized part of the local square dance community.

Nora and I were comfortable at this location. In fact, we still held membership in the San Angelo Square and Round Dance Club, and Nora was still its treasurer. It was a seventeen-year tenure for us to that point in time.

When the class of six couples graduated in March, the dancers had membership decisions to make. Some joined our Star Promenaders, some joined the San Angelo Square and Round Dance Club, and some joined both. It was proclaimed a success.

In the summer of 1996, we learned that the San Angelo Square and Round Dance Club had elected to do its own lessons on the only night that the hall was available. Here we go again, beating the streets for a place to conduct lessons.

This time, we found a vacant nightclub location, up a long flight of stairs (twenty-eight steps, I counted) and with a carpet floor, but at the crossroads of commerce in the city. With the help of our members, a count of about thirty at that time (in number, not in age), and lots of TV exposure and newspaper ads, we managed to put lessons together once again in the fall of 1996. It was our largest class to date.

Our classes were going well, and club spirits were great, so Nora and I arrived at a decision: get a place of our own and be no longer at the mercy of situations. We wanted to hold club dances and have lessons under one roof—ours!

I could write a book about our search for a suitable building in our price range. (I promise, I won't write that book!) In fact, we concluded there was no such place within city limits, and very few beyond.

It was now mid-summer 1996. While driving on West

Washington Street, that short space between Abe and Kohenheim, the premier arterial throughway of central San Angelo, Nora said, "There's a lot for sale. Let's look at it."

I drove around the block, wondering what the heck she was thinking, and stopped across the street from this forlorn-looking vacant lot on the fringe of the business district. We walked the length and width of the lot. It was big. It was kitty-corner across the back lane from our friends and club members Jim and Beverly Grenda. It was also directly across the back lane from our old square dance caller friends Bob and Minnie Turner. By now, Nora had let her intentions be known. "Let's build a square dance hall!"

I learned from Jim and Beverly that this was a distress sale and made a bid of 60 percent of asking price. It was accepted.

———◆—◆—◆———

Thus it was that we chartered and funded a corporation and built Promenade Square. It was activated in April 1997.

This building stands at what today is 412 West Washington Street. It featured a hardwood floor, oak-paneled walls, a kitchen, great acoustics, a little office for Nora, and my place in the sun on a raised six-by-ten-foot podium. The podium featured a beautiful backlighted stained-glass replica of our club symbol. Yep, it was our contribution to the architectural finesse of San Angelo. At last, we were home!

We held a grand opening, with the mayor cutting the ribbon and all that great ceremony stuff with help from the Chamber of Commerce. That just happened to be on the afternoon of the evening on which we started, for the first time, summer lessons.

The club grew; we prospered. We built an addition to the hall in 1999, danced on Saturday evenings, and held lessons on Tuesday evenings. The hall also hosted a clogging club on Mondays and a line-dance club on Thursdays. We rented the club for various activities during the day on unscheduled evenings.

Yes, it was a beautiful feeling to be able do what we wanted, when we wanted, and if we wanted. Our dream had come true, and we were to spend many retirement years involved in our chosen recreation of square dancing.

Now for more of the story.

CHAPTER 54

NORA'S FINAL ROMANCE

The opportunity for indiscretions often
overcomes one's power of resistance.

I have spoken of Promenade Square, our contribution to the architectural finesse of San Angelo. Our activity-center business was prospering. Into this picture of achievement there crept the proverbial worm in the apple.

Our club was well attended, dancers were skilled, and there was a blessed aura of peace and contentment within the club. From my position behind the mic, I saw all but did not comprehend all. A pattern that was discreetly being pointed out by others began to emerge from my denial to relevance.

Since the opening of the hall, Nora had attended the door each dance night, receiving admissions and welcoming the guests. She would accept their refreshment offerings and place them behind the kitchen counter. If she was busy, Glen would be there to help by taking the refreshment offerings to the kitchen for her. When the traffic slowed down, she sat at the nearest table to the door, beside Glen.

A relationship became evident. Glen, whose wife did not attend dances, sat at that first table beside Nora. Always beside Nora! It seemed to be preordained that *that* was *his* chair.

During the second tip, Nora would place refreshments on the kitchen counter, with help from Glen. After that second tip, tables were cleared of paper plates and such, mostly by Nora and Glen as I called that third tip. When I called set-in-order for the fourth tip, directly in front of me, the first couple in the square and always holding hands was … Nora and Glen. They made no pretense of hiding their mutual feelings and would dance together the remainder of the evening.

Between some tips I played music, and Nora led line-dance routines. At other times I played and sang two-step tunes or waltzes, or just played country and western dance music. I kept close to the podium.

After several months—too many months—my patience was eroding. I had never brought up the subject of Glen with Nora since she would have perceived it to be criticism, or an accusation, and she did not take either well.

Finally, one night, on the second tip break, I put on recorded music and decided to intervene in that little table-one clique. I went to the counter, selected a plate of refreshments, and went to the table where Nora and Glen, and others, sat. I expected an invitation to pull up a chair at the end of the table and join them.

No one extended that invitation. There was a brief embarrassing silence as people at the table looked at each other with that *what do we do now?* expression.

With hazy, uncertain thoughts I returned to the kitchen and, with a meaningful slam, dumped my plate of food into the garbage. I wanted to hide and quickly left through the back door. I was distraught.

Walking to the dark end of the building by the alley, I sat on a box, put my face in my hands, and sobbed—real harsh, body-shaking sobs! *Dear God, why?* I asked myself.

I composed myself and returned through the front door. No one seemed to have noticed I was gone. While finishing the dance, I hoped those dramatic moments of absence had gone unobserved. Apparently, they did.

The following week, Nora and I worked together on a full slate of hall bookings. She never spoke of seeing me leave the building or that the second break on dance night had been somewhat extended by my absence.

During that week, I came to a heartbreaking conclusion. I was depressed, and I could not go on. One week later, as I called the last tip, between the patter and singing call I told all the dancers to hold the horseshoe thank-you while I made an announcement.

As the horseshoe formed, with Nora and Glen holding hands in the middle of it, I set my records aside and announced, "Folks, it has been a long run of fun, and I would like to once again thank you for making it so, but this is my last dance. I need a rest. I need to reassess my goals and values. I will miss you all!"

The most shocked person in the crowd was Nora!

With that, the Star Promenaders Square Dance Club came to an end. It was the year 2004.

Time passed. We quit taking bookings and listed Promenade Square for sale.

Everything in life happens for a reason. Every act of every person is to fulfill an obligation, a need, or a raw nature-driven desire. Nora's attraction to Glen should not have mystified me. I once understood her need for comfort from others because of my extensive absences and apparent emotional neglect. I never did develop a manner of expressing love and affection, and Nora obviously had a need for it.

Was that, then, her attraction to Glen? Was that why she was prepared to give herself to him body and soul in full view of our friends? Was he that important to her?

I had chosen to not believe Nora was philandering and had, in fact, long been in denial. I hypothesized that perhaps she was just enjoying making me envious. Then it struck me: she was savoring Glen's craving for <u>her</u> affections. Fulfilling <u>his</u> needs triggered impassioned desires of her own.

Mutual gratification promotes covert sensuous activity.

Many months later, Nora and I were shopping in the kitchenware section of Walmart. Suddenly, Nora was walking away, toward the grocery aisles. There, in the distant produce section, was Glen.

I watched them embrace and commence a cheerful but earnest conversation. After a few minutes, I started toward the checkout with a heavy, torn heart. I was going home. I did not know what else to do. I didn't even look back.

While waiting at the checkout, Nora caught up with me and said, "I just had a nice visit with Glen."

I replied, "I noticed."

On the way home, she asked, "Were you going to leave me there?"

I simply said, "Yes."

We rode the rest of the way in silence.

The lyrics by Peter Yarrow and Phillip Jarrell still hurt me when I hear their song "Torn Between Two Lovers "on the car radio.

Four years later, March 2008, Glen's obituary appeared in the San Angelo *Standard-Times*. As I passed the paper to Nora at the breakfast counter, I said nothing, but I took note of her reaction when she spotted it. She was noticeably affected.

Later, as I disposed of that paper, I noticed that the obituary had been cut out.

CHAPTER 55

THE RETURN TO
SQUARE DANCING

*Let them praise his name with dancing and make
music to him with timbrel and harp.—Psalm 149:3*

After the sale of Promenade Square, I continued contract calling for clubs in Odessa, Midland, Ozona, Brownwood, Eastland, Temple, and so forth. I did skip calling at a couple of annual state festivals and even yielded a couple of annual square dance exhibitions at the Christmas at Old Fort Conch celebrations to fellow caller Ed Hart.

We took part in very little square dance activity above and beyond my contract calling, but Nora always danced while I called and did love to do so. She was a truly graceful dancer with the poise and balance of a ballerina. In most clubs, men made it a point to dance with the caller's wife. Nora enjoyed that!

In these idle years, we did take one last trip to Europe for a visit with our son and his family. We traveled to East Berlin, where the replacement of rickety Soviet-built tenements was still in progress. Following that, we visited and danced with former club members now stationed in Bad Kreuznach.

Little by little, the memories of Nora's romance wore off. I had long forgiven her, but it takes time to ease the burden of acrimony.

———◆•◆•◆———

Time moves along. This is true retirement. No business, no jobs, just us, enjoying the comforts of doing nothing ... but our lives were missing a purpose. The purpose of life is to have a purpose, is it not?

Whether by instinct or a need for a purpose, one night at dinner, Nora, not looking directly at me and in a hesitant voice, said, "Let's start a club." Her love of square dancing was daring her to broach a delicate subject. She must have wondered, had I absolved her of her transgressions from another point in time?

To live in peace, we must forgive those who trespass against us. While I had not excused her actions. I had long relieved myself of the burden of animosity. "Yes," I said. "We do need to do something."

In January 2007, I made a presentation to the Woodsmen of the World (WOW) board of governors to use their run-down hall on Locust Street. It was barely habitable but located near the intersection of highways US-67 and US-87—the crossroads of San Angelo. The neighborhood was dismal, the location perfect. They accepted my proposal.

There were other buildings on this one-block-long street. They were abandoned, housed homeless people, stray cats, rats, and cockroaches. Most were overgrown with prickly pear, mesquite, and stirrup-high prairie grass, but the WOW hall featured a spacious hardwood floor, a dais, and a functional kitchen. It was climate-controlled and had operational washrooms. The price was right, and it fulfilled our needs.

The usual TV and radio talk-show guest appearances and newspaper ads brought good results. We had a class!

Our history at WOW was brief. We graduated the current class, formed a club, now called Promenade Squares (to reflect the name of our still existing corporation), and we put another class together in the fall. I was increasing my contract calling, had called at a National Square Dance Convention, was calling at annual Texas State Square and Round Dance Festivals, and enjoying a second wave of prominence in the square dance world.

Then a shoe dropped. I was informed that the WOW building was for sale. Was I interested? The short answer was no. (It had asbestos-shingle siding, and I was not about to touch that!)

⸻ ◆ ⸻

On a following summer evening after a dance, in the fading light of day, I spotted Nora looking into the windows of the abandoned Boy Scouts of America building next door. She had waded through the uncut grass and was quite focused on the structure. Returning to the car, she said, "That's big enough for a dance club." She continued, "It even has a fireplace."

Oh no! Here we go again.

Yes, we bought that old concrete-block Boy Scout building. It had six rooms, three at each end bracketing a main hall. The partitions were concrete block, some of which had to be removed. I sawed what was needed with a masonry saw, and Nora pushed those walls over with much glee. (She was playing Superwoman!)

We piled those blocks into dumpsters and had them taken away. The bare cement block walls, we paneled. We then laid hardwood floors, painted the inside trim, built a podium, installed a kitchen, made space for new washrooms and such. Finally, we had a dance hall! We opened the doors in February 2008.

Our new club had a home, nestled on a half-acre lot cradled in the bend of the quiet Concho River. The location was sheltered from the bustle of city traffic, and the well-manicured riverside Picnic Park beyond River Drive gives the location an air of serenity.

There were no flashing neon signs or other commercial distractions—just a square dancer's silhouette on the end of the

319

white-painted cement block building facing River Drive. It alerted passersby to our existence.

———◆◆◆———

Thankfully, to accommodate our breathing of life into this eyesore corner of San Angelo, the city tore down four abandoned buildings and kept the vacant lots mowed. A new high school had been built across the Houston Hart (US-87) throughway, giving the neighborhood an air of respectability.

Be it ever so humble, there is no place like home.

Our little hall by the river became the focal point of square dancing in San Angelo. Nora relished the roll of hostess. She had the dancers' respect and was living a life of social prominence.

We took pleasure and pride in maintaining the grounds of that building. We were doing it for a purpose—our purpose. The club members became our support, our community family. And family is synonymous with loyalty, love, and trust.

CHAPTER 56

THE FINAL CURTAIN

*He will send his angel with you and will make
your mission successful.*—*Genesis 24:40*

T he creation and maintenance of any organization is not a
sporadic activity. It is an ongoing process. Thus, Nora and
I undertook to sustain square dancing in San Angelo for the
duration of our capabilities. It was a '*we*' undertaking. We won some,
we lost some, but we played.

The Promenade Squares Square Dance Club would last for
fourteen years, some good, some great. Our club made many
exhibition appearances at public and private events and entertained
at the Christmas celebrations of Old Fort Concho for all those years.

For four of those years, I wrote the script, produced, and
directed the Old Fort Concho Frontier Ball. Nora supervised the
decorations of the old stone stable building with coal oil lamps
and much traditional paraphernalia. The stage was adorned with
decorated Christmas trees, and she dressed the part for the rich
ceremonies of tradition. (Sadly The Frontier Ball is no more.)

A short list of some past club activities would include an
appearance at the governor-for-a-day celebration under the legislative
dome in Austin and being featured in the *San Angelo Lifestyle*
magazine, seven pages of print and photos.

We were regulars in the annual full costume dance appearances at the Texas Independence Day celebrations in the Paseo de Santa Anna and entertained at the annual Silver Bluebonnet's Day in the state park. One year, we were featured in the rodeo parade on a twenty-foot float featuring seventeen dancers. Our colorful costumed dancers were a credit to the San Angelo Scene.

In January 2017, Nora and I attended a Texas State Federation of Square and Round Dance event in Ozona, where I was awarded the Prestige Award by the Texas State Callers Hall of Fame. Nora proudly stood beside me during the presentation.

Life with our little club on the river went on, and in 2017, Nora and I celebrated our anniversary at a theater presentation of *All Hands on Deck*. We were seated just four rows from the front, and at intermission, as the light came on, an announcer came in front of the curtain and asked the audience to remain seated for a few minutes.

He proceeded to ask, "Where are Mr. and Mrs. Geen seated?" When I raised my hand, he simply said, "Please stand." He then announced our sixty fifth anniversary and, kneeling on one knee, sang an old Al Jolson love song.

The audience was then dismissed, and Nora and I were the center of much attention in the lobby. (I never found out who put the cast up to that. There were several square dancers in the audience.)

Next day was Sunday. We arose early, ate breakfast, proceeded to enjoy our usual Sunday things like watching a hockey game, then had dinner.

After dinner, and after we'd watched the news and *60 Minutes*, Nora, seated in her recliner, said, "I have chest pains."

Looking at her, I saw that she was ashen, and I said, "We're going the hospital!"

Nora went to the bedroom, put on a sweater, and brought her purse to the car. I began to speed to Shannon Hospital. Within a few blocks, Nora heaved a great bodily pulse, made a deep vocal sound, and settled into her seat. It was the last sound she ever made.

On the rest of the frantic ride to the hospital, I talked to her, encouraging her to stay with me. She did not respond to my voice or touch. Entering the emergency entrance, I loudly announced, "My wife is in the car and had a heart attack." There was much scrambling getting her on a gurney and into some emergency chamber.

After heroic attempts by the hospital staff, at three in the morning, Nora was pronounced dead.

I received comfort counseling from a padre and arrived home just before daybreak.

I was not taking this well. I cried profusely.

For sixty-five years, my partner, my companion, my wife and I had faced this life together. I was not prepared for it to end. Many little things began to plague me. After my first night of fitful sleep, I entered the kitchen and reality dawned upon me. I was home alone.

I made a single piece of toast, poured one cup of coffee, and consumed them beside an empty chair. A sinking feeling told me that this was for real. A hollow feeling engulfed me. This was how it would ever be.

Nora's memorial service was well attended. Our children came from Canada, Maine, and Dallas. Square dancers came from near and far. Nora loved flowers and often wore one in her hair. The funeral parlor overflowed with flowers. A eulogy was given by our youngest son, Glen, and many gave testaments of respect. I was too despairing to speak.

Services were conducted by a club member, the Reverend Daniel Maynard. His wife rendered songs of worship.

Nora's cremated ashes will go with me to my grave in the San Angelo Fairmont Cemetery.

———◆———

I pressed on with running the club. Our daughter, Gail, had now assumed the role of my caregiver. We held regular dances until the deadly COVID came to town. In February 2020, the club went dark.

I reopened the club in February 2021, but illnesses and other needs of absence decreased the attendance to the point that it was not practical to continue. On December 3, 2021, I closed the club.

The square dance community of Texas was far-flung and expansive. Nora and I traveled far and wide to gala festivals where we were not strangers, just friends with a liking for fun and a love of tradition. I am proud we had the tenure of some forty years in that community. It all began when we arrived in Texas, and over the years, our enthusiasm progressed from a curiosity to a passion. We became involved in a recreation we both truly loved.

She shared the heartbeat of the San Angelo square dance community and was part of it for thirty-seven years. She was dedicated to it. She motivated me to keep this community whole. Yes, that hallowed little hall at 618 Locust Street was her pride. I wish I could once again make it active.

When traveling the Texas Highways and byways, I often spotted a roadside memorial to the loss of a life—perhaps a few flowers lovingly placed in remembrance, perhaps a humble cross or wooden slab with a name etched in an indelible ink, a symbolic indication that a loved one is missed and remembered.

When Nora passed, she was, by choice, cremated. There was no grave, no headstone with her name and life duration, no location for future visits to relive memories.

The ladies of the local square dance community felt that there should be a memorial placed by some path or roadside, a place where passers-by could be reminded that she was once here amongst us and journeyed to the trail's end. They decided that a bronze plaque by a noble live oak tree would be appropriate and pursued and funded it. The question arose, where to place it? Many locations were considered, many were deemed worthy, but as the second anniversary of her passing approached, a decision was finally made.

The recently developed Heritage Park in the heart of downtown San Angelo was selected. There, visitors are informed by sight and sound of the historic significance of our growing city in the heart of south-central Texas.

Finally, her roadside memorial would have a home. It was dedicated on the anniversary of her passing. Her tree and plaque will henceforth remind passersby that her life of fun, fitness, and fellowship ended here, in a land she came to love.

Passersby will only see
Her name beneath a noble tree
And wonder just who she may be.
She now rests in eternity.

CHAPTER 57

REFLECTIONS OF JOHN

*There is no fear in love, but perfect love
casts out fear. For fear has to do with
punishment, and whoever fears has not
been perfected in love.—1 John 4:18*

I am no longer the person I was, or will ever be again, I am no longer a person of purpose, significance, meaning, or even of value.

I am an old man. I have no further dreams to fulfill, only memories of achievements.

I am no longer a person who people thank for rendering unto them a service. I now thank those who render unto me a needed service.

I am no longer a person recognized on the street by strangers, but a person from whom a stranger may turn and not notice.

I will no longer ever reach any significant summits of achievement, but I do enjoy the view from where I am. If given a choice, would I have lived my life differently?

Yes. I now possess wisdom and feelings I once did not have.

Our children are scattered hither and yon throughout the world. We influenced their educational plateaus and selection of careers, but they pursued their own destiny. In my youth, I was probably influenced in some small way by grandfather Geen's choice to seek a fortune in pursuit of placer gold. Mine was to seek independence from family influence.

My late wife, Nora, may well have been influenced by her Mennonite heritage, wherein a woman's life is made to center around the needs of men. Until recent times, they closely followed the biblical philosophy of Genesis 3:16.

She married me, a nomadic individual who went when and where many others would not go just to prove my worth,.

For a high school graduation gift, we bought each of our children the best luggage we could afford. The message was, go seek your fortune wherever you can find it. I encouraged them to never turn down an opportunity; it may not be offered again. Go where chance offers the greatest rewards.

They did just that.

Did we encourage our children to abandon us, or did we in fashion and fact abandon our children?

I'm not too sure either way.

My life has not been without regrets—many regrets. During the early period of my life, a man was expected to be the household breadwinner, and a woman was expected to be the household bread-baker. While during my lifetime social systems changed, I took my time in doing so.

I made choices to best accommodate needs that were not necessarily the immediate interests or comforts of my wife and family. Some economically influenced decisions I made were outright abusive.

Yes, it brought us monetary comfort and independence, but often the family paid a price. There is no restitution for such callousness, and they seek it not.

Have they forgiven me? In attitudes and actions, yes. In mind, I can only presume.

It is Sunday morning. I am alone in the easy chair of my bedroom contemplating, well, nothing. This chair, and the floor lamp behind me, were gifts from my departed neighbor, Nancy. She looked to me for spiritual support and comfort during the last days of her husband, John. She followed him a year later.

I hear the sound of Gail in the kitchen and know I will soon have breakfast.

I draw comfort from the trove of relics around me. I see faces and hear voices from the past as I view an old rickety table fashioned like a shamrock that stands in the corner. Beside it, a battered violin case holds an ancient instrument. They were brought to the new world from Ireland by my mother's family. On the table stands a candlestick telephone rescued from some dial-conversion job in Ontario, Canada, and beside it is a delicate doll dressed in a hand-sewn square dance costume given to us by a club member who just wanted us to have it.

There is a foot-trestle sewing machine nearby that Nora's mother sat beside in Altona, Manitoba, making suitable school clothes for her family. It complements the walnut-finished pine bedroom suite we purchased at Sears Roebuck in Albany, New York, for our master bedroom in the new house in Johnstown. It reflects the elegant beauty of traditional craftmanship.

Atop a chest of drawers sits a rare and valued Eichwald vase, a wedding gift to my parents. Mother had used it to store buttons. At the foot of the bed is a Lane cedar chest, purchased at a two-for-the-price-of-one sale. The second one we gifted to Gail and Jim; it is now located in her room at the far end of the house. Mine holds spare bedding and a treasured unframed photo of Mother and Dad standing in front of the windmill at the Geen homestead in Thomasburg, Ontario.

Hanging on the wall is a large needlework creation by Nora. It pictures a round end table by a chair with a lap blanket hanging over one arm. The chair sits beside a window with a reclining cat on the sill. It reflects the beauty, pride, and effort she put into every stich.

Also featured on the wall is a framed 1979 photo of a full eclipse of the sun. Its ghostly image appears to be suspended over the up-reaching hand of The Golden Boy that stands atop of the legislative buildings in Winnipeg, Manitoba. It was a gift to us from Nora's Aunt Kay, the last living soul she knew in her family. She was never informed of Aunt Kay's passing—when or where or why.

The bedside table holds a glass-based tri-lamp given to us by our son Glen after he assumed residence in Dallas. That was at the launching of his long and highly successful career. Beside it sits a radio/alarm clock purchased from the company store forty years ago, while Glen was still in school. It still works!

Near my bedside sits a small chest that holds the cremated ashes of Nora. It awaits burial with me in my gravesite in Fairmont Cemetery. Together we will rest there eternally.

Yes, here in this room are so many items that have touched my life, and the lives of those I love. I cannot take all these articles to my grave, but I will take their memory to my eternity.

Memories are precious. Skills and energy may fade, but memories we cherish. Let me now share one last one with you.

Sunday mornings, prior to church, I visit Heritage Park at the corner of Twohig and Oak Street, San Angelo Texas. There, on the peripheral boundaries of that little park, I stand for a few moments to remember, to ponder, and to reminisce. A bronze plaque beneath a maturing tree reads, "San Angelo Square Dance Community—In memory of Nora Geen, 1933–2017."

Her roadside memorial will long be observed by friends and strangers alike. They will know she was precious to many.

EPILOGUE

Soon I will lay me down to rest
I thank my God that I've been blessed.

I have shared with you many of my thoughts, ideas, experiences, and beliefs. I have expressed my faith in God and my rejection of Bible stories that defy rational, science-based explanations. Yes, the Bible once was public law, enforced by popes, priests, and bishops. We now live by legislated laws enforced by heads of state, police, and judges.

I also recognize that well-researched knowledge has replaced many faith-based suppositions. Does that make me a hopeless agnostic or a practical academic? Your choice!

There have been many occurrences about and during my life influencing me to say, or muse, "Who will ever know, who will ever care, whatever difference have I really made?" I now have the answer. I do know, I do care, and I have made a difference! Do my recollections involve anyone who remembers my name, who remembers who I was or who shared my joys, emotions, opinions, or regrets? I believe so, but at this point, does it really matter?

I did not write this memoir to enumerate my triumphs, share my disappointments, or seek forgiveness, but I do remain eternally grateful that I have found the strength to forgive all who have trespassed against me.

All through my life, there have been unexplainable solutions to potentially disastrous situations. Has this been a God-sent rescue or just good luck? For example:

- As I faced unemployment in Winnipeg in 1951, a lady who had no need to do so found me a job that would become my life's profession. Was she a guardian angel looking out for me?
- An auto accident that had me plunging down a twenty-foot cliff allowed me to walk away unscathed. Did a power I do not understand protect me?
- I quitt a secure job in Salmon Arm, British Columbia, to seek a job at a General Telephone–owned company in Vancouver. My educational achievements did not qualify me for that job but I was hired. Was it because some unknown person in some unknown office location had some God-given courage to override a company policy and employ me anyway?
- Did this same person, or perhaps some other persons, influence the company to place me in a temporary warehouse job shortly after a general lay-off, so I might feed my family and make my house payments?
- And who was the individual who recognized my experience and background were needed to fill a prominent installation position in the Brockville, Ontario, manufacturing plant?
- When the Automatic Electric plant in Brockville came under the shadow of a doubtful future, a person well known to me in the personal office called me in to tell me of an open position in the General Telephone Company of Upstate New York. He advised me to take a transfer. Why did he think he owed me that? Was some divine intervention involved?
- When the General Telephone Company of Upstate New York was sold ten years later, why was I whisked off to the General Telephone Company of Texas before the

deal closed? Here I would finish my thirty-year General Telephone Company career.

Never have I been able to give myself full credit for any of this. Most of my rescues and moves came about through the efforts of others. To this, I give full credit to a power beyond my comprehension. I cannot accept that all this as just plain old-fashioned good luck.

I have chosen to attribute it to the hand of God.

Ingram Content Group UK Ltd.
Milton Keynes UK
UKHW012122060323
418148UK00013B/456/J